Reverse Engineering of Object Oriented Code

Monographs in Computer Science

Paolo Tonella
Alessandra Potrich

Reverse Engineering of Object Oriented Code

Paolo Tonella and Alessandra Potrich
ITC-irst
Via Sommarive
Povo, Trent 38050
ITALY

Series Editors

David Gries
Department of Computer Science
Cornell University
4130 Upson Hall
Ithaca, NY 14853-7501
USA

Fred P. Schneider
Department of Computer Science
Cornell University
4130 Upson Hall
Ithaca, NY 14853-7501
USA

Cover illustration: Verona-climbing the tower. Photo courtesy Philip Greenspun, http://philip.greenspun.com.

ISBN 978-1-4419-2325-7   e-ISBN 978-0-387-23803-6
Printed on acid-free paper.

9 8 7 6 5 4 3 2 1

springeronline.com

To Silvia and Chiara
    – Paolo

To Bruno
– Alessandra

Contents

Contents ix

Foreword

There has been an ongoing debate on how best to document a software system ever since the first software system was built. Some would have us writing natural language descriptions, some would have us prepare formal specifications, others would have us producing design documents and others would want us to describe the software thru test cases. There are even those who would have us do all four, writing natural language documents, writing formal specifications, producing standard design documents and producing interpretable test cases all in addition to developing and maintaining the code. The problem with this is that whatever is produced in the way of documentation becomes in a short time useless, unless it is maintained parallel to the code. Maintaining alternate views of complex systems becomes very expensive and highly error prone. The views tend to drift apart and become inconsistent.

The authors of this book provide a simple solution to this perennial problem. Only the source code is maintained and evolved. All of the other information required on the system is taken from the source code. This entails generating a complete set of UML diagrams from the source. In this way, the design documentation will always reflect the real system as it is and not the way the system should be from the viewpoint of the documentor. There can be no inconsistency between design and implementation. The method used is that of reverse engineering, the target of the method is object oriented code in C++, C#, or Java. From the code class diagrams, object diagrams, interaction diagrams and state diagrams are generated in accordance with the latest UML standard. Since the method is automated, there are no additional costs. Design documentation is provided at the click of a button.

This approach, the result of many years of research and development, will have a profound impact upon the way IT-systems are documented. Besides the source code itself, only one other view of the system needs to be developed and maintained, that is the user view in the form of a domain specific language. Each application domain will have to come up with it's own language to describe applications from the view point of the user. These languages may range from natural languages to set theory to formal mathematical notations.

What these languages will not describe is how the system is or should be constructed. This is the purpose of UML as a modeling language. The techniques described in this book demonstrate that this design documentation can and should be extracted from the code, since this is the cheapest and most reliable means of achieving this end. There may be some UML documents produced on the way to the code, but since complex IT systems are almost always developed by trial and error, these documents will only have a transitive nature. The moment the code exists they are both obsolete and superfluous. From then on, the same documents can be produced cheaper and better from the code itself. This approach coincides with and supports the practice of extreme programming.

Of course there are several drawbacks, as some types of information are not captured in the code and, therefore, reverse engineering cannot capture them. An example is that there still needs to be a test oracle – something to test against. This something is the domain specific specification from which the application-oriented test cases are derived. The technical test cases can be derived from the generated UML diagrams. In this way, the system as implemented will be verified against the system as specified. Without the UML diagrams, extracted from the code, there would be no adequate basis of comparison.

For these and other reasons, this book is highly recommendable to all who are developing and maintaining Object-Oriented software systems. They should be aware of the possibilities and limitations of automated post documentation. It will become increasing significant in the years to come, as the current generation of OO-systems become the legacy systems of the future. The implementation knowledge they encompass will most likely be only in the source and there will be no other means of regaining it other than through reverse engineering.

Trento, Italy, July 2004   *Harry Sneed*
Benevento, Italy, July 2004   *Aniello Cimitile*

Preface

Diagrams representing the organization and behavior of an Object Oriented software system can help developers comprehend it and evaluate the impact of a modification. However, such diagrams are often unavailable or inconsistent with the code. Their extraction from the code is thus an appealing option. This book represents the state of the art of the research in Object Oriented code analysis for reverse engineering. It describes the algorithms involved in the recovery of several alternative views from the code and some of the techniques that can be adopted for their visualization.

During software evolution, availability of high level descriptions is extremely desirable, in support to program understanding and to change-impact analysis. In fact, location of a change to be implemented can be guided by high level views. The dependences among entities in such views indicate the proportion of the ripple effects.

However, it is often the case that diagrams available during software evolution are not consistent with the code, or – even more frequently – that no diagram has altogether been produced. In such contexts, it is crucial to be able to reverse engineer design diagrams directly from the code. Reverse engineered diagrams are a faithful representation of the actual code organization and of the actual interactions among objects. Programmers do not face any misalignment or gap when moving from such diagrams to the code.

The material presented in this book is based on the techniques developed during a collaboration we had with CERN (Conseil Européen pour la Recherche Nucléaire). At CERN, work for the next generation of experiments to be run on the Large Hadron Collider has started in large advance, since these experiments represent a major challenge, for the size of the devices, teams, and software involved. We collaborated with CERN in the introduction of tools for software quality assurance, among which a reverse engineering tool.

The algorithms described in this book deal with the reverse engineering of the following diagrams:

Class diagram: Extraction of inter-class relationships in presence of weakly typed containers and interfaces, which prevent an exact knowledge of the actual type of referenced objects.

Object and interaction diagrams: Recovery of the associations among the objects that instantiate the classes in a system and of the messages exchanged among them.

State diagram: Modeling of the behavior of each class in terms of states and state transitions.

Package diagram: Identification of packages and of the dependences among packages.

All the algorithms share a common code analysis framework. The basic principle underlying such a framework is that information is derived *statically* (no code execution) by performing a propagation of proper data in a graph representation of the object flows occurring in a program. The data structure that has been defined for such a purpose is called the Object Flow Graph (OFG). It allows tracking the lifetime of the objects from their creation along their assignment to program variables.

UML, the Unified Modeling Language, has been chosen as the graphical language to present the outcome of reverse engineering. This choice was motivated by the fact that UML has become the standard for the representation of design diagrams in Object Oriented development. However, the choice of UML is by no means restrictive, in that the same information recovered from the code can be provided to the users in different graphical or non graphical formats.

A well known concern of most reverse engineering methods is how to filter the results, when their size and complexity are excessively high. Since the recovered diagrams are intended to be inspected by a human, the presentation modes should take into account the cognitive limitations of humans explicitly. Techniques such as focusing, hierarchical structuring and element explosion/implosion will be introduced specifically for some diagram types.

The research community working in the field of reverse engineering has produced an impressive amount of knowledge related to techniques and tools that can be used during software evolution in support of program understanding. It is the authors' opinion that an important step forward would be to publish the achievements obtained so far in comprehensive books dealing with specific subtopics.

This book on reverse engineering from Object Oriented code goes exactly in this direction. The authors have produced several research papers in this field over time and have been active in the research community. The techniques and the algorithms described in the book represent the current state of the art.

Trento, Italy   *Paolo Tonella*
July 2004   *Alessandra Potrich*

1

Introduction

Reverse engineering aims at supporting program comprehension, by exploiting the source code as the major source of information about the organization and behavior of a program, and by extracting a set of potentially useful views provided to programmers in the form of diagrams. Alternative perspectives can be adopted when the source code is analyzed and different higher level views are extracted from it. The focus may either be on the structure, on the behavior, on the internal states, or on the physical organization of the files. A single diagram recovered from the code through reverse engineering is insufficient. Rather, a set of complementary views need to be obtained, addressing different program understanding needs.

In this chapter, the role of reverse engineering within the life cycle of a software system is described. The activities of program understanding and impact analysis are central during the evolution of an existing system. Both activities can benefit from sources of knowledge about the program such as reverse engineered diagrams.

The reverse engineering techniques presented in the following chapters are described with reference to an example program used throughout the book. In this chapter, this example program is introduced and commented. Then, some of the diagrams that are the object of the following chapters are provided for the example program, showing their usefulness from the programmer's point of view. The remaining parts of the book contain the algorithmic details on how to recover them from the source code.

1.1 Reverse Engineering

In the life cycle of a software system, the maintenance phase is the largest and the most expensive. Starting after the delivery of the first version of the software [35], maintenance lasts much longer than the initial development phase. During this time, the software will be changed and enhanced over and over. So it is more appropriate to speak of *software evolution* with reference to the whole life cycle, in which the initial development is only a special case where the existing system is empty.

Software evolution is characterized by the existence of the source code of the system. Thus, the typical activity in software evolution is the implementation of a program change, in response to a *change request*. Changes may be aimed at correcting the software (*corrective* maintenance), at adding a functionality (*perfective* maintenance), at adapting the software to a changed environment (*adaptive* maintenance), or at restructuring it to make future maintenance easier (*preventive* maintenance) [35].

During software evolution, the most reliable and accurate description of the behavior of a software system is its source code. In fact, design diagrams are often outdated or missing at all. Such a valuable information repository may not directly answer all questions about the system. Reverse engineering techniques provide a way to extract higher level views of the system, which summarize some relevant aspects of the computation performed by the program statements. Reverse engineered diagrams support program comprehension, as well as restructuring and traceability.

When an existing code base is worked on, the micro-process of *program change* can be decomposed into localizing the change, assessing the impact, and implementing the change. All such activities depend on the knowledge available about the program to be modified. In this respect, reverse engineering techniques are a useful support. Reverse engineering tools provide useful high level information about the system being maintained, thus helping programmers locate the component to be modified. Moreover, the relationships (dependencies, associations, etc.) that connect the entities in reverse engineered diagrams provide indications about the impact of a change. By tracing such relationships the set of entities possibly affected by a change are obtained.

Object Oriented programming poses special problems to software engineers during the maintenance phase. Correspondingly, reverse engineering techniques have to be customized to address them. For example, the behavior of an Object Oriented program emerges from the interactions occurring among the objects allocated in the program. The related instructions may be spread across several classes, which individually perform a very limited portion of the work locally and delegate the rest of it to others. Reverse engineered diagrams capture such collaborations among classes/objects, summarizing them in a single, compact view. However, recovering accurate information about such collaborations represents a special challenge, requiring major improvements to the available reverse engineering methods [48, 100].

When a software system is analyzed to extract information about it, the fundamental choice is between static and dynamic analysis. *Dynamic* analysis requires a tracer tool to save information about the objects manipulated and the methods dispatched during program execution. The diagrams that can be reverse engineered in this way are partial. They hold valid for a single, given execution of the program, with given input values, and they cannot be easily generalized to the behavior of the program for any execution with any input. Moreover, dynamic analysis is possible only for complete, executable systems, while in Object Oriented programming it is typical to produce incomplete sets of classes that are reused in different contexts. On the contrary, a *static* analysis produces results that are valid for all executions and for all inputs. On the other side, static analyses may be over-conservative. In fact, it is undecidable to determine if a statically possible path is *feasible*, i.e., if there exists an input value allowing its traversal. Static analysis may conservatively assume that some paths are executable, while they are actually not so. Consequently, it may produce results for which no input value exists. In the following chapters, the advantages and disadvantages of the two approaches will be discussed for each specific diagram, illustrating them on an executable example.

UML (Unified Modeling Language) [7, 69] has become the standard graphical language used to represent Object Oriented systems in diagrammatic form. Its specifications have been recently standardized by the Object Management Group (OMG) [1]. UML has been adopted by several software companies, and its theoretical aspects are the subject of several research studies. For these reasons, UML was chosen as the graphical representation that is produced as the output of the reverse engineering techniques described in this book. However, the choice of UML is by no means limiting: while the information reverse engineered from the code can be represented in different graphical (or non graphical) forms, the basic analysis methods exploited to produce it can be reused unchanged in alternative settings, with UML replaced by some other description language.

An important issue reverse engineering techniques must take into account is usability. Since the recovered views are for humans and not for computers, they must be compatible with the cognitive abilities of human beings. This means that diagrams convey useful information only if their size is kept small (while 10 entities may be fine, 100 starts being too much and 1000 makes a diagram unreadable). Several approaches can be adopted to support visualization and navigation modes making reverse engineered information usable. They range from the possibility to focus on a portion of the system, to the expand/collapse or zoom in/out operations, or to the availability of an overall navigation map complemented by a detailed view. In the following chapters, ad hoc methods will be described with reference to the specific diagrams being produced.

1.2 The *eLib* Program

The *eLib* program is a small Java program that supports the main functions operated in a library. Its code is provided in Appendix A. It will be used in the remaining of this book as the example.

In *eLib*, libraries are supposed to hold an archive of documents of different categories, properly classified. Each document can be uniquely identified by the librarian. Library users can request some of these documents for loan, subjected to proper access rules. In order to borrow a document, users must be identified by the librarian. For example, this could be achieved by distributing library cards to registered users.

As regards the management of the documents in the *eLib* system, the librarian can insert new documents in the archive and remove documents no longer available in the library. Upon request, the librarian may need to search the archive for documents according to some search criterion, such as title, authors, ISBN code, etc. The documents held by a library are of several different kinds, including books, journals, and technical reports. Each of them has specific properties and specific access restrictions.

As far as user management is concerned, a set of personal data (name, address, phone number, etc.) are maintained in the archive. A special category of users consists of internal users, who have special permission to access documents not allowed for loan to normal users.

The main functionality of the *eLib* system is loan management. Users can borrow documents up to a maximum number. While books are available for loan to any user, journals can be borrowed only by internal users, and technical reports can be consulted but not borrowed.

Although this is a small application, by going through the source code of the *eLib* program (see Appendix A) it is not so easy to understand how the classes are organized, how they interact with each other to fulfill the main functions, how responsibilities are distributed among the classes, what is computed locally and what is delegated. For example, a programmer aiming at understanding this application may have the following questions:

- What is the overall system organization?
- What objects are updated when a document is borrowed?
- What classes are responsible to check if a given document can be borrowed by a given user?
- How is the maximum number of loans handled?
- What happens to the state of the library when a document is returned?

Let us assume the following change request (perfective maintenance):

> When a document is not available for loan, a user can reserve it, if it has not been previously reserved by another user. When a document is returned to the library, the user who reserved it is contacted, if any is associated with the document. The user can either borrow the document that has become available or cancel the reservation. In both cases, after this operation the reservation of the document is deleted.

the programmer who is responsible for its implementation may have the following questions about the system:

- Does the overall system organization need any change?
- What classes need to collaborate to realize the reservation functionality?

- Is there any possible side effect on the existing functionalities?
- What changes should be made in the procedure for returning documents to the library?
- How is the new state of a document described?
- Is there any interaction between the new rules for document borrowing and the existing ones?

In the following sections, we will see how UML diagrams reverse engineered from the code can help answer the program understanding and impact analysis questions listed above.

1.3 Class Diagram

The class diagram reverse engineered from the code helps understand the overall system's organization and the kind of interclass connections that exist in the program.

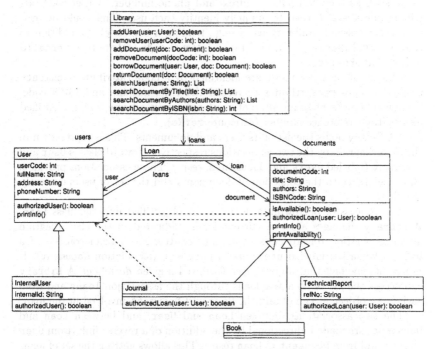

Fig. 1.1. Class diagram for the *eLib* program.

Fig. 1.1 shows the class diagram of the *eLib* program, including all interclass dependencies. The UML graphical language has been adopted, so that dashed lines indicate a dependency, solid lines an association and empty arrows inheritance. The exact meaning of the notation will be clarified in the following chapters. An intuitive idea is sufficient for the purposes of this section. Only some attributes and methods inside the compartments of each class have been selected for display.

The overall architecture of the system is clear from Fig. 1.1. The class Library provides the main functionalities of the *eLib* program. For example, library users are managed through the methods addUser and removeUser, while documents to be archived or dismissed are managed through addDocument and removeDocument. The objects that respectively represent users and documents belong to the two classes User and Document. As apparent from the class diagram, there are two kinds of users: normal users, represented as objects of the base class User, and internal users, represented by the subclass InternalUser. Library documents are also classified into categories. A library can manage journals (class Journal), books (class Book), and technical reports (class TechnicalReport). All these classes extend the base class Document.

The attributes of class User aim at storing personal data about library users, such as their full name, address and phone number. A user code (attribute userCode) is used to uniquely identify each user. This could be read from a card issued to library users (e.g., reading a bar code). In addition to that, internal users are identified by an internal code (attribute internalId of class InternalUser).

Objects of class Document are identified by a code (attribute documentCode), and possess attributes to record the title, authors and ISBN code. Technical reports obey an alternative classification scheme, being identified also by their reference number (attribute refNo).

A Library holds the list of its users and documents. This is represented in the class diagram by the two associations respectively toward classes User and Document (labeled users and documents, resp.). These associations provide a stable reference to the collection of documents and the set of users currently handled.

The process of borrowing a document is objectified into the class Loan. A Library manages a set of current loans, indicated in the class diagram as an association toward class Loan (labeled loans). A Loan consists of a User (association labeled user) and a Document (association document). It represents the fact that a given *user* borrowed a given *document*. A Library can access the list of its active loans through the association loans and from each Loan object, it can obtain the User and Document involved in the loan.

The two associations, between Loan and User, and between Loan and Document, are made bidirectional by the addition of a reverse link (from User to Loan and from Document to Loan resp.). This allows getting the set of loans of a given user and the loan (if any exists) associated to a given document. The chain from users to documents, and vice versa, can thus be closed. Given a user, it is possible to access her/his loans (association loans), and from each loan, the related Document object. In the other direction, given a Document, it is possible to see if it is borrowed (association loan leads to a non-null object), and in case a Loan object exists, the user who borrowed the document is accessible through the association user (from Loan to User).

Class Library establishes the relationships between users and documents, through Loan objects, when calls to its method borrowDocument are issued. On the contrary, the method returnDocument is responsible for dropping Loan objects, thus making a document no longer connected to a Loan object, and diminishing the number of loans a user is associated with. When a document is requested for loan by a user, the Library checks if it is available, by invoking the method isAvailable of class Document, and if the given user is authorized to borrow the document, by invoking the method authorizedLoan inside class Document. Since loan authorization depends also on the kind of user issuing the request (normal vs. internal user), a method authorizedUser is provided inside the class User to distinguish normal users from users with special loan privileges. The method authorizedLoan is overridden when the default authorization policy, implemented by the base class Document, needs be changed in a subclass (namely, TechnicalReport and Journal). Similarly, the default authorization rights of normal users, defined in the base class User, are redefined inside InternalUser.

Search facilities are available inside the class Library. Users can be searched by name (method searchUser), while documents can be searched by title (method searchDocumentByTitle), authors (method searchDocument-ByAuthors), or ISBN code (method searchDocumentByISBN). Retrieved users can be associated with the documents they borrowed and retrieved documents can be associated with the users who borrowed them (if any) as explained above.

Print facilities are available inside classes Library, User, Document, and Loan (for clarity, some of them are not shown in Fig. 1.1). The method printInfo is a function to print general information available from the classes User and Document. The method printAvailability inside class Document emits a message stating if a given document is available or was borrowed. In the latter case, information about the user who borrowed it is also printed.

The mutual dependencies between classes User and Document (dashed lines in Fig. 1.1) are due to the invocation of methods to gather information that is displayed by some printing function. For example, the method printInfo of class User displays personal user data, followed by the list of borrowed documents. Information about such documents is obtained by traversing the two associations loans and document, leading to a Document object for each borrowed item. Then, calls to get data about each Document (e.g., method getTitle) are issued. Hence, the dependency from User to Document. Symmetrically, method printAvailability of class Document accesses user data (e.g., calling method getName), in case a User borrowed the given Document. This happens when the association loan is non-null. The direct invocation from Document to User is the cause of the dependency between these two classes.

Authorization to borrow documents is handled in a straightforward way inside the classes Document and TechnicalReport, which return a constant value (resp. true and false) and do not use at all the parameter user received upon invocation of authorizedLoan. On the other side, the class Journal returns a value that depends on the privileges of the parameter user. This is achieved by calling authorizedUser from authorizedLoan inside Journal. This direct call from Journal to User explains the dependency between these two classes in the class diagram.

Chapter 3 provides an algorithm for the extraction of the class diagram in a context similar to that of the *eLib* program, where weakly typed containers and interfaces are used in attribute and variable declarations.

1.4 Object Diagram

The object diagram focuses on the objects that are created inside a program. Most of the object creations for the classes in the *eLib* program are performed inside an external driver class, such as that reported in Appendix B.

The *static* object diagram represents all objects and inter-object relationships possibly created in a program. The *dynamic* object diagram shows the objects and the relationships that are created during a specific program execution.

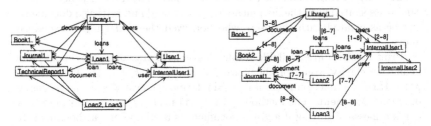

Fig. 1.2. Static (left) and dynamic (right) object diagram for the *eLib* program.

Fig. 1.2 depicts both kinds of object diagrams for the *eLib* program. In the static object diagram, shown on the left, each object corresponds to a distinct allocation statement in the program. Thus, for the *eLib* program under analysis (Appendixes A and B), there is one allocation point for creating objects of the classes Library, Book, Journal, TechnicalReport, User, InternalUser. No object of class Document is ever allocated, while objects of class Loan are allocated by three different statements inside the class Library. One such allocation (line 60) belongs to the method borrowDocument, and produces the object named Loan1, another one (line 70) is inside returnDocument and produces Loan2, while the third one (line 78), inside isHolding, produces Loan3.

As apparent from the diagram in Fig. 1.2 (left), the object allocated inside borrowDocument (Loan1) is contained inside the list of loans possessed by the object Library1, which represents the whole library. Loan1 references the document and the user participating in the loan. These are objects of type Book, Journal, TechnicalReport and User, InternalUser respectively, as depicted in the static object diagram. In turn, they have a reference to the loan object (bidirectional link in Fig. 1.2). On the contrary, the objects Loan2 and Loan3 are not accessible from the list of loans held by Library1. They are temporary objects created to manage the deletion of a loan (method returnDocument, line 70) and to check the existence of a loan between a given user and a given document (method isHolding, line 78). However, none of them is in turn referenced by the associated user/document (unidirectional link in Fig. 1.2).

The dynamic object diagram on the right of Fig. 1.2 was obtained by executing the *eLib* program under the following scenario:

Time	Operation
1	An internal user is registered into the library.
2	Another internal user is registered.
3	A book is archived into the library
4	Another book is archived.
5	A journal is archived into the library.
6	The journal archived at time 5 is borrowed by the first registered user.
7	The journal borrowed at time 6 is returned to the library and the loan is closed.
8	The librarian verifies that the loan was actually closed.

The time intervals indicating the life span of the inter-object relationships are in square brackets. The objects InternalUser1, InternalUser2 represent the two users created at times 1 and 2, while Book1, Book2, Journal1 are the objects created when two books and a journal are archived into the library, at times 3, 4, 5 respectively. When a loan is opened between InternalUser1 and Journal1 at time 6, the object Loan1 is created, referencing, and referenced by, the user and document involved in the loan. At time 7 the loan is closed. Correspondingly, the life interval of all associations linked to Loan1 is [6-7], including the association from the object Library1, representing the presence of Loan1 in the list of currently active loans (attribute loans of the object Library1). Loan deletion is achieved by looking for a Loan object (indicated as Loan2 in the object diagram) in the list of the active loans (Library1.loans). Loan2 references the document (Journal1) and the user (InternalUser1) that are participating in the loan to be removed. Being a temporary object, Loan2 disappears after the loan deletion operation is finished, together with its associations (life span [7-7]). The object Loan3 has a similar purpose. It is temporarily created to verify if Library1.loans contains a Loan which references the same user and document (resp., InternalUser1 and journal1) as Loan3. After the check is completed, Loan3 and its associations are dismissed (life span [8-8]).

Static and dynamic object diagrams provide complementary information, extremely useful to understanding the relationships among the objects that are actually allocated in a program. The existence of three different roles played by the objects of class Loan is not visible in the class diagram. It becomes clear once the object diagram for the *eLib* application is built. Moreover, the analysis of the dynamically allocated objects during the execution of a specific scenario allows understanding the way relationships are created and destroyed at run time. Temporary objects and relationships, used only in the scope of a given operation, can be distinguished from the stable relationships that characterize the management of users, documents and loans performed by the library. Moreover, the dynamics of the inter-object relationships that take place when a document is borrowed or returned also become explicit. Overall, the structure of the objects instantiated by the *eLib* program and of their mutual relationships, which is somewhat implicit in the class diagram, becomes clear in the object diagrams recovered from the code and from the program's execution.

Static and dynamic object diagram extraction is thoroughly discussed in Chapter 4.

1.5 Interaction Diagrams

The exchange of messages among the objects created by a program can be displayed either by ordering them temporally (sequence diagrams) or by showing them as labels of the inter-object relationships (collaboration diagrams). These are the two forms of the interaction diagrams. Each message (method call) is prefixed by a Dewey number (sequence of dot-separated decimal numbers), which indicates the flow of time and the level of nesting. Thus, a method call numbered 3.2 will be the second call nested inside another call, numbered 3.

Fig. 1.3 clarifies the interactions among objects that occur when a document is borrowed by a library user. The first three operations shown in the collaboration diagram in Fig. 1.3 (numbered 1, 2, 3) are related to the rules for document loaning implemented in the *eLib* program. In fact, the first operation (call to numberOfLoans) is issued from the Library object to the user who intends to borrow a document. The result of this operation is the number of loans currently held by the given user. The borrowing operation can proceed only if this number is below a predefined threshold (constant MAX_NUMBER_OF_LOANS in class Library).

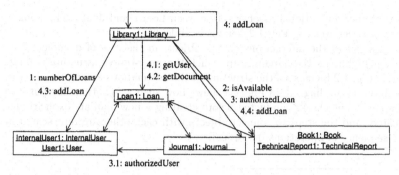

Fig. 1.3. Collaboration diagram focused on method `borrowDocument` of class `Library`.

The second check is about document availability (call to `isAvailable`). Of course, the document must be available in the library, before a user can borrow it.

The third check implements the authorization policy of the library. Not all kinds of users are allowed to borrow all kinds of documents. The call to `authorizedLoan`, issued from the `Library` object, is processed differently by different targets. When the target is a `Book` or a `TechnicalReport` object, it is processed locally. Actually, in the first case the constant `true` is returned (books can be borrowed by all kinds of users), while in the second case, `false` is always returned (technical reports cannot go out of the library). When the target of `authorizedLoan` is a `Journal`, a nested call to the method `authorizedUser`, numbered 3.1, is made, directed to the user requesting the loan. Since the actual target can be either a `User` (normal user) or an `InternalUser`, two different return values are produced in these two cases. The constants `false` and `true` are two such values, meaning that normal users are not allowed to borrow journals, as are internal users.

If all checks (messages 1, 2, 3) give positive answers, document borrowing can be completed successfully. This is achieved by calling the method `addLoan` from class `Library` (call number 4). The parameter of this method is a new `Loan` object, which references the user requesting the loan and the document to be borrowed. Inside `addLoan`, such a parameter is queried to get the `User` and `Document` involved in the loan (method calls numbered 4.1 and 4.2). Then, the operation `addLoan` is invoked both on the `User` (call 4.3) and on the `Document` (call 4.4) object. The effect of `addLoan` on the user (`User` or `InternalUser`) is the creation of a reverse link with the `Loan` object (see bidirectional association between `Loan1` and `InternalUser1`, `User1` in Fig. 1.2, left). This is achieved by adding the `Loan` object to the list of loans held by the given user. Similarly, the effect of `addLoan` on the document (`Journal`, `Book` or `TechnicalReport`), is the creation of a reference link to the `Loan` object, so that the bidirectional association between **Loan1** and **Journal1**, **Book1**, **TechnicalReport1** in Fig. 1.2 (left) is completed.

Analysis of the interactions among objects in the case of document borrowing highlights the dynamics by which the inter-object structure is built. While Fig. 1.2 focuses on the structure of the associations among the objects, the interaction diagram in Fig. 1.3 shows how such associations are put into existence. The checks conducted before creating a new loan are explicitly indicated, and the steps to connect objects with each other are represented in the sequence of operations performed.

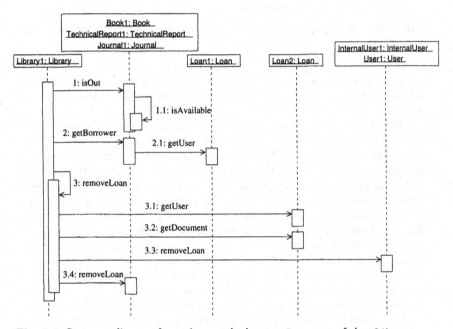

Fig. 1.4. Sequence diagram focused on method **returnDocument** of class **Library**.

The sequence diagram in Fig. 1.4 represents the interactions occurring over time among objects when a borrowed document is returned to the library. First of all, a check is made to see if the returned document is actually recorded as a borrowed document in the library (call to **isOut**, number 1). Another method of the class **Document** is exploited to get the answer (nested call **isAvailable**, number 1.1).

If the returned **Document** happens to be actually out, the operation **returnDocument** can proceed. Otherwise it is interrupted. The user holding the document being returned is obtained by calling the method **getBorrower** on the given document. This call is numbered 2. In turn, the **Book**, **TechnicalReport** or **Journal** objects that receive such a call do not have any direct

reference to the user who borrowed them. However, they have a reference to
the related Loan object. Thus, they can request the Loan object (Loan1) to
return the borrowing user (nested call 2.1, getUser).

Once information about the Document and User objects participating in
the loan to be closed have been gathered, it is possible to call the method
removeLoan from class Library and actually delete all references to the related Loan object. In order to identify which Loan object to remove, the
method removeLoan needs a temporary Loan object to be compared with
the Loan objects recorded in the Library. In Fig. 1.4, such a temporary Loan
object is named Loan2, while Loan objects stored in the Library are named
Loan1.

Deletion of the Loan object in the Library that is equal to Loan2 is
achieved by means of a call to the method remove of class Collection (see
line 52), which in turn uses an overridden version of method equals (see class
Loan line 146). Deletion of the references to the Loan object from Document
and User objects requires a few nested calls. First of all, the two referencing objects are made accessible inside the method removeLoan, by calling
getUser and getDocument (calls numbered 3.1 and 3.2) on the temporary
Loan object (Loan2). Then, deletion of the references to the Loan object is
obtained by invoking removeLoan on both User (InternalUser1 or User1)
and Document (Book1, TechnicalReport1, Journal1) objects (calls numbered 3.3 and 3.4). At this point, deletion of the bidirectional association
between Library and User and of that between Library and Document is
completed.

With reference to the static object diagram in Fig. 1.2 (left), the sequence diagram in Fig. 1.4 clarifies the dynamics by which the associations of
Library1 with the other objects are dropped. As one would expect, returning
a document to the library causes the removal of the association with Loan1,
the Loan object referenced by the Library object Library1, and the removal
of the reverse references from User (InternalUser1 or User1) and Document
(Book1, TechnicalReport1, Journal1). The only check being applied verifies whether the returned document is actually registered as a borrowed document (with associated loan data). Since the data structure used to record
the loans inside class Library is a Collection, an overridden version of the
method equals can be used to match the Loan to be removed with the actually recorded Loan. Two Loan objects are considered equal if in turn the
referenced User and Document objects are equal (see lines 148, 149 in class
Loan). This requires that the method equals be overridden by classes User
and Document as well (see lines 295 and 172).

The sequence diagram in Fig. 1.4 helps programmers to clarify the operations carried out when documents are returned. Reading the source code
with such a diagram available simplifies the program understanding activity,
in that method calls spread throughout the code are concentrated in a single
diagram. Of course, the diagram itself cannot tell everything about the behavior of specific methods, so that a look at their body is still necessary. However,

the overall picture assumes a concrete form – the sequence diagram – instead of existing only in the mind of the programmer who understands the code. For larger systems, the support coming from these diagrams is potentially even more important, given the cognitive difficulties of humans confronted with a large number of interacting entities.

The construction of collaboration and sequence diagrams is presented in Chapter 5. An algorithm for the computation of the Dewey numbers associated with the method calls is described in the same chapter. It determines the flow of the events in sequence diagrams. A focusing method to produce diagrams for specific computations of interest is also provided.

1.6 State Diagrams

State diagrams are used to represent the states possibly assumed by the objects of a given class, and the transitions from state to state possibly triggered by method invocations. The joint values of an object's attributes define its "complete" state. However, it is often possible to select a subset of all the attributes to characterize the state. Moreover, the set of all possible values can usually be abstracted into a small set of symbolic values. In this way, the size of the state diagrams can be kept limited, fitting the cognitive abilities of humans.

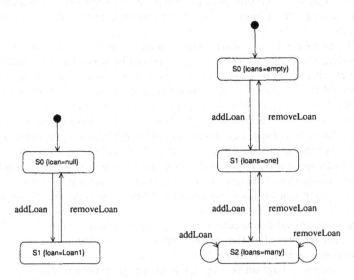

Fig. 1.5. State diagram for class Document (left) and User (right).

The state of an object of class Document of the *eLib* program can be characterized by the physical presence/absence of the related item in the library.

Different behaviors are obtained by invoking methods on a Document object, when such an object is available for loan, rather than being out, borrowed by some library user.

Among the attributes of class Document, the one which characterizes the state of its objects is loan. In fact, a null value of loan indicates that the document is available for loan, while a non null value indicates that the document is currently borrowed, with the related Loan object referenced by the attribute loan.

Fig. 1.5 (left) shows the state diagram reverse engineered from the code of class Document. Its two states S_0 and S_1 indicate respectively the situation where the document is available for loan (tagged value *loan=null* in braces) or is loaned (tagged value *loan=Loan1*). Initially, the document is available (edge from the initial state, indicated as a small solid filled circle, to S_0).

Interesting information conveyed by Fig. 1.5 (left) regards the states in which method calls can be accepted. In state S_0 (document available) the only admitted operation is addLoan. It is not possible to request the removal of a loan associated to the given Document in state S_0. On the other side, when the document is loaned (state S_1), the only admitted operation is the closure of the loan (removeLoan), and no request can be accepted to borrow the given document (no call of addLoan admitted). This is consistent with the intuitive semantics of document borrowing: it makes no sense returning available documents as well as borrowing loaned documents.

The state of the objects that belong to the class User is identified by the values of the attribute loans, which records the set of loans a given library user has made. Since this attribute is a container of objects of the type Loan, it is possible to abstract its concrete values into three symbolic values: *empty* (no element in the container), *one* (exactly one element in the container) and *many* (more than one element in the container).

Fig. 1.5 (right) shows the state transitions that characterize the lifetime of the objects of class User. Initially, they are associated to no loan (edge from the small solid filled circle to S_0). In this state the removeLoan operation is not admitted, and the only possibility is to add a new loan, by invoking the method addLoan. This corresponds to the expected behavior of a User object, which initially can only be involved in borrowing documents, and not in returning them.

When the User object contains exactly one Loan (state S_1), it is possible to close it, by returning the related document (call to removeLoan) and moving it back to state S_0, or to add another loan (call to addLoan), moving it to the state S_2, which represents more than one document loaned by a given user.

Finally, in state S_2 the addition of further loans does not modify the state of the given object, while the closure of a loan (removeLoan) may either trigger the transition to state S_1, if after the removal only one loan remains, or to S_2 itself.

Similar to the class Document, some preconditions on the admitted method invocations are revealed by the state diagram for class User. In particular, no call to `removeLoan` is accepted in the state assumed by a `User` object after its creation (S_0), when no loan has yet been created by the given user.

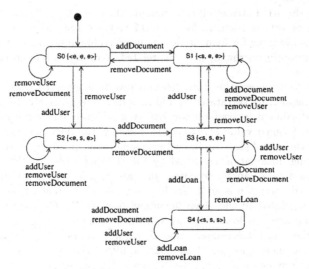

Fig. 1.6. State diagram for class `Library`.

The state of the objects of the class `Library` is characterized by the joint values assumed by the class attributes `documents`, `users` and `loans`. The attribute `documents` contains a mapping from document identifiers (`documentCode`) to the related `Document` objects stored in the library. Similarly, `users` holds the mapping from user identifiers (`userCode`) to `User` objects. Thus, they can be regarded as containers, storing documents possessed by the library and the users registered in the library.

The attribute `loans` is a container of type `Collection`, which maintains the set of currently active loans in the library. A `Loan` references the library user who requested the document as well as the borrowed document.

Since the three attributes `documents`, `users` and `loans` are containers of other objects, it is possible to abstract the values they can assume by means of two symbolic values: e, indicating an *empty* container, and s, indicating that *some* (i.e., one or more) objects are stored inside the container. Thus, the joint values of the three considered attributes is represented by a triple, such as $< e, s, e >$, whose elements correspond respectively to `documents`, `users` and `loans` (thus, $< e, s, e >$ should read *documents = empty, users = some, loans = empty*).

Fig. 1.6 shows the state diagram of class `Library`, characterized by the triples of joint values of `documents`, `users` and `loans`. When no user is yet registered and no document is available in the library, invocations of addDocument and addUser change the initial state S_0 into S_1 or S_2 respectively. Addition of a new user in S_1 or of a document in S_2 moves the library into state S_3, where some users are registered and some documents are available. Transitions among the states S_0, S_1, S_2, S_3 are achieved by calling methods addUser, removeUser, addDocument, removeDocument. No special constraint is enforced with respect to such method invocations. Of course, removal methods have no effect when containers are empty (e.g., removeDocument in state S_1).

Overall, the four topmost states in Fig. 1.6 describe the management of users and documents. The librarian can freely add/remove users and documents, changing the library state from S_0 to S_1, S_2, S_3.

Creation or deletion of a loan is possible only in state S_3, where some documents are available in the library and some users are registered. This is indicated by the absence of edges labeled addLoan in the states S_0, S_1, S_2 of the state diagram and by the presence of such an edge in the state S_3 (as well as S_4). Actually, the corresponding precondition on the invocation of addLoan is checked by the calling methods. In the source code for the *eLib* program (see Appendix A), the only invocation to addLoan is at line 61 inside borrowDocument. This call is preceded by a check to verify that the involved User object and Document object (parameters of borrowDocument obtained from the library at lines 438, 439) be not null. This ensures that no call to addLoan is issued when no related user or document data are stored in the library.

Another interesting information that can be obtained from the state diagram in Fig. 1.6 is about the methods that can be invoked in S_4. In this state, the library holds some documents, it has some registered users, and some loans are active. It is not possible to reach any of the states S_0, S_1, S_2 directly from S_4. The only reachable state is S_3, which becomes the new state of the library when all active loans are removed. In other words, the state diagram constrains the legal sequences of operations that jointly modify users, documents and loans. Before removing all of the users or documents from the library, it is necessary to close all of the active loans.

The code implements the rules described above by performing some checks before proceeding with the removal of the given item from the respective container. As regards the method removeUser, at line 17, the number of loans associated with the user being removed is requested, and if it is greater than zero, the removal operation is aborted. Similarly, inside removeDocument, at line 33 the removal operation is interrupted if the document is out (i.e., some loan is associated with it). Thus, before deleting a user, all of the related loans must be closed, i.e., users can unregister from the library only if all of the documents they borrowed have been returned. Dually, documents can be dismissed only after being returned by the users who borrowed them. These two constraints on the joint values of the attributes document, users, loans are revealed by the transitions outgoing from state S_4 in the state diagram.

State diagrams and their recovery from the source code are presented in detail in Chapter 6.

1.7 Organization of the Book

The remainder of the book describes the algorithms that can be used to produce the diagrams presented in the previous sections for the *eLib* program, starting from its source code.

Most of the static analyses used to reverse engineer these diagrams share a common representation of the code called the Object Flow Graph (OFG). Such a data structure is presented in Chapter 2. This chapter contains the rules for the construction of the OFG and introduces a generic flow propagation algorithm that can be used to infer properties about the program's objects. Specializations of the generic algorithm are defined for specific properties.

The basic algorithm for the recovery of the *class diagram* is presented at the beginning of Chapter 3. Here, the rules for the recovery of the various types of associations, such as dependencies and aggregations, are discussed. One problem of the basic algorithm for the recovery of the class diagram is that declared types are an approximation of the classes actually referenced in a program, due to inheritance and interfaces. An OFG based algorithm is described that improves the accuracy of the class diagram extracted from the source code, when classes belonging to a hierarchy or implementing interfaces are referenced by class attributes. Another problem of the basic algorithm is related to the usage of weakly typed containers. Associations determined from the types of the container declarations are in fact not meaningful, since they do not specify the type of the contained objects. It is possible to recover the information about the contained objects by exploiting a flow analysis defined on the OFG.

Chapter 4 describes a technique for the static identification of class instances (*objects*) in the code. The allocation points in the code are used to approximate the set of objects created by a program, while the OFG is used to determine the inter-object relationships. A dynamic method for the production of the object diagram is also presented. Then, the differences between static and dynamic approach are discussed.

Interaction diagrams are obtained by augmenting the object diagram with information about message exchange (method invocations). In Chapter 5, the sequence of method dispatches is considered and their ordering is represented in the two forms of the interaction diagrams: either as *collaboration diagrams*, which emphasize the message flows over the structural organization of the objects, or as *sequence diagrams*, which emphasize the temporal ordering. The numbering algorithm, used to order events temporally, is also described in this chapter. In order for the approach to scale to large systems, it is complemented by an algorithm to handle incomplete systems, and by a focusing technique that can be used to locate and visualize only the interactions of interest.

Chapter 6 deals with the partitioning of the possible values of an object's attributes into equivalence classes, vital to testing, which are approximated by means of static code analysis. The effects of method invocations on the class attributes determine the state transitions, i.e., the possibility that a given method invocation changes the state of the target object. The usage of abstract interpretation techniques for *state diagram* recovery is presented in detail in this chapter.

Chapter 7 is focused on the *package diagram*. Packages represented in the package diagram are groupings of design entities (typically classes) identified in the previous steps. The relationships that hold among such entities are abstracted into dependences among the packages they belong to. Techniques for the identification of cohesive groups of classes, including clustering and concept analysis, are presented in this chapter.

The last chapter contains some considerations on the development of tools that implement the techniques presented in the previous chapters. Then, the *eLib* program is considered once again, to describe the usage of reverse engineering after change implementation. Reverse engineered diagrams help understand the overall program organization and locate the code portions subjected to change. They are also useful after implementing the change, in that they can be compared with the initial diagrams, thus revealing the impact of the change at the design level, possibly indicating the opportunity of refactoring interventions. Furthermore, they support testing by providing information for the generation of class and integration test cases. Reverse engineered diagrams for the *eLib* program obtained after its modification are commented in this chapter. Finally, a survey of the existing support and of the current practice in reverse engineering is provided in the last section, where a discussion on the future trends and perspectives concludes the book.

All central chapters (2 through 7) have a similar structure: after a theoretical presentation of the analysis algorithms, which usually includes small code fragments used as examples, the *eLib* program is used as input for the described techniques and a step by step execution of the algorithms is conducted on this program. A discussion of related work concludes each chapter.

2

The Object Flow Graph

The Object Flow Graph (OFG) is the basic program representation for the static analysis described in the following chapters. The OFG allows tracing the flow of information about objects from the object creation by allocation statements, through object assignment to variables, up until the storage of objects in class fields or their usage in method invocations.

The kind of information that is propagated in the OFG varies, depending on the purposes of the analysis in which it is employed. For example, the type to which objects are converted by means of *cast* expressions can be the information being propagated, when an analysis is defined to statically determine a more precise object type than the one in the object declaration. Thus, in this chapter a flow propagation algorithm is described, with a generic indication of the object information being processed.

In the first section of this chapter, the Java language is simplified into an abstract language, where all features related to the object flow are maintained, while the other syntactic details are dropped. This language is the basis for the definition of the OFG, whose nodes and edges are constructed according to the rules given in Section 2.2. Objects may flow externally to the analyzed program. For example, an object may flow into a library container, from which it is later extracted. Section 2.3 deals with the representation of such external object flows in the OFG. The generic flow propagation algorithm working on the OFG is described in Section 2.4. Section 2.5 considers the differences between an object insensitive and an object sensitive OFG. Details of OFG construction are given for the *eLib* program in the next Section. A discussion of the related works concludes this chapter.

2.1 Abstract Language

The static analysis conducted on Java programs to reverse engineer design diagrams from the code is data flow sensitive, but control flow insensitive. This means that programs with different control flows and the same data flows are associated with the same analysis results. Data flow sensitivity and control flow insensitivity are achieved by defining the analyses with reference to a program representation called the Object Flow Graph (OFG). A consequence of the control flow insensitivity is that the construction of the OFG can be described with reference to a simplified, abstract version of the Java language. All Java instructions that refer to data flows are properly represented in the abstract language, while instructions that do not affect the data flows at all are safely ignored. Thus, all control flow statements (conditionals, loops, etc.) are not part of the simplified language. Moreover, in the abstract language name resolution is also simplified. All identifiers are given fully scoped name, being preceded by a dot separated list of enclosing packages, classes and methods. In this way, no name conflict can ever occur.

The choice of a data flow sensitive/control flow insensitive program representation is motivated by two main reasons: computational complexity and the "nature" of the Object Oriented programs. As discussed in Section 2.4, the theoretical computational complexity and the practical performances of control flow insensitive algorithms are substantially superior to those of the control flow sensitive counterparts. Moreover, the Object Oriented code is typically structured so as to impose more constraints on the data flows than on the control flows. For example, the sequence of method invocations may change when moving from an application which uses a class to another one, while the possible ways to copy and propagate object references remains more stable. Thus, for Object Oriented code, where the actual method invocation sequence is unknown, it makes sense to adopt control flow insensitive/data flow sensitive analysis algorithms, which preserve the way object references are handled.

Fig. 2.1 shows the abstract syntax of the simplified Java language. A Java program P consists of zero or more occurrences of declarations (D), followed by zero or more statements (S). The actual ordering of the declarations and of the statements is irrelevant, due to the control flow insensitivity. The nesting structure of packages, classes and methods is completely flattened. For example, statements belonging to different methods are not divided into separate groups. However, the full scope is explicitly retained in the names (see below). Consequently, a fine grain identification of the data elements is possible, while this is not the case for the control elements (control flow insensitivity).

Transformation of a given Java program into its abstract language representation is an easy task, that can be fully automated. Program transformation tools can be employed to achieve this aim.

2.1.1 Declarations

Declarations are of three types: attribute declarations (production (2)), method declarations (production (3)) and constructor declarations (4). An attribute declaration consists just of the fully scoped name a of the attribute, that is, a dot-separated list of packages, followed by a dot-separated list of

$$
\begin{array}{llll}
(1) & P & ::= & D^* S^* \\
(2) & D & ::= & a \\
(3) & & | & m(f_1, ..., f_k) \\
(4) & & | & cs(f_1, ..., f_k) \\
(5) & S & ::= & x = \text{new } c(a_1, ..., a_k); \\
(6) & & | & x = y; \\
(7) & & | & [x =] \, y.m(a_1, ..., a_k);
\end{array}
$$

Legend:
Metasymbols: * (repetition), | (alternative), [ ] (optional part).
Non terminals: upper case letters
Fully scoped identifiers: lower case letters
Terminals: all the other symbols

Class scoped identifiers:

a: class attribute name	$<attr>$
m: method name	$<meth>$
$f_1, ..., f_k$: formal parameters	$<param>$
x, y: program locations	$<progloc>$
$a_1, ..., a_k$: actual parameters	$<progloc>$
cs: class constructor	$<constr>$
c: class name	$<class>$

where:

$<attr>$: attribute	$[<ppref>] \, <cpref> \, <vid>$
$<meth>$: method	$[<ppref>] \, <cpref> \, <mid>$
$<param>$: parameter	$[<ppref>] \, <cpref> \, <mid> \, . \, <vid>$
$<constr>$: class constructor	$[<ppref>] \, <cpref> \, <cid> \, (. \, <cid>)^*$
$<class>$: class name	$[<ppref>] \, <cid> \, (. \, <cid>)^*$
$<locvar>$: local variable	$[<ppref>] \, <cpref> \, <mid> \, . \, <vid>$
$<progloc>$: program location	$<locvar> \, | \, <attr> \, | \, <param>$
$<ppref>$: package prefix	$<pid> \, (. \, <pid>)^* \, .$
$<cpref>$: class prefix	$<cid> \, (. \, <cid>)^* \, .$
$<pid>$: package identifier	
$<cid>$: class identifier	
$<mid>$: method identifier	
$<vid>$: variable identifier	

Fig. 2.1. Abstract syntax of the simplified Java language.

classes, followed by the attribute identifier. A method declaration consists of the fully scoped method name m (constructed similarly to the class attribute name a), followed by the list of formal parameters $f_1, ..., f_k$. In turn, each formal parameter f_i has m (the fully scoped method name) as prefix, and the parameter identifier as dot-separated suffix. Constructors have an abstract syntax similar to that of methods, with class names ($<cid>$) instead of method names ($<mid>$). Declarations do not include type information, since this is not required for OFG construction.

_____eLib example _____

Let us consider the class `Library` of the *eLib* program (see Appendix A). The abstraction of its attribute `loans`, of type `Collection` (line 6), consists just of the fully scoped attribute name:

`Library.loans`   <*attr*>

The declaration of its method `borrowDocument` (line 56) is abstracted into:

`Library.borrowDocument(Library.borrowDocument.user,`
`              Library.borrowDocument.doc)`   <*method*>

The declaration of its implicit constructor (with no argument) is abstracted into:

`Library.Library()`   <*constr*>

2.1.2 Statements

Statements are of three types (see Fig. 2.1): allocation statements (production (5)), assignment statements (production (6)) and method invocations (production (7)). The left hand side x of all statements (optional for method invocations) is a program location. The right hand side y of assignment statements, as well as the target y of method invocations, is also a program location. Program locations (<*progloc*>) are either local variables, class attributes or method parameters. The former have a structure identical to that of formal parameters: dot-separated package/class prefix, followed by a method identifier, followed by variable identifier. Chains of attribute accesses are replaced by the last field only, fully scoped (e.g., `a.b.c` becomes `B.c`, assuming `b` of class `B` and class `B` containing field `c`). The actual parameters $a_1, ..., a_k$ in allocations and method invocations are also program locations (<*progloc*>). The variable identifier (<*vid*>) that terminates a program location admits two special values: `this`, to represent the pointer to the current object, and `return`, to represent the return value of a method. Program locations (including formal and actual parameters) of non object type (e.g., `int` variables) are omitted in the chosen program representation, in that they are not associated to any object flow. Class names in allocation statements (production (5)) consist of a dot-separated list of packages followed by a dot-separated list of classes.

_____ _eLib_ example _____

The body of the second **if** statement of method `borrowDocument` (class `Library` of the _eLib_ program, lines 60-62) is represented as the following abstract lines of code:

```
Library.borrowDocument.loan =
    new Loan(Library.borrowDocument.user,
            Library.borrowDocument.doc);

Library.borrowDocument.this.
    Library.addLoan(Library.borrowDocument.loan);
```

Conditional and return statements have been skipped, and only allocations, assignments and invocations have been maintained (actually, one allocation, one invocation, and no assignment). Variable names are expanded to fully scoped names (no packages are used in this application). In the method call (second line above), the method name is prefixed by the class name. The implicit target object (**this**) is made explicit, and prefixed according to the rules for the program locations.

Return values are represented by an explicit location, which we call **return** and which is prefixed by the fully scoped method name. Thus, the values returned by `getUser` (line 42) and `getDocument` (line 43) inside method `addLoan` of class `Library` and assigned respectively to the local variables `user` and `doc` are abstractly represented as:

```
Library.addLoan.user = Loan.getUser.return;
Library.addLoan.doc  = Loan.getDocument.return;
```

Unique names are assumed for all program entities. This is the reason why in the abstract grammar, package, class, method, and variable _identifiers_ (_<pid>_, _<cid>_, _<mid>_, _<vid>_) are indicated instead of their names. Given the source of a Java program, it is always possible to transform it so as to make its names unique [30]. Names of overloaded methods belonging to the same class can be augmented with an incremented integer suffix, to make them unique. The same can be done for methods of different classes with the same name. Calling statements are transformed correspondingly. The called method(s) can be resolved with all statically type-compatible possibilities.

2.2 Object Flow Graph

The Object Flow Graph (OFG) is a pair (N, E), comprising of a set of nodes N and a set of edges E. A node is added to the OFG for each _program location_ (i.e., local variable, attribute or formal parameter, according to the definition in Fig. 2.1).

─────────────────────────eLib example ─────────────────────────

The OFG for the class `Library` of the *eLib* program contains, for example, a node associated with the class attribute `loans` (line 6), labeled:

`Library.loans`

Two nodes are associated with the formal parameters of method `borrow-Document` (line 56):

`Library.borrowDocument.user`
`Library.borrowDocument.doc`

The local variable `loan` (line 60) is associated with node:

`Library.borrowDocument.loan`

The current object inside method `borrowDocument` is also associated with an OFG node:

`Library.borrowDocument.this`

(1)	P	$::=$	$D^* S^*$	$\{\}$
(2)	D	$::=$	a	$\{\}$
(3)		|	$m(f_1, ..., f_k)$	$\{\}$
(4)		|	$cs(f_1, ..., f_k)$	$\{\}$
(5)	S	$::=$	$x = \text{new } c(a_1, ..., a_k);$	$\{(a_1, f_1) \in E, ..., (a_k, f_k) \in E, (cs.this, x) \in E\}$
(6)		|	$x = y;$	$\{(y, x) \in E\}$
(7)		|	$[x =] y.m(a_1, ..., a_k);$	$\{(y, m.this) \in E, (a_1, f_1) \in E, ..., (a_k, f_k) \in E,$ $(m.return, x) \in E\}$

Fig. 2.2. OFG edges induced by each abstract Java statement.

Edges are added to the OFG according to the rules specified in Fig. 2.2 (right). They represent the data flows occurring in the analyzed program. The set of OFG edges E contains all and only the pairs that result from at least one rule in Fig. 2.2.

When a constructor or a method are invoked (statements (5) and (7), resp.), edges are built which connect each actual parameter a_i to the respective formal parameter f_i. In case of constructor invocation, the newly created object, referenced by *cs.this* (with *cs* the constructor called by *new c(...)*), is paired with the left hand side x of the related assignment (see statement

(5)). In case of method invocation, the target object y becomes $m.this$ inside the called method, generating the edge $(y, m.this)$, and the value returned by method m (if any) flows to the left hand side x (pair $(m.return, x)$).

_____*eLib* example _____

The following invocations, taken from class Library (lines 60, 61):

```
Library.borrowDocument.loan =
        new Loan(Library.borrowDocument.user,
                Library.borrowDocument.doc);

Library.borrowDocument.this.
        Library.addLoan(Library.borrowDocument.loan);
```

generate the following OFG edges:

```
(Library.borrowDocument.user, Loan.Loan.usr)
(Library.borrowDocument.doc, Loan.Loan.doc)
(Loan.Loan.this, Library.borrowDocument.loan)
(Library.borrowDocument.this, Library.addLoan.this)
(Library.borrowDocument.loan, Library.addLoan.loan)
```

Plain assignments (statement (6) in Fig. 2.2) generate an edge that connects the right hand side to the left hand side. Thus, the following abstract statements, taken from the constructor of class Loan (lines 137-138):

```
Loan.user     = Loan.Loan.usr;
Loan.document = Loan.Loan.doc;
```

generate the following edges:

```
(Loan.Loan.usr, Loan.user)
(Loan.Loan.doc, Loan.document)
```

2.3 Containers

Edges in the OFG account for all data flows occurring in a program. While some of them are associated with specific Java instructions, such as the assignment or the method call, others may be related to the usage of library classes. Each time a library class introduces a data flow from a variable x to a variable y, an edge (x, y) must be included in the OFG.

A category of library classes that introduces additional, external data flows is represented by containers. In Java, an example is any class implementing the interface Collection, such as the classes Vector, LinkedList, HashSet, and `TreeSet`. Another example is the interface `Map`, implemented by classes `Hashtable`, `HashMap`, and `TreeMap`.

Classes implementing the `Collection` interface provide public methods to insert objects into a container and to extract objects from it. One such insertion method is `add`, while extraction can be achieved by requesting an `Iterator` object, that is successively used to sequentially access all objects in the container (method `next` in interface `Iterator`).

Classes implementing the `Map` interface offer similar facilities, with the difference that contained objects are accessed by key. Thus, method `put` can be used to insert an object and associate it to a given key, while method `get` can be used to retrieve the object associated to a given key.

Abstractly, container objects provide two basic operations that alter the data flows in a program: *insert*, to add an object to a container, and *extract*, to access an object previously inserted into a container. Thus, for a program with containers, the two basic cases that have to be handled in OFG construction are the following:

(1) *c.insert(x);*
(2) *x = c.extract();*

where c is a container and x is an object. In the first case there is a data flow from the object x to the container c, while in the second case the data flow is reversed. Correspondingly, the following edges are introduced in the OFG:

(1) *c.insert(x);* $(x, c) \in E$
(2) *x = c.extract();* $(c, x) \in E$

The same edges would be introduced in the OFG in presence of the following assignments:

(1) $c = x;$
(2) $x = c;$

For this reason, in the abstract program representation we have adopted, insertion and extraction methods associated with container objects are accounted for by transforming the related statements into assignment statements, such as those given above.

───────────────────────*eLib* example ───────────────────────

Examples of containers used in the *eLib* program are the attributes `documents`, `users`, and `loans` of the class `Library` (lines 4, 5, 6). The attribute `loans`, of type `Collection`, is initialized with a `LinkedList` object. Its method `addLoan` contains the following statement (line 44) :

```
loans.add(loan);
```

where loan is the formal parameter of the method. Its abstract syntax representation is therefore:

```
Library.loans = Library.addLoan.loan;
```

The invocation of the insertion method add on the container loans is transformed into an assignment that captures the data flow from the inserted object (loan) to the container.

An example of extraction from a container is available from the same class, method printAllLoans (lines 120-122), where the following loop is used to access the Loan objects previously inserted into the loans container:

```
Iterator i = loans.iterator();
while (i.hasNext()) {
   Loan loan = (Loan)i.next();
}
```

The related abstract representation, which preserves the data flows between container and contained objects is:

```
Library.printAllLoans.i    = Library.loans;
Library.printAllLoans.loan = Library.printAllLoans.i;
```

The first assignment accounts for the data flow from the container (loans) to the iterator (i). The second assignment accounts for the access to a contained object by means of the iterator (invocation of method next), and the assignment of this object to the local variable loan.

Another example available from the Library class is the attribute users, of type Map, initialized by a HashMap. Methods addUser (line 8) and getUser (line 21) contain respectively insertion and extraction instructions. Specifically, a User object is inserted into the container users by means of the following statement, taken from method addUser (line 10):

```
users.put(new Integer(user.getCode()), user);
```

which is transformed into the following abstract statement:

```
Library.users = Library.addUser.user;
```

Symmetrically, the following extraction statement, taken from method getUser (line 22):

```
return (User)users.get(new Integer(userCode));
```

is transformed into:

```
Library.getUser.return = Library.users;
```

In OFG construction, this is interpreted as the existence of a data flow from the container users to the value returned by the method getUser.

Other examples of external data flows possibly affecting the nodes and the edges in the OFG are associated with the usage of dynamic loading (e.g., through Java reflection) and with the access to modules written in other programming languages (e.g., through the Java native interface, JNI). In these cases, a semi-automated analysis of the data flows can still be conducted, provided that the external flows are (manually) modeled in a similar way as done above for the containers. The involvement of the user is required in the specification of the code fragments where such flows take place and of the program locations affected by them. Other language features not addressed explicitly in this section, such as exception handling and multi-threading, require minor extensions (e.g., identifying the throw-catch chains [76]) that can be fully automated.

2.4 Flow Propagation Algorithm

The OFG represents all data flows involving objects. It is thus possible to exploit it to analyze the program's behavior, by propagating proper information according to the same flows along which objects are possibly propagated. In the next chapters some examples of the kind of information to be propagated will be given. The type to which an object is cast is one such example. The allocation of an object at a given program point is another one. However, in general it can be assumed that some interesting piece of information, taken from a set V, is propagated along the OFG. Correspondingly, a flow propagation algorithm can be given, independent of the specific elements in V.

Fig. 2.3 shows the pseudocode of the generic flow propagation algorithm. It is a specific instance of the flow analysis framework described in [2], applied to the OFG instead of the control flow graph. Each node n of the OFG stores the incoming and outgoing flow information respectively inside the sets $in[n]$ and $out[n]$, which are initially empty. Moreover, each node n generates the set of flow information items contained in the $gen[n]$ set, and prevents the elements in the $kill[n]$ set from being further propagated after node n. Incoming flow information is obtained from the predecessors of node n as the union of the respective out sets (*forward* propagation). For some analyses, it may be appropriate to propagate flow information following the OFG edges in reverse order (*backward* propagation). This is obtained by collecting the incoming information from the out sets of the successors. In other words, the pseudo-statement 7 becomes:

```
1    for each node n ∈ OFG
2        in[n] = ∅
3        out[n] = gen[n] ∪ (in[n] \ kill[n])
4    end for
5    while any in[n] or out[n] changes
6        for each node n ∈ OFG
7            in[n] = ⋃_{p∈pred(n)} out[p]
8            out[n] = gen[n] ∪ (in[n] \ kill[n])
9        end for
10   end while
```

where $pred(n)$ is the set of predecessors of node n.

Fig. 2.3. Pseudocode of the flow propagation algorithm (*forward* propagation).

$$7' \qquad in[n] = \bigcup_{p \in succ(n)} out[p]$$

in case of *backward* propagation. Incoming flow information (*in[n]*) is transformed into outgoing information *out[n]* by removing the elements in the set *kill[n]* and adding those in *gen[n]*. Flow information is repeatedly propagated inside the OFG until the fixpoint is reached: no incoming and no outgoing information changes, in any OFG node.

Assuming an upper bound for the flow information propagated in the OFG, the algorithm in Fig. 2.3 is ensured to converge in polynomial time. The actual performance can be greatly improved by choosing a proper ordering of the nodes in the OFG. In absence of loops, the best ordering is the partial order induced by the graph edges. When loops are present, a good strategy consists of propagating the flow information inside the loop before considering the nodes following the loop.

The solution produced by the algorithm in Fig. 2.3 has the property of being valid for all program executions that give rise to the data flows represented in the OFG. Since the OFG has been defined in order to take into account all statically possible data flows, the resulting solution is conservative (safe), in that no data flow can ever occur at run time which is not represented by a path in the OFG. However, in general it is impossible to decide statically if a path is feasible or not (i.e., if it can actually be executed for some input). Thus, the solution produced by the algorithm might be over-conservative, in that it may permit flow propagation along infeasible paths. Consequently, if a flow information is present at a node, there *may* be an execution of the program that actually produces it, while if it is absent, it is ensured that no execution can ever produce it.

2.5 Object sensitivity

According to the abstract syntax in Fig. 2.1, class attributes, method names, program locations, etc., are scoped at the class level. This means that it is possible to distinguish two locations (e.g., two class attributes) when they belong to different classes, while this cannot be done when they belong to the same class but to different class instances (objects). In other words, the OFG constructed according to the rules given in Section 2.2 is object insensitive. While this may be satisfactory for some analyses, in some cases the ability to distinguish among locations that belong to different objects might improve the analysis results substantially.

An object sensitive OFG can be built by giving all non-static program names an object scope instead of a class scope (static attributes and program locations that belong to static methods maintain the class scope). Objects can be identified statically by their allocation points, thus, in an object sensitive OFG, non-static class attributes and methods (including their parameters and local variables) are replicated for every statically identified object. Syntactically, an object allocation point in the code is determined by statements of the kind (5) in Fig. 2.1. For each such allocation point, an object identifier is created, and all attributes and methods in the class of the allocated object are replicated for it. Replicated program locations become distinct nodes in the OFG.

Construction of the OFG edges becomes more complicated when locations are object sensitive. For example, in presence of method calls, sources and targets of OFG edges can be determined only if the current object (pointed to by this) and the objects pointed by the reference variable used as invocation target are known. Chapter 4 provides the details of an algorithm to infer such an information.

--------------------- *eLib* example ---------------------

Let us consider two statements, one from the method getUser (line 141) and the other from getDocument (line 144) of class Loan. Their abstract syntax, with class scoped names, is:

```
Loan.getUser.return     = Loan.user;
Loan.getDocument.return = Loan.document;
```

Assuming that two Loan objects are created in the program, their identifiers being Loan1 and Loan2, the two statements, with object scoped names, become:

```
Loan1.getUser.return     = Loan1.user;
Loan2.getUser.return     = Loan2.user;
Loan1.getDocument.return = Loan1.document;
Loan2.getDocument.return = Loan2.document;
```

The effect of object sensitivity on the accuracy of the OFG consists of
a finer grain edge construction, resulting in a more precise propagation of
information along the data flows. In fact, information is not mixed when
propagated along different objects, in an object sensitive OFG. Let us consider
the following code fragment, inside a hypothetical method main of class Main:

```
User u1 = new User("J. Smith", "", "");
Document d1 = new Document("The Story");
Loan l1 = new Loan(u1, d1);
Document d2 = new Document("Mother");
Loan l2 = new Loan(u1, d2);
Document doc = l1.getDocument();
```

in addition to the body of Loan.Loan (line 136) and Loan.getDocument
(line 143) represented as:

```
Loan.user              = Loan.Loan.usr;
Loan.document          = Loan.Loan.doc;
Loan.getDocument.return = Loan.document;
```

Five objects are allocated in total inside the code fragment above. We will
identify them as User1, Document1, Loan1, Document2, Loan2 respectively.

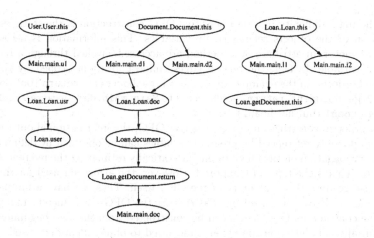

Fig. 2.4. Object insensitive OFG.

Figures 2.4 and 2.5 contrast object insensitive and object sensitive OFGs
for the code given above. Object flows in Fig. 2.5 capture the data flows
occurring in the code fragment more accurately than those in Fig. 2.4. For
example, the two variables d1 and d2 are assigned a Document object created
at two distinct allocation points. While in the OFG of Fig. 2.4 incoming

edges come from a same node (`Document.Document.this`), in Fig 2.5 the edge for the first object comes from node `Document1.Document.this` and ends at `Main.main.d1`, while the second edge goes from `Document2.Document.this` to `Main.main.d2`. In this way, the data flows related to these two objects are kept separated.

Similarly, the two `Loan` objects assigned to l1 and l2 belong to two different flows in Fig. 2.5 (bottom), while they share the same flow in Fig. 2.4. In the object sensitive OFG (Fig. 2.5), `Main.main.d1` flows into `Loan1.Loan.doc`, due to parameter passing, while `Main.main.d2` flows into `Loan2.Loan.doc`. These two flows are mixed in Fig. 2.4. When `getDocument` is called on object l1, a single location (`Loan.getDocument.return`) stores the return value in Fig. 2.4, combining both flows from `Main.main.d1` and `Main.main.d2`. On the contrary, two return locations are represented in Fig. 2.5, namely `Loan1.getDocument.return` and `Loan2.getDocument.return`. Since the call is issued on l1, and this variable can reference `Loan1` only, an OFG edge is created from `Loan1.getDocument.return` to `Main.main.doc`, but not from `Loan2.getDocument.return`.

The potential advantages of an object sensitive OFG construction are apparent from the example above. In practice, the actual benefits depend on the purposes for which the successive analysis is conducted.

The main difficulty in object sensitive OFG construction is the static estimation of the objects referenced by variables. This information is necessary whenever an attribute or a method are accessed/invoked through a reference variable. In fact, the related edges connect locations scoped by the pointed objects. In the example above, `Loan1.getDocument.return` (but not `Loan2.getDocument.return`) is connected to `Main.main.doc`, because l1 references `Loan1` (but not `Loan2`).

In order to construct an object sensitive OFG, the information about the objects possibly referenced by program variables can be obtained by defining a flow propagation on the OFG aiming at statically estimating the referenced objects. This is the topic of Chapter 4. However, the algorithm used for this purpose assumes the availability of the OFG itself. Thus, we have a mutual dependence. It can be solved by constructing the OFG edges incrementally. On the contrary, all OFG nodes can be constructed from the very beginning.

Initially, all allocations points are associated to object identifiers, used to scope the names of non-static program locations. This produces the set of all OFG nodes. As regards edges, only internal edges can be built at this stage, that is, edges involving constructor/method parameters or local variables, that are replicated for every object scope (boxes in Fig. 2.5).

Invocation of methods and access to class attributes require knowledge about the objects referenced by variables and by the special location `this`. Such information is approximated by a first round of flow propagation. At the

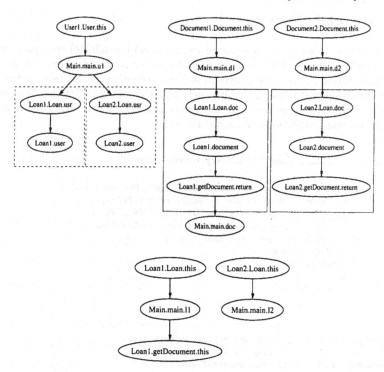

Fig. 2.5. Object sensitive OFG. Dashed (resp. solid) boxes indicate a method body replicated for each allocated object.

end of the propagation, edges can be added to the OFG for method calls and attribute accesses, using the objects pointed to by the related variables, as determined by the flow propagation. On the new version of the OFG obtained in this way, including the edges produced by the result of the previous flow propagation, a better estimate of the objects pointed by variables can be obtained. Refinement of the OFG can continue, until a stable one is produced (it should be noted that the incremental construction is monotone, in that edges are possibly added, but never removed).

Complete construction of an object sensitive OFG is possible only if the whole program is available (including the *main*), since all allocation points of all involved objects must be part of the code under analysis. In Object-Oriented programming this may not be the case, since incomplete systems are often produced and classes are often reused in different contexts. In these situations, an object insensitive OFG construction may be more appropriate.

2.6 The *eLib* Program

Let us consider the object insensitive (with no *main* available) construction of the OFG for the *eLib* program given in Appendix A. The first step consists of transforming the original program, written according to the Java syntax, into a program that respects the abstract syntax provided in Fig. 2.1. During the transformation, containers are taken into account by converting insertion and extraction instructions into assignments.

```
_____method Library.borrowDocument _____

56    public boolean borrowDocument(User user, Document doc) {
57        if (user == null || doc == null) return false;
58        if (user.numberOfLoans() < MAX_NUMBER_OF_LOANS &&
59            doc.isAvailable() && doc.authorizedLoan(user)) {
60          Loan loan = new Loan(user, doc);
61          addLoan(loan);
62          return true;
63        }
64        return false;
65    }


Library.borrowDocument(Library.borrowDocument.user,
                        Library.borrowDocument.doc)
Library.borrowDocument.user.numberOfLoans();
Library.borrowDocument.doc.isAvailable();
Library.borrowDocument.doc.authorizedLoan(Library.borrowDocument.user);
Library.borrowDocument.loan = new Loan(Library.borrowDocument.user,
                                        Library.borrowDocument.doc);
Library.borrowDocument.this.addLoan(Library.borrowDocument.loan);
```

Fig. 2.6. Concrete (top) and abstract (bottom) syntax of method borrowDocument from class Library.

Fig. 2.6 shows the translation of method borrowDocument from class Library (line 56) into its abstract representation. An abstract declaration of the method is generated first. The method name is prefixed by the class name, and all parameter names are fully scoped, being prefixed by class and method name. Then, abstract statements are generated only for statements that involve object flows. Thus, the first conditional statement is skipped. From the second conditional statement, only the method invocations contained in the condition need be transformed. Correspondingly, the abstract representation contains the invocation of numberOfLoans (class User), isAvailable (class Document), and authorizedLoan (class Document). Targets of these invocations are parameters of borrowDocument. They are abstracted into their fully

—————————————————method `Library.addLoan`—————————————————

```
40      private void addLoan(Loan loan) {
41        if (loan == null) return;
42        User user = loan.getUser();
43        Document doc = loan.getDocument();
44        loans.add(loan);
45        user.addLoan(loan);
46        doc.addLoan(loan);
47      }
```

```
Library.addLoan(Library.addLoan.loan)
Library.addLoan.user = Library.addLoan.loan.getUser();
Library.addLoan.doc = Library.addLoan.loan.getDocument();
Library.loans = Library.addLoan.loan;
Library.addLoan.user.addLoan(Library.addLoan.loan);
Library.addLoan.doc.addLoan(Library.addLoan.loan);
```

—————————————————method `User.addLoan`—————————————————

```
314     public void addLoan(Loan loan) {
315        loans.add(loan);
316     }
```

```
User.addLoan(User.addLoan.loan)
User.loans = User.addLoan.loan;
```

—————————————————method `Document.addLoan`—————————————————

```
202     public void addLoan(Loan ln) {
203        loan = ln;
204     }
```

```
Document.addLoan(Document.addLoan.ln)
Document.loan = Document.addLoan.ln;
```

Fig. 2.7. Concrete and abstract syntax of methods `addLoan` from classes `Library`, `User` and `Document`.

scoped names. The same holds for the actual parameter of `authorizedLoan` (see Fig. 2.6).

The next statement that is abstracted is the allocation of a `Loan` object (line 60). The local variable to which the allocated object is assigned is fully scoped, similarly to the method parameters. Finally, the call to method `addLoan` (line 61) from the same class (`Library`) is given an abstract representation in which the target of the call is the special location `this`, indicating explicitly that the method is called on the current object.

Other abstractions for the *eLib* program are reported in Fig. 2.7. Note that the same method name `addLoan` has been left in more than one class, instead of introducing method identifiers (such as addLoan1, addLoan2, addLoan3), just to improve the readability. However, method calls are assumed to be uniquely solved when OFG edges are constructed (e.g., the statement at line 45 inside Library.addLoan is a call to User.addLoan, while the statement at line 46 is a call to Document.addLoan).

Methods getUser and getDocument, invoked inside addLoan in class Library (lines 42, 43), have a return value, which is assigned to a left hand side variable. Correspondingly, their abstract representations are assignments with the invocation in the right hand side and the fully scoped variable as left hand side (see Fig. 2.7). The method add is called at line 44 on the class attribute loans, a Collection type object. Since this is an insertion method, the related abstract representation is an assignment with the parameter of the call (loan) on the right hand side, and the container (loans) on the left hand side. It should be noted that the fully scoped name of the class attribute loans consists of class name and attribute name only. The last two calls inside Library.addLoan are similar to the first two ones, without any return value.

The body of method addLoan from class User is transformed (see Fig. 2.7) into an assignment, associated with a container insertion, where the container is the attribute loans (of type Collection) of class User. Finally, the body of method addLoan from class Document is abstracted into an assignment with the fully scoped method's parameter on the right hand side and the class field loan on the left hand side.

Transforming the remainder of the *eLib* program into its abstract syntax representation is quite straightforward, along the lines given above for the examples in Fig 2.6 and 2.7. Once the program's abstraction is completed, it is possible to construct the OFG by applying the rules in Fig. 2.2.

Fig. 2.8 shows the OFG nodes and edges that are induced by the abstract code in Fig. 2.6 and 2.7. The number labeling each edge refers to the statement that generates it. Method calls cause an edge whose target is a this location (properly prefixed). For example, the first two statements (following the declaration) in the abstract code of Fig. 2.6 (method calls: numberOfLoans() and isAvailable() at lines 58 and 59) generate respectively the edges (Library.borrowDocument.user, User.numberOfLoans.this) and (Library.borrowDocument.doc, Document.isAvailable.this), labeled 58 and 59. Parameter passing induces edges that end at formal parameter locations. For example, the third abstract statement in Fig. 2.6 (associated with line 59) is a call to the method authorizedLoan with actual parameter Library.borrowDocument.user and formal parameter Document.authorizedLoan.user. Correspondingly, in Fig. 2.8 the topmost edge labeled 59 connects these two locations.

Allocation statements, such as the fourth abstract statement in Fig. 2.6 (line 60), induce edges between actual and formal parameters, similarly to method calls. In addition, they induce an edge between the constructor's this location and the left hand side location. In our example, Loan.Loan.this

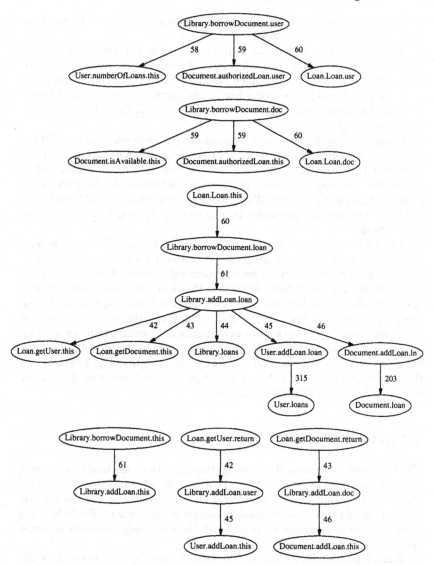

Fig. 2.8. OFG associated with the abstract code in Fig. 2.6 (method `borrowDocument` in class `Library`) and 2.7 (method `addLoan` in classes `Library`, `User`, `Document`).

and the allocation's left hand side variable, `Library.borrowDocument.loan` (Fig. 2.8 center, edge labeled 60).

An example of a method call with a return value is provided by the first abstract statement (after the declaration) of method `Library.addLoan` (see Fig. 2.7 top, line 42). The left hand side location (`Library.addLoan.user`) is the target of an edge outgoing from `Loan.getUser.return`, the location associated with the value returned by the method call (see Fig. 2.8 bottom, edge labeled 42).

Container operations are also responsible for some edges in the OFG of Fig. 2.8. For example, the body of `User.addLoan` contains just an insertion statement (line 315). The container `User.loans`, into which a `Loan` object is inserted, becomes the target of an edge starting at the inserted object location, `User.addLoan.loan` (Fig. 2.8 center, edge labeled 44). This indicates an object flow from the parameter `loan` of method `addLoan` into the container `User.loans`.

The OFG constructed for the code in Fig. 2.6 and 2.7 shows the data flows through which objects are propagated from location to location. Thus, the parameter `user` of method `borrowDocument` becomes the current object (`this`) inside `numberOfLoans`, while it is the parameter `user` inside method `authorizedLoan` and it is the parameter `usr` inside the constructor of class `Loan`, as depicted at the top of Fig 2.8. Similarly, the other parameter of `borrowDocument`, `doc`, flows into `isAvailable` and `authorizedLoan` as `this`, and into the constructor of class `Loan` as the parameter `doc`. The object of class `Document` returned by `Loan.getDocument` (bottom-right of Fig. 2.8) flows into the local variable `doc` of `Library.addLoan`, and then becomes the current object (`this`) inside `Document.addLoan`.

2.7 Related Work

The OFG and the related flow propagation algorithms are based on research conducted on pointer analysis [3, 21, 47, 49, 60, 68, 81, 86]. The aim of pointer analysis is to obtain a static approximation of any points-to relationship that may hold at run-time between pointers and program locations. Similarly, when Object-Oriented programs are considered, the relationship between reference variables and objects is analyzed.

Pointer analysis algorithms can be divided into flow/context sensitive [21, 47, 60] and flow/context insensitive [3, 81]. Flow/context sensitive algorithms produce fine grained and accurate results, in that a points-to relationship is determined that holds at every program statement. Moreover, different invocation contexts can be distinguished. However, the computational complexity involved in these approaches is high, and in practice their performance does not scale to large software systems. Flow/context insensitive algorithms have lower complexity and scale well. On the other side, they produce results that hold for the whole program, and the points-to relationships they derive cannot be distinguished by statement or invocation context. Flow/context sensitive analyses are defined with reference to the control flow graph [2] of a program, while flow/context insensitive algorithms define the analysis semantics at the statement level.

The algorithm most similar to ours is [3]. Originally described for the C language, it has been recently extended to Java [49, 68]. Differently from the approach followed in this book, no explicit data structure, such as the OFG, is used in [3] as a support for the flow propagation: data flows are represented as set-inclusion constraints.

The improvement of a control flow insensitive pointer analysis obtained by introducing object sensitivity was proposed in [57], where the possibility of parameterizing the degree of object sensitivity is also discussed.

3

Class Diagram

The class diagram is the most important and most widely used description of an Object Oriented system. It shows the static structure of the core classes that are used to build a system. The most relevant features (attributes and methods) of each class are provided in the class diagram, together with the optional indication of some of their properties (visibility, type, etc.). Moreover, the class diagram shows the relationships that hold among the classes in a system. This gives a static view of the structural connections that have been designed to allow communication and interaction among the classes. Thus, the class diagram provides a very informative summary of many design decisions about the system's organization.

Recovery of the class diagram from the source code is a difficult task. The decision about what elements to show/hide profoundly affects the usability of the diagram. Moreover, interclass relationships carry semantic information that cannot be inferred just from the analysis of the code, being strongly dependent on the domain knowledge and on the design rationale.

A basic algorithm for the recovery of the class diagram can be obtained by a purely syntactic analysis of the source code, provided that a precise definition of the interclass relationships is given. For example, an association can be inferred when a class attribute stores a reference to another class. One problem of the basic algorithm for the recovery of the class diagram is that declared types are an approximation of the classes actually instantiated in a program, due to inheritance and interfaces. An OFG based algorithm can be defined to improve the accuracy of the class diagram extracted from the code, in presence of subclassing and interface implementation. Another problem of the basic algorithm is related to the usage of weakly typed containers. Associations determined from the types of the container declarations are in fact not meaningful, since they do not specify the type of the contained objects. It is possible to recover information about the contained objects by exploiting a flow analysis defined on the OFG.

The basic rules for the reverse engineering of the class diagram are given in Section 3.1. Accuracy of the associations in presence of inheritance and in-

terfaces is discussed in Section 3.2, where an algorithm is provided to improve
the results of a purely syntactic analysis. The problems related to the usage
of weakly typed containers and an OFG based algorithm to address them are
described in Section 3.3. Recovery of the class diagram is conducted on the
eLib application in Section 3.4. Related works are discussed in the last section
of this chapter.

3.1 Class Diagram Recovery

The elements displayed in a class diagram are the classes in the system under
analysis. Internal class features, such as attributes and methods, can be also
displayed. Properties of the displayed features, as, for example, the type of
attributes, the parameters of methods, their visibility and scope (object vs.
class scope), can be indicated as well. This information can be directly obtained by analyzing the syntax of the source code. Available tools for Object
Oriented design typically offer a facility for the recovery of class diagrams
from the code, which include this kind of syntactic information.

_____*eLib* example _____

User
userCode: int
fullName: String
address: String
phoneNumber: String
loans: Collection
nextUserCodeAvailable: int

User(name: String, addr: String, phone: String)
equals(obj: Object): boolean
authorizedUser(): boolean
getCode(): int
getName(): String
getAddress(): String
getPhone(): String
addLoan(loan: Loan)
numberOfLoans(): int
removeLoan(loan: Loan)
printInfo()

Fig. 3.1. Information gathered from the code of class User.

Fig. 3.1 shows the UML representation recovered from the source code of
class User, belonging to the *eLib* example (see Appendix A). The first compartment below the class name shows the attributes (userCode, fullName,
etc.). Static attributes (nextUserCodeAvailable) are underlined. Class op-

erations are in the bottom compartment. The first entry is the constructor, while the other methods provide the exported functionalities of this class.

Relationships among classes are used to indicate either the presence of abstraction mechanisms or the possibility of accessing features of another class. Generalization and realization relationships are examples of abstraction mechanisms commonly used in Object Oriented programming that can be shown in a class diagram. Aggregation, association and dependency relationships are displayed in a class diagram to indicate that a class has access to resources (attributes or operations) from another class.

A *generalization* relationship connects two classes when one inherits features (attributes and methods) from the other. The subclass can add further features and can redefine inherited methods (overriding). A *realization* relationship connects a class to an interface if the class implements all methods declared in the interface. Users of this class are ensured that the operations in the realized interface are actually available.

Generalization and realization relationships satisfy the substitutability principle: in every place in the program where a location of the superclass/interface type is declared and used, an instance of any sublass/class realizing the interface can actually occur.

Relationships of access kind hold between pairs of classes each time one class possesses a way to reference the other. Conceptually, access relationships can be categorized by relative strength. A quite strong relationship is the *aggregation*. A class is related to another class by an aggregation relationship if the latter is a part-of the former. This means that the existence of an object of the first class requires that one or more objects of the other class do also exist, in that they are an integral part of the first object. Participants in aggregation relationships may have their own independent life, but it is not possible to conceive the whole (first class) without adding also the parts (second class). An even stronger relationships is the *composition*. It is a form of aggregation in which the parts and the whole have the same lifetime, in that the parts, possibly created later, can not survive after the death of the whole.

A weaker relationship among classes than the aggregation is the *association*. Two classes are connected by a (bidirectional) association if there is the possibility to navigate from an object instantiating the first class to an object instantiating the second class (and vice versa). Unidirectional associations exist when only one-way navigation is possible. Navigation from an object to another one requires that a stable reference exists in the first object toward the other one. In this way, the second object can be accessed at any time from the first one.

An even weaker relationship among classes is the *dependency*. A dependency holds between two classes if any change in one class (the target of the dependency) might affect the dependent class. The typical case is a class that uses resources from another class (e.g., invoking one of its methods). Of course, aggregation and association are subsumed by dependency.

3.1.1 Recovery of the inter-class relationships

From the implementation point of view, there is no substantial difference between aggregation and association. Both relationships are typically implemented as a class attribute referencing other objects. Attributes of container type are used whenever the multiplicity of the target objects is greater than one. In principle, there would be the possibility to approximately distinguish between composition and aggregation, by analyzing the life time of the referenced objects. However, in practice implementations of the two relation variants have a large overlap.

In the implementation, dependencies that are not associations or aggregations can be distinguished from the latter ones because they are accesses to features of another class performed through program locations that, differently from class attributes, are less stable. For example, a local variable or a method parameter may be used to access an object of another class and invoke one of its methods. In such cases, the reference to the accessed object is not stable, being stored in a temporary variable. Nevertheless, any change in the target class potentially affects the user class, thus there is a dependency.

Relationships	*Code*
Association/aggregation `A` → `B`	Class attribute: `class A { B b; }`

Dependency
`A` --→ `B`
	Local variable/parameter:
	
	`class A { void f(B b) {b.g();} }`
	`class A { void f() {B b; ... b.g();} }`

Generalization `A` —▷ `B`	 `class A extends B {...}`
Realization `A` --▷ `B`	 `class A implements B {...}`

Table 3.1. Reverse engineering of inter-class relationships.

Table 3.1 summarizes the inter-class relationships and the rules for their recovery. Generalization and realization are easily determined from the class declaration, by looking for the keywords **extends** and **implements**, respectively. The declared type of the program locations (attributes, local variables, method parameters) involved in associations (including aggregations) and dependencies is used to infer the target of such relationships. In the next two sections we will see that this simple method may potentially give rise to in-accuracies in the presence of inheritance, interfaces or containers. Improved class diagrams can be obtained by refining the declared type into more precise information by means of flow propagation in the OFG.

_____*eLib* example _____

In the *eLib* example (see Appendix A), class **Loan** has two association relationships with classes **User** and **Document**, which can be easily reverse engineered from its code given the presence of two attributes, **user** and **document** (lines 134, 135), of the two target classes. Conceptually, they could be regarded as aggregations, rather than associations, in that a loan has a user and a bor-rowed document as its integral constituents. However, from the analysis of the source code there is no way to distinguish this case from the plain association. In the following, no distinction is made between aggregation and association, and the latter will be used as possibly inclusive of the former.

The class **Library** performs method invocations on objects of class **User** and **Document** through parameters (resp. at line 10 inside **addUser** and at line 26 inside **addDocument**) or local variables (resp. at line 17 inside **removeUser** and at line 33 inside **removeDocument**). Thus, there is a depen-dency between **Library** and **User**, and between **Library** and **Document**.

_____

3.2 Declared vs. actual types

The declared type of attributes, local variables and method parameters is used to determine the target class of associations and dependencies. It is quite typical that the declared type is the root of a sub-tree in the inheritance hierarchy or it is an interface. For example, attributes **user** and **document** of class **Loan** in the *eLib* program are respectively declared to be of type **User**, which has **InternalUser** as a subclass, and **Document**, which has **Book**, **Journal**, and **TechnicalReport** as subclasses. A hypothetical *binary search tree* program may contain a class **BinaryTreeNode** with an attribute **obj** to store the information to be associated with each tree node. Its declared type could be **Comparable**, i.e., the interface implemented by objects that can be totally ordered by means of the method **compareTo**.

When the declared type is the root of an inheritance sub-tree, an associa-tion or dependency is inferred from the given class to the root of the sub-tree. In the *eLib* example, two of the inferred relationships connect **Loan** to **User** and Document. If the application program uses only a portion of the inheritance sub-tree, the target of the association/dependency is inaccurate. A more precise target class would consist of the classes of the actually allocated objects. For example, if in a specific instance of the library application only documents of type Book are handled, an association should connect Loan to Book instead of Document.

The problem is exacerbated with interfaces. Let us consider the *binary search tree* example sketched above. The presence of an attribute obj of type Comparable would generate an association from BinaryTreeNode to Comparable. Since the interface Comparable is not user-defined, such an association is typically not included in the class diagram of the system, since only relationships among user-defined classes are of interest. Let us assume that the application program using the binary search tree defines a class Student which implements the interface Comparable. Objects of type Student are allocated in the program and are assigned to the field obj of BinaryTreeNode objects. In the class diagram for this application, one would expect to see an association from BinaryTreeNode to Student. If the basic reverse engineering method described in Section 3.1 is applied, no such association is actually recovered from the code. Thus, usage of an interface as the type of a class field results in an inaccurate recovery of the class diagram.

In general, there might be a mismatch between the type declared for a program location and the actual types of the objects that are possibly assigned to such a location. In fact, the declared type might be a superclass of, or an interface implemented by, the actual object types. In these cases, a precise recovery of the class diagram can be achieved only by determining the type of the actually allocated objects that are possibly referenced by the program locations under analysis. The flow propagation algorithm presented in Chapter 2 can be used for this purpose.

3.2.1 Flow propagation

Specialization of the generic flow propagation algorithm to refine the declared type of variables requires the specification of the sets *gen* and *kill* of each OFG node. Fixpoint of the flow information on the OFG is achieved by the generic procedure given in Chapter 2. Fig. 3.2 shows how the *gen* set is determined for the OFG nodes. Only nodes of type *cs.this* have non empty *gen* set. All other OFG nodes have an empty *gen* set. All *kill* sets are empty in this analysis specialization.

Given an object allocation such as statement (5) of Fig. 3.2, the flow information that has to be propagated in the OFG is the exact type of the allocated object. This is the reason why the class name c is inserted into the *gen* set. The OFG location where the propagation of this flow information starts is the this pointer of the constructor. In fact, that is the very first location holding a reference to the newly allocated object. Thanks to the OFG edges, constructed according to the algorithm described in Chapter 2, this

$$
\begin{array}{llll}
(1) & P & ::= & D^*S^* \\
(2) & D & ::= & a \\
(3) &   & \mid & m(f_1, ..., f_k) \\
(4) &   & \mid & cs(f_1, ..., f_k) \\
(5) & S & ::= & x = \text{new } c(a_1, ..., a_k); \quad gen[cs.this] = \{c\} \\
(6) &   & \mid & x = y; \\
(7) &   & \mid & [x =] \ y.m(a_1, ..., a_k);
\end{array}
$$

where in (5) cs is the invoked constructor for class c.
$gen[n] = \emptyset$ for all locations different from $cs.this$
$kill[n] = \emptyset$ for all locations

Fig. 3.2. Flow propagation specialization to determine the type of actually allocated objects referenced by program locations.

information is propagated to the right hand side x of the allocation statement (5), and from this location it can reach other program locations, according to the object flows. In the end, the class names that reach class attributes indicate the improved targets of association relationships. Similarly, the class names associated with local variables or method parameters allow the refinement of dependency relationships.

3.2.2 Visualization

Since flow propagation in the OFG according to the specialization in Fig. 3.2 results in a set of referenced object types for each program location, instead of a single type, a postprocessing that simplifies the output might be appropriate. Each time the types inferred for a location x, and available from $out[x]$ after the fixpont, are coincident with all descendants of a user-defined class A, a single relationship can be produced toward class A, which is assumed to imply a relationship with all subclasses. In this way, the class diagram is not cluttered by relationships toward all subclasses. However, the disadvantage of this graphical representation is that it makes it impossible to distinguish between a relationship with class A only and a relationship with A and all its subclasses.

In the *eLib* example, if the result of flow propagation is: $out[\texttt{Loan.user}]$ = {User, InternalUser}, it is possible to draw just one association in the class diagram, between Loan and User. However, this makes the diagram indistinguishable from one produced for a program where no InternalUser is ever allocated. Such an inaccuracy becomes acceptable when the diagram is large and drawing relationships toward all subclasses makes it not understandable and usable. Otherwise, the diagram with more precise relationships should be preferred.

As a general rule, when several relationships are directed from a class to a set of classes, an option to reduce the visual cluttering is replacing them with a single relationship toward the Least Common Ancestor (LCA) of the target classes. The diagram becomes less precise but easier to read.

_____*binary search tree* example _____

The importance of applying the flow propagation algorithm to determine the targets of associations and dependencies becomes even more evident when interfaces are used in the program. Let us consider the *binary tree* example once more. The code fragments relevant to our analysis are the following:

```
class BinaryTreeNode {
  BinaryTreeNode left, right;
  Comparable obj;
  public BinaryTreeNode(Comparable x) {
    obj = x;
  }
  ...
}
class UniversityAdmin {
  static BinaryTree students = new BinaryTree();
  ...
  public static addStudent(Student s) {
    BinaryTreeNode n = new BinaryTreeNode(s);
    students.insert(n);
  }
  public static void main(String args[]) {
    ...
    Student s = new Student("J. Smith");
    addStudent(s);
    ...
  }
}
```

The abstract syntax of the statements above follows:

```
BinaryTreeNode.obj = BinaryTreeNode.BinaryTreeNode.x;
UniversityAdmin.students = new BinaryTree();
UniversityAdmin.addStudent.n =
             new BinaryTreeNode(UniversityAdmin.addStudent.s);
UniversityAdmin.students.insert(UniversityAdmin.addStudent.n);
UniversityAdmin.main.s = new Student();
UniversityAdmin.addStudent(UniversityAdmin.main.s);
```

The related OFG is shown in Fig. 3.3. The only non empty *gen* sets of its nodes are:

gen[Student.Student.this] = {Student}
gen[BinaryTreeNode.BinaryTreeNode.this] = {BinaryTreeNode}
gen[BinaryTree.BinaryTree.this] = {BinaryTree}

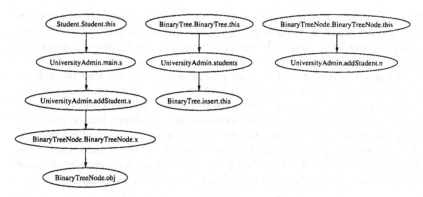

Fig. 3.3. OFG for the binary search tree example.

After flow propagation, the following *out* set is determined for the attribute obj of class BinaryTreeNode:

$$out[\texttt{BinaryTreeNode.obj}] = \{\texttt{Student}\}$$

Thus, an association can be drawn in the class diagram from BinaryTreeNode to Student. On the contrary, the analysis of the declared type would miss completely this interclass relationship, because the declared type of BinaryTreeNode.obj is Comparable.

As apparent from the example above, the declared types of variables are a good starting point to infer the relationships that hold among the user-defined classes represented in a class diagram. However, they may lead to imprecise diagrams, where some of the existing relationships are absent. One of the main reasons for the inaccuracy is the declaration of program locations whose type is an interface. In this case, the declared type is not very informative. An OFG based analysis of the actual object types can be used to obtain a more accurate class diagram.

3.3 Containers

Containers are classes that implement a data structure to store, manage, and access other objects. Classical examples of such data structures are: list, tree, graph, vector, hash table, etc. *Weakly typed* containers are containers that collect objects the type of which is not declared. With the current version of Java, that does not yet support genericity, all containers are weakly typed.

Thus, an object x of type List that is used to store objects from class A is declared as: "List x;", without any explicit mention of the contained object type, A. Knowledge about the kind of objects that can be inserted into x and that are retrieved from x is not part of the program's syntax.

Weakly typed containers expose programmers to errors that are not detected at compile time, and are typically due to a wrong type assumed for contained objects. Moreover, they make reverse engineering a difficult task. In fact, interclass relationships, such as associations and dependencies, are determined from the type declared for attributes, local variables and parameters. When containers are involved, the relationships to recover should connect the given class to the classes of the contained objects. However, information about the contained object classes is not directly available in the program.

─────────────────────────────eLib example─────────────────────────────

Let us consider the eLib example. Class Library has an attribute loans (line 6) of declared type Collection, and two attributes, users and documents (lines 4, 5), of type Map. Since both Collection and Map are interfaces, the algorithm described in Section 3.2 can be applied to determine a more accurate type for these class attributes. The result does not help reverse engineer the associations implemented through these attributes. In fact, the classes that implement the Collection and Map interfaces and are actually used for the corresponding attributes of class Library are respectively LinkedList and HashMap, that is, two weakly typed containers. Since HashMap and LinkedList are library classes, no relationship is drawn in the class diagram for them (only user defined classes are considered). However, a closer inspection of the source code reveals that the attribute documents holds the mapping between a document code and the corresponding Document object. Similarly, the attribute users associates a user code to the related User object. The attribute loans stores the list of all active loans of the library, represented as objects of the class Loan. Thus, three association relationships are missed when only declared types are considered, one between Library and Document, another one between Library and User, and a third one between Library and Loan. Correspondingly, the reverse engineered class diagram is very poor and does not show important information such as the way to access the Document objects managed by the Library, the library users (User objects), and the loans (missing association with class Loan).

───

3.3.1 Flow propagation

It is possible to define a specialization of the flow propagation algorithm presented in Chapter 2, aimed at estimating the type of the contained objects for weakly typed containers. The basic idea is that before insertion into a container each object has to be allocated, and allocation requires the full specification of the object type. Symmetrically, after extraction from a container each object has to be constrained to a specific type, in order to be manipulated with type-dependent operations. Flow propagation of the pre-insertion and post-extraction type information results in a static approximation of the contained object types. Such information can be used to refine the class diagrams extracted from the code, by recovering some of the otherwise missing relations between classes.

Container classes offer two basic functionalities to user classes: *insertion* methods, to store objects into the container, and *extraction* methods, to retrieve objects out of a container. During OFG construction, these functionalities are abstracted by the two methods *insert* and *extract*. Their effects on the object flows are accounted for by replacing their invocations with assignment statements, equivalent to the method calls from the point of view of the data flows (see Chapter 2, Section 2.3).

Given the OFG produced by taking container flows into account, a specialization of the flow propagation algorithm to determine the type of the contained objects is obtained by defining *gen* and *kill* sets of each OFG node. Two different kinds of flow information can be used to infer the type of contained objects: the type of *inserted* objects can be obtained from their allocation, while the type of *extracted* objects can be obtained from their type coercion. For example, (abstract) statements such as "$x = new\ A();\ c.insert(x);$" can be exploited to estimate the contained object type as that of the allocation, while the coerced type in a statement such as "$x = (A)c.extract();$", where "(A)" is the syntax for type coercion, can be exploited to associate type A to container c. Correspondingly, two executions of the flow propagation algorithm have to be conducted, with two different sets of *gen* and *kill* sets associated with OFG nodes. Moreover, the direction of flow propagation changes when insertion vs. extraction information is used.

$$
\begin{array}{llll}
(1) & P & ::= & D^* S^* \\
(2) & D & ::= & a \\
(3) & & | & m(f_1, ..., f_k) \\
(4) & & | & cs(f_1, ..., f_k) \\
(5) & S & ::= & x = new\ c(a_1, ..., a_k); \quad gen[cs.this] = \{c\} \\
(6) & & | & x = y; \\
(7) & & | & x = y.m(a_1, ..., a_k); \\
\end{array}
$$

where in (5) cs is the invoked constructor for class c.
$gen[n] = \emptyset$ for all other locations
$kill[n] = \emptyset$ for all locations

Fig. 3.4. Flow propagation specialization to determine the type of objects stored inside weakly typed containers, accounting for object insertions and based on allocation information. Forward propagation.

Fig. 3.4 provides the *gen* and *kill* sets to use when the contained object type is estimated from insertion information. Object allocation statements provide the precise type of allocated objects. This information is propagated from object constructors to the containers, according to the fixpoint algorithm described in Chapter 2. The direction of propagation is forward, so that incoming information of each node ($in[n]$) is obtained from the predecessors. It can be noted that the same flow analysis specialization has been used to refine associations when declared types are superclasses of actual types or interfaces (see Fig. 3.2).

(1)	P	::=	$D^* S^*$	
(2)	D	::=	a	
(3)		$\mid$	$m(f_1, ..., f_k)$	
(4)		$\mid$	$cs(f_1, ..., f_k)$	
(5)	S	::=	$x = \text{new } c(a_1, ..., a_k);$	
(6)		$\mid$	$x = (c)y;$	$gen[y] = \{c\}$
(7)		$\mid$	$x = (c)y.m(a_1, ..., a_k);$	$gen[m.return] = \{c\}$

where (c) indicates type coercion.
$gen[n] = \emptyset$ for all other locations
$kill[n] = \emptyset$ for all locations

Fig. 3.5. Flow propagation specialization to determine the type of objects stored inside weakly typed containers, accounting for object extractions and based on type coercion. Backward propagation.

Fig. 3.5 gives *gen* and *kill* sets for the second execution of the flow propagation algorithm, exploiting extraction information. The abstract syntax given in Chapter 2 has been enriched with a type coercion operator, "*()*". Each time a type coercion occurs on a program location or on the value returned by a method, the related type information is generated at the corresponding OFG node. In order to reach the container from which an object has been extracted, this type information has to be propagated *backward* in the OFG, that is, from the successors of a node to the node itself. In fact, type coercion occurs after an object has flown out of a container up to a given location. Such data flow has to be reversed to propagate the coerced type back to the container.

After the two flow propagations are complete, the two respective *out* sets of each container location hold the contained object types computed by the two specializations described above. The union of these two *out* sets gives the final results, i.e., the set of types estimated for the contained objects. If several classes from an inheritance subtree are included in the *out* set of a container, it may be appropriate to replace them with the LCA, thus reducing the number of connections among entities in the class diagram, and improving its readability.

_____*eLib* example _____

Let us consider the *eLib* program in Appendix A, and in particular, let us focus on methods `addUser` (line 8) and `searchDocumentByTitle` (line 90) of class `Library`. Their abstract statements are respectively:

```
Library.users = Library.addUser.user;
```

where the assignment has been obtained by transforming the insertion method put invoked on `Library.users` at line 10, and:

```
Library.searchDocumentByTitle.i = Library.documents;
Library.searchDocumentByTitle.doc =
                (Document)Library.searchDocumentByTitle.i;
Library.searchDocumentByTitle.doc.getTitle();
Library.searchDocumentByTitle.docsFound =
                Library.searchDocumentByTitle.doc;
Library.searchDocumentByTitle.return =
                Library.searchDocumentByTitle.docsFound;
```

where the first and second assignments are the result of transforming invocations of extraction methods (`iterator` at line 92 and `next` at line 94, resp.), while the fourth assignment results from the conversion of an insertion (invocation of `add` on `docsFound` at line 96). For completeness, let us consider a code fragment from class `Main` (Appendix B), that performs a user insertion into the library:

```
347      class Main {
348          static Library lib = new Library();
             ...
379          public static void addUser(String cmd) {
             ...
382              User user = new User(args[0], args[1], args[2]);
383              lib.addUser(user);
                 ...
386          }
             ...
536      }
```

The abstract statements of this code fragment are:

```
Main.lib = new Library();
Main.addUser.user = new User();
Main.lib.addUser(Main.addUser.user);
```

Fig. 3.6 shows (a portion of) the OFG associated with the abstract statements above. Sets *gen1* and *gen2* have been obtained according to the rules in Fig. 3.4 and 3.5 respectively. Thus, *gen1* is used during the first, forward propagation, while *gen2* is used in the second, backward flow propagation. The cumulative result is:

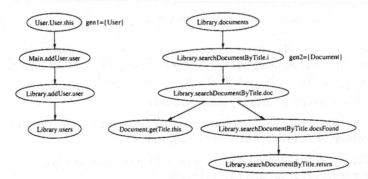

Fig. 3.6. OFG for a portion of the *eLib* program. Set *gen1* is used during forward flow propagation, while *gen2* is used for backward propagation.

```
out[Library.users] = {User}
out[Library.documents] = {Document}
```

This allows a precise estimation of the contained object types. The attribute **users** of class **Library** contains objects of type **User**, so that an association can be drawn in the class diagram between **Library** and **User**. Similarly, the class attribute **documents** has been found to contain objects of type **Document**, resulting in the recovery of an association between **Library** and **Document**. Both associations are completely missed if container analysis is not performed.

3.4 The *eLib* Program

Fig. 3.7 shows the class diagram obtained by applying the basic reverse engineering method described in Section 3.1, which takes only declared types into account, to the *eLib* program. Since typically interconnections due to dependencies that are not associations tend to make the class diagram less readable, they have not been considered in Fig. 3.7. Only the two most important interclass relationships, associations and generalizations, are displayed. Moreover, class attributes and methods are hidden, to simplify the view, and only class names are shown.

Apparently, the class **Library** holds no stable reference toward the other classes in the system. In fact, it is an isolated node in Fig. 3.7. This is due to the usage of Java containers to implement associations with multiplicity greater than one. Specifically, its fields **documents**, **users** and **loans** are

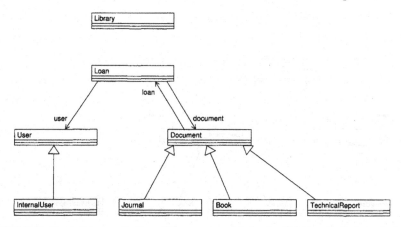

Fig. 3.7. Class diagram for the *eLib* program, obtained without container analysis.

Java containers (the declared type is the interface Map for the first two, and Collection for the latter).

A bidirectional association exists between classes Loan and Document, in that a Loan object holds a reference toward the borrowed Document object, and vice versa, a borrowed Document has access to the Loan object with data about the loan. While one would expect a similar bidirectional association between Loan and User, such a connection seems to be unidirectional, according to the class diagram in Fig. 3.7. The reason for the missing association between User and Loan is that the related multiplicity is greater than 1 (a user can borrow several documents). From the implementation point of view, the problem is the usage of a container (actually, a Collection) for the field loans of class User. On the contrary, since a document can be borrowed by exactly one user, the association from Document to Loan has the multiplicity one, and is implemented as a plain reference, that can be easily reverse engineered from the code.

To summarize, the class diagram depicted in Fig. 3.7 does not represent associations with multiplicity greater than one, since they are implemented through containers. Execution of the container analysis algorithm described in Section 3.3 is thus of fundamental importance for this program.

Fig. 3.8 shows the class diagram for the *eLib* program, produced by taking into account the estimated classes of the objects stored inside containers. The previously missing association between User and Loan has now been correctly recovered. This is achieved by considering the set out [User.loans] = {Loan} after flow propagation for container analysis.

Class Library is no longer a disconnected node in the diagram. Its container attributes have been analyzed, and the type determined for the contained objects allows drawing association relationships toward User, Loan and Document. They correspond to an intuitive model of a library, where the list

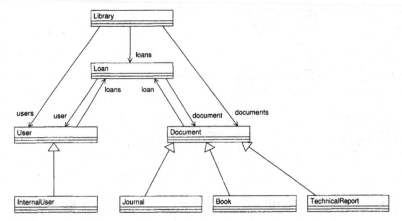

Fig. 3.8. Class diagram for the *eLib* program, obtained after performing container analysis.

of registered users is available, as well as the archive of the documents and the set of loans currently active. The class diagram in Fig. 3.8 is much more informative and accurate than that in Fig. 3.7. A programmer that has to understand this application will find it much easier to map intuitive notions about a library to software components by means of the diagram in Fig 3.8.

Fig. 3.9 completes the class diagram in Fig. 3.8 with the dependency relationships, which are shown only if they connect two classes otherwise not connected by an association (association is subsumed by dependency). Class User iteratively accesses Document objects (through the association with Loan) inside method printInfo (line 323), where code and title of borrowed documents are printed (line 332). The related method calls (getCode and getTitle) are the reasons for the dependency from User to Document. In the reverse direction, the dependency is due to calls of methods getCode and getName, issued at lines 220 and 221 inside printAvalability (line 215). When a document is not available, the code and name of the user who borrowed it are printed. The User object on which calls are made is obtained from the Loan object (attribute loan) reachable from Document, which is non-null in case the document is borrowed (not available).

The dependency from Journal to User is due to the implementation of method authorizedLoan in class Journal (line 253). The base implementation of this method, in class Document, returns the constant true: every user is authorized to borrow any document. This implementation is overridden by the class TechnicalReport, returning the constant false (technical reports can be consulted, but not borrowed). The class Journal also overrides it, delegating the authorization to class User (hereby, the dependency), in that only internal users (class InternalUser) are authorized to borrow journals (line 254).

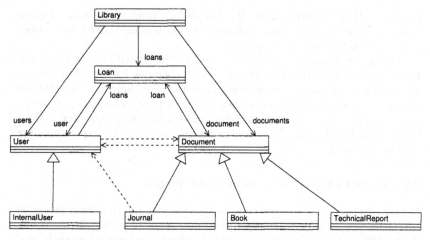

Fig. 3.9. Class diagram for the *eLib* program including dependency relationships.

3.5 Related Work

Usage of points-to analysis to improve the accuracy of the interclass relationships is described in [56], where the type of pointed-to objects is used to replace the declared type. The results obtained by points-to analysis are comparable to those obtained by the OFG based algorithm to handle inheritance, given in Section 3.2. Both approaches exploit the object type used in allocation points to infer the actual type of referenced objects. As discussed in [56], this represents a substantial improvement over the Class Hierarchy Analysis (CHA) [17], which determines all direct and transitive subclasses of the declared type as possibly referenced by a given program location. CHA becomes particularly imprecise in the presence of interfaces as declared types. In fact, it is quite typical that a large number of classes implement general purpose interfaces (such as the Comparable interface). If all of them are accounted for as possible targets of interclass relationships, a completely unusable class diagram is derived from the code. In [56], the output of two points-to analysis algorithms, described respectively in [68] and [57], is used to determine the possibly pointed-to locations for each variable in the given program. The experimental data show that such information is crucial to refine the inter-class relationships associated with dynamic binding.

In [18], container types are analyzed with the purpose of moving to a hypothetical strongly typed version of the Java containers. A set of constraints is derived on the type parameters that are introduced for each potentially generic class (e.g., containers). A templated instance of the original class which respects such constraints can safely replace the weakly typed one, thus making most of the downcasts unnecessary and allowing for a deeper static check of the code. Although based on a different algorithm, this approach is comparable to that described in Section 3.3. In fact, more accurate information about the type of objects inserted into containers is inferred from type-related statements in the code under analysis.

An empirical study comparing the results obtained with and without container analysis is described in [87]. The class diagrams for the subsystems in a large C++ code base were reverse engineered. The number of associations missed in the absence of container analysis turned out to be high, and the visual inspection of the related class diagrams revealed that container analysis plays a fundamental role in reverse engineering, when weakly typed container libraries are used.

3.5.1 Object identification in procedural code

In this chapter, reverse engineering of the class diagram has been presented with reference to Object Oriented programs. A lot of work [12, 13, 51, 75, 80, 88, 102] has been conducted within the reverse engineering research community, aimed at identifying abstract data types in *procedural* code. Thus, classes are tentatively reverse engineered from procedural (instead of Object Oriented) code.

The purpose of the analyses considered in these works is supporting the migration from procedural to Object Oriented programming. It was recognized that this migration process cannot be fully automated and the results available in the literature provide local approaches which help in some cases, but not in others. If a software system was built around data types in the first place, it is possible to identify and extract them as objects. If not, it is hard to retrofit objects into the system and, until now, no one has come up with a general, automated solution for transforming procedural systems into Object Oriented ones. In such a case, the output of reverse engineering may be only the starting point for a highly human-intensive reengineering activity.

In [51] the main methods for class identification are classified as global-based or type-based, respectively when functions are clustered around globally accessible objects or formal parameter and return types. A new identification method – based on the concept of receiver parameter type – is also proposed. The approach presented in [12], which considers accesses to global variables, uses an internal connectivity index to decide which functions should be clustered around the recognized class. Such a method is extended in [13] to include type-based relations and it is combined with the strong direct dominance tree to obtain a more refined result. The recovery technique described in [102] builds a graph showing the references of the procedures to the internal fields of structures. Accesses to global variables drive the recognition of classes.

In [27] the *star diagram* is proposed as a support to help programmers restructure programs by improving the encapsulation of abstract data types. Another decomposing and restructuring system is described in [58]. Both of them provide sophisticated interaction means to assist the user in the process of analyzing and restructuring a program.

Several works [50, 75, 80, 88] on identification and remodularization of abstract data types are based on the output produced by *concept analysis* [25]. The relation between procedures and global variables is analyzed by means of concept analysis in [50]. The resulting lattice is used to identify module candidates. Concept analysis is used in [75] to identify modules, by considering both positive and negative information about the types of the function arguments and of the return value. An example of how to identify class candidates from a C implementation of two tangled data structures is provided in [75]. Concept analysis succeeds in separating them into two distinct classes. In [88], encapsulation around dynamically allocated memory locations and module restructuring are considered. Points-to analysis is used to determine dynamic memory accesses, while concept analysis permits grouping functions around the accessed dynamic locations. Concept analysis is exploited in [80] to reengineer class hierarchies. A context describing the usage of a class hierarchy is the starting point for the construction of a concept lattice, from which redesign possibilities are derived.

4

Object Diagram

This chapter describes a technique to statically characterize the behavior of an object oriented system by means of diagrams which represent the class instances (objects) and their mutual relationships.

Although the class diagram is the basic view for program understanding of Object Oriented systems, it is not very informative of the behavior that a program will exhibit at run time, being focused on the static relationships among classes. On the contrary, the *object diagram* represents the instances of the classes and the related inter-object relationships. This program representation provides additional information with respect to the class diagram on the way classes are actually used. In fact, while the class diagram shows all possible relationships for all possible class instances, the object diagram takes into consideration the specific object allocations occurring in a program, and for each class instance it provides the specific relationships a given object has with other objects. While in the class diagram a single entity represents a class and summarizes the properties of all of its instances, in the object diagram different instances are represented as distinct diagram nodes, with their own properties. Thus, the dynamic layout of objects and inter-object relationships emerges from the object diagram, while it is only implicit in the class diagram.

A static analysis of the source code based on the flow propagation in the OFG can be exploited to reverse engineer information about the objects allocated in a program and the inter-object relationships mediated by the object attributes. The allocation points in the code are used to approximate the set of objects created by a program, while the OFG is used to determine the inter-object relationships. Resulting diagrams approximate statically any run-time object creation and inter-object relationship, in a conservative way.

A second, dynamic technique that can be considered to produce the object diagram is based on the execution of the program on a set of test cases. Each test case is associated with an object diagram depicting the objects and the relationships that are instantiated when the test case is run. The diagram can be obtained as a postprocessing of the program traces generated during each execution.

The static and the dynamic techniques are complementary, in that the first is safe with respect to the objects and relationships it represents, but it cannot provide precise information on the actual multiplicity of the allocated objects (e.g., in presence of loops), nor on the actual layout of the relationships associated with the allocated objects (e.g., in presence of infeasible paths). The dynamic view is accurate with concern to the number of instances and the relationship layout, but it is (by definition) partial, in that it holds for a single test run. Therefore, it is useful to contrast the dynamic and static view, to determine the portion of the latter that was explored with the available test suite and to refine it with information suggested by the dynamic views.

This chapter is organized as follows: after a summary presentation of the object diagram elements, given in Section 4.1, Section 4.2 describes a static method for object diagram recovery. It is a specialization of the general purpose framework defined in Chapter 2. Section 4.3 provides the details of an object sensitive OFG algorithm for the recovery of the object diagram. The dynamic technique for object diagram recovery is presented in Section 4.4. At the end of this section, static and dynamic analysis views are contrasted, highlighting advantages and disadvantages of both, and providing hints on how they can complement each other. Static and dynamic extraction of the object diagram is conducted on the *eLib* program in Section 4.5. Related works are discussed in Section 4.6.

4.1 The Object Diagram

The object diagram represents the set of objects created by a given program and the relationships holding among them. The elements in this diagram (objects and relationships) are *instances* of the elements (classes and associations, resp.) in the class diagram. The difference between an object diagram and a class diagram is that the former instantiates the latter. As a consequence, the objects in the object diagram represent specific cases of the related classes. Their attributes are expected to have well defined values and their relationships with other objects have a known multiplicity. For each class in the class diagram there may be several objects instantiating it in the object diagram. For each relationship between classes in the class diagram there may be object pairs instantiating it and pairs not related by it.

The usefulness of the object diagram as an abstract program representation lies in the information specific to the instantiation of the classes that it shows. While the class diagram summarizes all properties that objects of a given class may have, the object diagram provides more details on the properties that specific instances of each class possess. Different instances may play different roles and may be involved in different relationships with other objects. While this is not apparent in the class diagram, the object diagram represents this kind of information explicitly.

Let us consider a hypothetical BinaryTree program. In its class diagram, there might be one BinaryTreeNode class, with two auto-associations named left and right for the two children, while a possible instance represented in the object diagram might include three objects of type BinaryTreeNode, playing three different roles (i.e., tree root, left child and right child). The relationships among these three elements are compliant with those in the class diagram, but provide more information on the layout of the related instances by showing a specific scenario (where the root references two children which have no further descendants). Moreover, the object diagram is the starting point for the construction of the interaction (collaboration and sequence) diagrams, where information about the message exchange between objects is added to the class instances, thus focusing the view on the dynamic behavior of a set of cooperating objects (a *collaboration*, in the UML terminology).

In the following text, two techniques are described for the recovery of the object diagram. The first exploits only static information and approximates the set of objects created in the program by analyzing the allocation (new) statements and propagating the resulting objects by means of the flow propagation algorithm described in Chapter 2. The second considers a set of execution traces, associated with the test cases available for a given program, and obtained by running an instrumented version of the given program. Execution traces include information about each object allocated by the program, uniquely identified, and its attributes. Object attributes which reference other objects are used to recover inter-object associations. These two techniques have advantages and disadvantages, and it is therefore desirable to be able to compute and integrate the results of both of them.

4.2 Object Diagram Recovery

The static computation of the object diagram exploits the flow propagation on the OFG to transmit information about the objects that are created in the program up to the attributes that reference them. Objects are identified by allocation site (i.e., the line of code containing the allocation statement), with no regard to the actual number of times it is executed (which is, in general, undecidable for a static analysis).

Fig. 4.1 shows the flow information that is propagated in the OFG to recover the object diagram. Each allocation site (statement of kind (5)) is associated with a unique object identifier, constructed as the class name c, subscripted by an incremented integer i (giving the object identifier c_i). Such flow information is propagated in the OFG according to the algorithm given in Chapter 2, in the forward direction.

Construction of the object diagram is a straightforward post-processing of the computation described above. Every object identifier c_i generates a

$$
\begin{array}{llll}
(1) & P & ::= & D^* S^* \\
(2) & D & ::= & a \\
(3) & & | & m(f_1, ..., f_k) \\
(4) & & | & cs(f_1, ..., f_k) \\
(5) & S & ::= & x = \text{new } c(a_1, ..., a_k); \quad gen[x] = \{c_i\} \\
(6) & & | & x = y; \\
(7) & & | & [x =] \, y.m(a_1, ..., a_k);
\end{array}
$$

where in (5) c_i is the object identifier associated with this allocation site.
$gen[n] = \emptyset$ for all locations different from the left hand side x in (5)
$kill[n] = \emptyset$ for all locations

Fig. 4.1. Flow propagation specialization to determine the set of objects allocated in the program that are referenced by each program location.

corresponding node in the object diagram. Every node in the OFG associated to an object attribute, i.e., having a prefix "c" and a suffix "$.a$", where a is an attribute of class c, is taken into consideration when inter-object associations are generated. The *out* set of such an OFG node (i.e., $out[c.a]$) gives the set of objects reachable from all objects c_i of class c along the association implemented through the attribute a. Such an association can thus be given the name of the attribute, a.

———————————————*binary search tree* example ———————————————

```
class BinaryTreeNode {
  BinaryTreeNode left, right;
  public void addLeft(BinaryTreeNode n) { left = n; }
  public void addRight(BinaryTreeNode n) { right = n; }
}

class BinaryTree {
  BinaryTreeNode root;
  public void build() {
    root = new BinaryTreeNode();
    BinaryTreeNode curNode = root;
    while (...) {
      ...
      curNode.addLeft(new BinaryTreeNode());
      ...
      curNode.addRight(new BinaryTreeNode());
    }
  }
  static public void main(String args[]) {
    BinaryTree bt = new BinaryTree();
    bt.build();
  }
}
```

The abstract syntax representation of the Java code fragment above is the following:

```
BinaryTreeNode.left = BinaryTreeNode.addLeft.n;
BinaryTreeNode.right = BinaryTreeNode.addRight.n;
BinaryTree.root = new BinaryTreeNode();
BinaryTree.build.curNode = BinaryTree.root;
BinaryTreeNode.addLeft.n = new BinaryTreeNode();
BinaryTreeNode.addLeft.this = BinaryTree.build.curNode;
BinaryTreeNode.addRight.n = new BinaryTreeNode();
BinaryTreeNode.addRight.this = BinaryTree.build.curNode;
BinaryTree.main.bt = new BinaryTree();
BinaryTree.build.this = BinaryTree.main.bt;
```

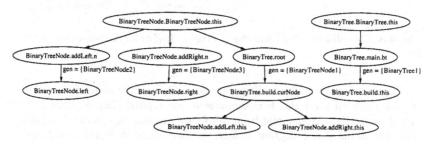

Fig. 4.2. Object flow graph for the binary tree example.

Fig. 4.2 shows the OFG derived from the abstract statements above. Non empty *gen* sets of OFG nodes are also shown. Objects of type `BinaryTreeNode` are allocated at three distinct program points, thus originating three object identifiers, `BinaryTreeNode1`, `BinaryTreeNode2` and `BinaryTreeNode3`, which are in the *gen* set of the respective left hand side locations (`BinaryTree-.root`, `BinaryTreeNode.addLeft.n` and `BinaryTreeNode.addRight.n`). Since there is just one allocation statement for `BinaryTree` objects, the only object identifier for this class is `BinaryTree1`, inserted into the *gen* set of the allocation left hand side, `BinaryTree.main.bt`.

After flow propagation, the following *out* sets are determined for the class attributes:

out[BinaryTree.root] = {BinaryTreeNode1}
out[BinaryTreeNode.left] = {BinaryTreeNode2}
out[BinaryTreeNode.right] = {BinaryTreeNode3}

Construction of the object diagram is now possible. Every object identifier becomes a node in the object diagram. Thus, in the example above four nodes are inserted into the diagram, three of class `BinaryTreeNode` and one of class `BinaryTree`. The *out* sets of the class attributes after flow propagation determine the inter-object associations. Thus, object `BinaryTree1` is associated with `BinaryTreeNode1` through the attribute `root`, used as the association name. All three objects of type `BinaryTreeNode` are associated with `BinaryTreeNode2` through a link named `left`, and with `BinaryTreeNode3` through a link named `right`.

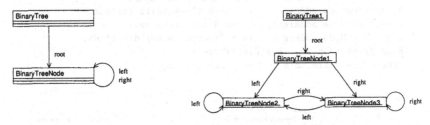

Fig. 4.3. Class diagram (left) and object diagram (right) for the binary tree example.

Fig. 4.3 shows the object diagram recovered from the code of the binary tree example on the right. For comparison, the related class diagram is depicted on the left. As apparent from this figure, the class diagram is less informative than the object diagram. In fact, the three elements `BinaryTreeNode1`, `BinaryTreeNode2`, `BinaryTreeNode3` of the object diagram are collapsed into a single element (`BinaryTreeNode`) in the class diagram, with two auto-associations (`left` and `right`). The object diagram makes it clear that the attribute `root` of class `BinaryTree` always references the object identified as `BinaryTreeNode1` (first allocation site), while attributes `left` and `right` reference respectively the objects `BinaryTreeNode2` (second allocation site) and `BinaryTreeNode3` (third allocation site).

4.3 Object Sensitivity

A more accurate estimate of the relationships among the objects allocated in a program can be obtained by means of an object sensitive analysis (see Chapter 2 for the general framework). Program locations are distinguished by the object they belong to instead of their class. Given the allocation sites in the program under analysis, an object identifier c_i is associated to each of them. A program location n originally scoped by class c, gives rise to a set of OFG nodes n', scoped by object identifiers c_i, when an object sensitive OFG is constructed. Specifically, for each object identifier c_i created for class c, a replication of the program location n scoped by c_i is inserted into the object sensitive OFG. This gives the complete set of OFG nodes. The main drawback is that construction of OFG edges becomes more complicated in case of object sensitive analysis.

(1)	P	::=	$D^\bullet S^\bullet$	$\{\}$
(2)	D	::=	a	$\{\}$
(3)		|	$m(f_1, ..., f_k)$	$\{\}$
(4)		|	$cs(f_1, ..., f_k)$	$\{\}$
(5)	S	::=	$x = \text{new } c(a_1, ..., a_k);$	$\{(a'_1, f'_1) \in E, ..., (a'_k, f'_k) \in E, (cs'.this, x') \in E\}$
(6)		|	$x = y;$	$\{(y', x') \in E\}$
(7)		|	$[x =] y.m(a_1, ..., a_k);$	$\{(y', m'.this) \in E, (a'_1, f'_1) \in E, ..., (a'_k, f'_k) \in E,$
				$(m'.return, x') \in E\}$

where, for each class scoped location x, x' represents the corresponding object scoped location. In (5), cs is the invoked constructor for class c.

1. In (5), $scope(cs') = c_i$, $scope(f'_1) = c_i$, ..., $scope(f'_k) = c_i$, with c_i the object identifier of the allocation site (5).

2. In (5), (6), (7), if $x, y, a_1, ..., a_k$ are local variables, current method's parameters, or current object's attributes, $scope(x') = c_j$, $scope(y') = c_j$, $scope(a'_1) = c_j$, ..., $scope(a'_k) = c_j$, with c_j the object identifier scoping the current method. If they are accesses to attributes of objects other than the current one, of the kind $p.a$, $scope(x') = c_k$, with c_k running over $out[p]$.

3. In (7), if $y.m$ is a call performed on the current object (y ends with this), $scope(m') = c_j$, $scope(f'_1) = c_j$, ..., $scope(f'_k) = c_j$, with c_j the object identifier scoping the current method. If it is a call performed on an object other than the current one, $scope(m') = c_k$, $scope(f'_1) = c_k$, ..., $scope(f'_k) = c_k$, with c_k running over $out[y]$.

Fig. 4.4. Incremental construction of OFG edges for object sensitive analysis.

Fig. 4.4 shows the rules for OFG edge construction, when an object sensitive analysis is conducted. Some object scoped locations connected by OFG edges can be computed directly from the abstract syntax of the code under analysis. This happens when the scope of the location is the object allocated at the current statement or the object scoping the current method. Let us consider statement (5) in Fig. 4.4. The scope of the invoked constructor cs is the currently allocated object c_i, so that all formal parameters $f'_1, ..., f'_k$, as well as the this location inside cs ($cs'.this$), will be scoped by c_i.

Class methods are replicated for each object of the given class allocated in the program. Inside such copies, a unique identifier c_j of the current object (this) is available. It defines the scope of local variables, method parameters, and attributes of the current object.

The most difficult case is when an attribute is accessed or a method is called through a location other than this. In fact, in such a case, the target attribute or method belongs to an object other than the current one. If the attribute access has the form $p.a$ and the method call has the form $p.m(...)$, the object scoping the related program locations is not directly available from the abstract statements. It can be obtained by executing the flow propagation algorithm for object analysis described in Section 4.2. However, such an algorithm requires the availability of the OFG, which has been built only partially. This is the reason why the rules in Fig. 4.4 have to be applied incrementally. During the first iteration of OFG construction, $out[p] = \emptyset$ for all locations p. Thus, only OFG edges connecting locations scoped by c_i or c_j (resp., the object allocated at current statement and the object scoping the current method) can be added to the OFG. Once this initial OFG is built, flow propagation for object analysis can be performed, giving a first estimate of the objects $c_k \in out[p]$. These objects can be used to scope the accesses to attributes of objects other than the current one, or method names and parameters, in case of an invocation to a target different from the current object. This allows adding more edges to the OFG, connecting locations scoped by c_k, an object different from the current one. The refined version of the OFG allows an improved estimation of the objects $c_k \in out[p]$ for each location p, thus possibly augmenting the set of edges added to the OFG, according to the rules in Fig. 4.4. At the end of this process, when no more edges are added to the OFG, the final, object sensitive OFG is obtained. OFG nodes will have *out* sets storing object identifiers determined through an object sensitive analysis. Thus, the object diagram derived from them is expected to be more accurate than the one constructed by an object insensitive analysis.

The algorithm described above produces quite precise object diagrams, since object flows are not mixed when they belong to the same class but to different objects. However, it requires replicating the program locations for all allocation sites, thus generating a larger OFG. Moreover, it assumes that the whole program is available for the analysis. In fact, if an allocation point for a class is not part of the code under analysis, some of the related edges in the OFG are missed, since $out[p]$ will remain empty during all OFG construction iterations. In other words, the result of the object sensitive analysis is still safe (conservative) only if the whole system is available for the analysis, including all object allocation statements.

_____*binary search tree* example _____

Let us consider the following Java code fragment for a *binary tree* program. Two binary tree data structures, bt1 and bt2, are created to handle two different kinds of data elements: objects of class A and objects of class B.

```
class BinaryTreeNode {
    BinaryTreeNode left, right;
    Comparable object;
```

```
    BinaryTreeNode(Comparable obj) {
        object = obj;
    }
    ...
}
class BinaryTree {
    BinaryTreeNode root;
    public void insert(BinaryTreeNode n) {
        if (root == null) {
            root = n;
        } else {
            root.insert(n);
        }
    }
    ...
}
class Main {
    public static void main(String args[]) {
        BinaryTree bt1 = new BinaryTree();
        BinaryTree bt2 = new BinaryTree();
        ...
        A a = new A();
        BinaryTreeNode n1 = new BinaryTreeNode(a);
        bt1.insert(n1);
        ...
        B b = new B();
        BinaryTreeNode n2 = new BinaryTreeNode(b);
        bt2.insert(n2);
    }
}
```

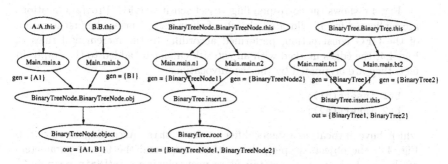

Fig. 4.5. Object insensitive OFG for object analysis.

Fig. 4.5 shows the object insensitive OFG built for the code fragment above. All program locations are scoped by the class they belong to. The *out* sets provided for some OFG nodes are those obtained after completing the flow propagation on the OFG. They will be used for the object diagram construction.

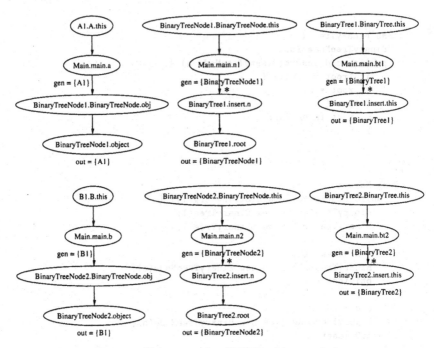

Fig. 4.6. Object sensitive OFG for object analysis.

Fig. 4.6 shows the corresponding object sensitive OFG. Program locations are replicated for all allocated objects of their class. During the first iteration of the OFG construction, performed according to the incremental rules in Fig. 4.4, the edges marked with an asterisk cannot be added to the graph. In fact, they are originated by the two invocations:

```
bt1.insert(n1);
bt2.insert(n2);
```

which have invocation targets different from **this**. According to rule 3 in Fig. 4.4, the objects scoping the method name and the formal parameters of the method are to be obtained respectively from *out*[Main.main.bt1] and *out*[Main.main.bt2], but both sets are initially empty. Consequently, an OFG is built with missing edges, associated with these two calls (asterisks in Fig. 4.6).

On the initial, partial OFG, the object analysis algorithm is run, and the result of the flow propagation at the two nodes of interest is:

out[Main.main.bt1] = {BinaryTree1}
out[Main.main.bt2] = {BinaryTree2}

This allows computing a proper scope for **insert** and its formal parameter n. Specifically, the invocation bt1.insert(n1) results in the addition of the two topmost edges marked with an asterisk in Fig. 4.6, since the target object of this invocation has been determined to be BinaryTree1 by the previous flow propagation step. Similarly, bt2.insert(n2) gives rise to the two asterisked edges at the bottom.

A new iteration of the flow propagation gives the final result of the object analysis. Some of the out sets obtained after this final flow propagation are shown in Fig. 4.6. They are exploited for the construction of the object diagram.

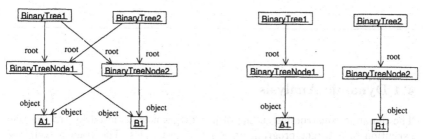

Fig. 4.7. Object diagram computed by an object insensitive analysis (left) and by an object sensitive analysis (right).

Object insensitive (Fig. 4.5) and object sensitive (Fig. 4.6) results are associated to the two object diagrams respectively on the left and on the right of Fig. 4.7. When object insensitive results are used for an object diagram construction, each class attribute is scoped by the class name, so that the relationships it induces are replicated for every object of that class. Thus, for example, the presence of BinaryTreeNode1 and BinaryTreeNode2 in the out set of BinaryTree.root originates the four associations labeled root in the object diagram on the left. Similarly, four associations labeled object are generated due to the output of BinaryTreeNode.object.

On the contrary, in the object sensitive OFG, class attributes are scoped by the object they belong to. Thus, the attribute root has two replications in Fig. 4.6, namely BinaryTree1.root and BinaryTree2.root, each with a different out set. Since only BinaryTreeNode1 is in the out of BinaryTree1.root, and only BinaryTreeNode2 is in the out of BinaryTree2.root, just two edges are constructed in the object diagram on the right for the association labeled `root`. Similarly, the output of `BinaryTreeNode1.object` and `BinaryTreeNode2.object` in the object sensitive OFG allows drawing the two associations labeled `object` in the object diagram on the right in Fig. 4.7.

The object diagram obtained by the object sensitive analysis conveys accurate information about the data elements stored in the two binary trees `bt1` and `bt2`. In fact, node `BinaryTreeNode1` has an attribute `object` that points to `A1`, while `BinaryTreeNode2` points to `B1` (see Fig. 4.7, right). This indicates that the first tree is used to manage objects of class `A` (created at allocation point 1), while the second tree has a different purpose: managing objects allocated as `B1`. On the contrary, the object insensitive diagram is less accurate and does not allow distinguishing the data elements stored in the two trees.

Both object diagrams in Fig. 4.7 are safe, that is, they represent a conservative superset of all inter-object relationships that may occur at run time. However, the object sensitive one is more precise. The object insensitive diagram contains spurious associations, but has the advantage of being computable even when not all object allocations are part of the code under analysis.

4.4 Dynamic Analysis

The dynamic construction of the object diagram is achieved by tracing the execution of a target program on a set of test cases. The tracing facilities required are basically the possibility to inspect the current object and its attributes each time a method is invoked on an object and its statements are executed. Trace data should include an object identifier for the current object and for any object referenced by the current object's attributes.

It is possible to obtain these dynamic data either by exploiting available tracing tools or by instrumenting the given program. In case of program instrumentation, the following additions are required:

- Classes are augmented with an object identifier, which is computed and traced during the execution of class constructors.
- Upon an attribute change, the identifier(s) of the object(s) referenced by the given attribute are added to the execution trace.
- Time stamps are produced and traced when either of the two events above occurs.

Each program execution is thus associated with an execution trace, the analysis of which produces an object diagram. Consequently, the outcome of the dynamic analysis is a set of object diagrams, each associated with a test case, providing information on the objects and the relationships that are instantiated in the test case. Their construction from the execution trace is straightforward. The identifier of each object in the execution trace is associated to a node in the dynamic object diagram. The identifiers of the objects referenced by the current object's attributes determine the relationships between the current object and the other ones.

Since the relationship between two objects on a given attribute may change over time, if such an attribute is successively reassigned, in the execution trace multiple target objects may be associated to the same attribute at different times, resulting in more than one association to be drawn in the object diagram for that attribute. Their interpretation is that there exists a time interval when each drawn relationship actually holds. The traced time stamps are exploited when the dynamic object diagram is built, to decorate objects and associations with the time interval that represents their life span (from creation time to deletion time). Snapshots of the object diagram at a given time point or for a given interval can also be derived from the overall diagram.

──────────────────*binary search tree* example ──────────────────

With reference to the binary tree example described in Section 4.3, let us assume that the tree is kept ordered according to the `compareTo` method available for the attribute `object` (inside class `BinaryTreeNode`), which implements the `Comparable` interface. A test case may consist in the creation of one or more `BinaryTreeNode` objects, with a `String` parameter assigned to the attribute `object`, and the insertion of the newly created node into a same `BinaryTree`. We can, for example, consider the following sequences of three strings as our test cases TC1, TC2, TC3. A node is created and inserted into the binary tree for each string encountered in the sequence:

TC1 ("a", "b", "c")
TC2 ("b", "a", "c")
TC3 ("c", "b", "a")

Test case	Relationships	Time int.
TC1	`BinaryTree1.root = BinaryTreeNode1`	[1-3]
	`BinaryTreeNode1.right = BinaryTreeNode2`	[2-3]
	`BinaryTreeNode2.right = BinaryTreeNode3`	[3-3]
TC2	`BinaryTree1.root = BinaryTreeNode1`	[1-3]
	`BinaryTreeNode1.left = BinaryTreeNode2`	[2-3]
	`BinaryTreeNode1.right = BinaryTreeNode3`	[3-3]
TC3	`BinaryTree1.root = BinaryTreeNode1`	[1-3]
	`BinaryTreeNode1.left = BinaryTreeNode2`	[2-3]
	`BinaryTreeNode2.left = BinaryTreeNode3`	[3-3]

Table 4.1. Relationships and time intervals gathered from the execution traces.

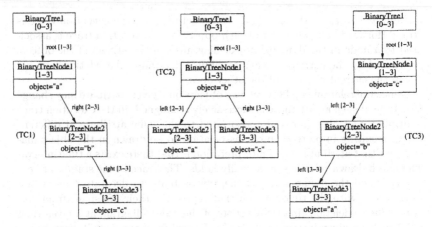

Fig. 4.8. Dynamic construction of object diagrams for test cases TC1, TC2 and TC3.

The execution traces for these three test cases contain the information in Table 4.1 (attributes with `null` value have been removed from the execution trace, being not relevant for the construction of the object diagram). Time intervals in which a given relation holds are given in square brackets.

The analysis of the three execution traces produces the three object diagrams depicted in Fig. 4.8. In TC1, all child nodes are added on the right. In TC2, the tree is balanced, while in TC3 only left children are present. The life span of objects and relationships is in square brackets.

4.4.1 Discussion

Static extraction and dynamic extraction of the object diagram produce different but complementary information about the instantiations of the classes performed by a program. The static object diagram gives a conservative view of the objects that are possibly created by the program and of the relationships that may exist between the objects. The number of objects reflects the number of program locations where an allocation statement is present. If such a statement is executed multiple times, the actual multiplicity of the related object is greater than the multiplicity indicated in the static object diagram (i.e., one). The presence of a relationship between two objects in the static object diagram indicates that there is some path in the program along which the first object may reference the second one (through some of its attributes). The existence of a path in the program does not imply that such a path is traversed in every execution. As a consequence, the relationships between objects indicated in the static object diagram are a conservative superset of those actually instantiated at run time. Moreover, it may happen that some of these relationships are associated to paths that can never be followed, for any input value. This is typical of static analysis: the solution is conservative, but may include infeasible parts, due to mutually exclusive conditions on the input values.

The dynamic object diagram complements the static one, in that objects are replicated in it each time a same allocation statement is re-executed, thus giving a better picture of their actual multiplicity. However, such a diagram is always partial, being based on a limited and necessarily incomplete set of test cases. An indication of the parts of the object diagram not yet explored can be obtained by contrasting it with the static object diagram. Objects and relationships in the static object diagram that are not represented in the dynamic one are associated respectively to allocation statements and execution paths not exercised by the available test cases.

_____*binary search tree* example _____

Test case	Static diagram	Dynamic diagram
TC1	BinaryTree1	BinaryTree1
	BinaryTreeNode1	BinaryTreeNode1
	BinaryTreeNode2	-
	BinaryTreeNode3	BinaryTreeNode2
		BinaryTreeNode3
TC2	BinaryTree1	BinaryTree1
	BinaryTreeNode1	BinaryTreeNode1
	BinaryTreeNode2	BinaryTreeNode2
	BinaryTreeNode3	BinaryTreeNode3
TC3	BinaryTree1	BinaryTree1
	BinaryTreeNode1	BinaryTreeNode1
	BinaryTreeNode2	BinaryTreeNode2
		BinaryTreeNode3
	BinaryTreeNode3	-

Table 4.2. Correspondence between statically and dynamically identified objects.

As depicted in Fig. 4.3 (right), the binary tree example has a static object diagram with 4 nodes and 7 edges. The first test case executed on it (Fig. 4.8, TC1) instantiates its objects in 3 out of the 4 locations identified statically. Allocation of a BinaryTreeNode in case of left insertion (addLeft) is not exercised in TC1. Consequently, the two edges leaving BinaryTreeNode2 in the static object diagram and the two incoming edges are not represented in the first dynamic object diagram. However, the first dynamic object diagram provides some additional information on the multiplicity of the object

BinaryTreeNode3 (Fig. 4.3), which appears to be greater than 1. On the contrary, a unitary multiplicity seems to be confirmed for BinaryTree1 and BinaryTreeNode1 (Fig. 4.3). Correspondence between the objects identified statically and those identified dynamically is as indicated in Table 4.2.

The second test case generates a dynamic object diagram (Fig. 4.8, TC2) in which all objects in Fig. 4.3 are represented. The last test case (Fig. 4.8, TC3) reveals that the multiplicity of BinaryTreeNode2 (Fig. 4.3) can also be greater than 1.

The comparison of the diagrams in Fig. 4.8 (right) with that in Fig. 4.3 highlights the different and complementary nature of the information they provide. The actual shape of the allocated objects (a tree) becomes clear only when the dynamic diagrams are considered. However, they cannot be taken alone, since they do not represent all possible cases that may occur in the program. Inspection of the static object diagram allows detecting portions of the code not yet exercised, which are relevant for the construction of the objects and of the inter-object relationships, and therefore could contribute to the understanding of the object organization in the program.

With reference to the diagram in Fig. 4.3, the relationship between BinaryTreeNode2 and BinaryTreeNode3 labeled right, and that between BinaryTreeNode3 and BinaryTreeNode2 labeled left, are not represented in any dynamic diagram (see Fig. 4.8). Two additional test cases can be defined to exercise them:

TC4 ("c", "a", "b")
TC5 ("a", "c", "b")

This highlights one of the advantages of combining the static and the dynamic method, consisting of the support given to the programmers in the production of the test cases.

4.5 The *eLib* Program

The code of the classes in the *eLib* program, provided in Appendix A, does not contain the statements allocating objects of type User, Book, etc. In fact, it is assumed that an external driver program performs such allocations. The classes in this appendix offer functionalities for general library management, but do not include a sample implementation of an actual library application. Appendix B contains an example of such an application, with a driver class (Main) that can be used to create a library, add/remove users and documents and manage the process of borrowing/returning documents. This is the list of commands that can be issued to the Main driver from the command prompt:

```
addUser name, address, phone
addIntUser name, address, phone, id
rmUser userId
addBook title, authors, ISBN
addReport title, ref, authors
addJournal title
rmDoc docId
borrowDoc userId, docId
returnDoc docId
searchUser name
searchDoc title
isHolding userId docId
printLoans
printUser userId
printDoc docId
exit
```

Each command is dispatched by the method `dispatchCommand` (line 504), triggering the execution of a proper method of class `Main` (the method name is coincident with the command name). In turn, the called method exploits the functionalities provided by the core classes of the *eLib* program to complete its task. Thus, for example, method `addUser` (line 379) creates a new `User` object, passing the parameters of the command (`name`, `address`, `phone`) to the constructor (line 382). The resulting object is added to the library by calling method `addUser` on the static attribute `lib` of class `Main` (line 383). Such an attribute references a statically allocated `Library` object, accessible to all methods of class `Main`.

A meaningful object diagram can be produced for the *eLib* program by analyzing both the code in the core classes (Appendix A) and that in the driver class (Appendix B). Actually, core classes perform just allocations of objects of type `Loan`, inside methods for loan management, such as `borrowDocument` (line 60), `returnDocument` (line 70) and `isHolding` (line 78). All the other object allocations are performed inside methods of class `Main` (Appendix B). Thus, if class `Main` is not included, a scarsely informative object diagram would be obtained, with only three nodes representing objects of type `Loan`, disconnected with each other.

4.5.1 OFG Construction

The OFG representing object allocations in the `Main` class and object propagation from allocation points to class attributes is shown in Fig. 4.9. Allocated objects are in the *gen* sets of the left hand side locations of allocation statements. The result of flow propagation is depicted only for nodes representing class attributes (`Library.users`, `Library.documents`, etc.). Their *out* sets contain the possibly referenced objects, according to the result of the static object analysis conducted on this OFG.

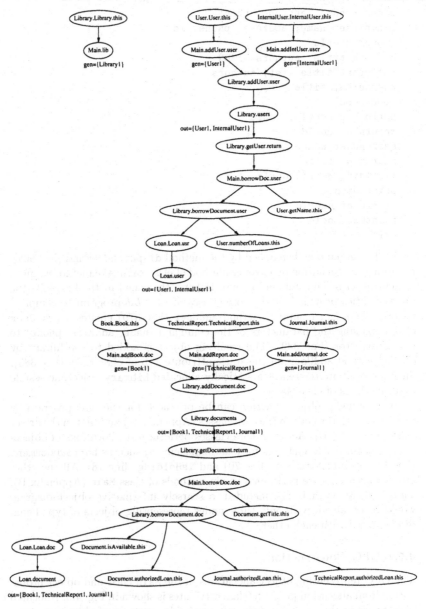

Fig. 4.9. OFG of the *eLib* program for object diagram recovery, driver class.

It can be noted that invocation of method `authorizedLoan` on the parameter `doc` of method `borrowDocument` (class `Library`) at line 59 is a polymorphic call. Consequently, the method actually invoked may be that defined in class `Document`, or that overridden by classes `Journal` and `TechnicalReport` (`Book` does not override it), depending on the actual type of the invocation target `doc`. Conservatively, edges in the OFG are drawn from the node associated with `doc` to the `this` location of all methods possibly invoked in the polymorphic call (see Fig. 4.9, bottom right edges).

Construction of the OFG in Fig. 4.9 requires a transformation of the statements involving containers, as described in Chapter 2. For example, the edge from `Library.addUser.user` to `Library.users` results from the invocation of method `put` on `Library.users`, an object of type `Map` (line 10).

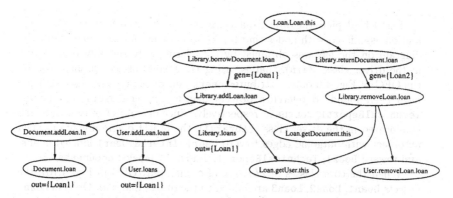

Fig. 4.10. OFG of the *eLib* program for object diagram recovery, core classes.

Fig. 4.10 contains the OFG for allocation points inside the core classes (Appendix A). Containers are handled similarly as for the OFG in Fig. 4.9. Only objects of type `Loan` are allocated inside core classes code. The `Loan` object allocated inside method `borrowDocument` at line 60 is named `Loan1`, the one allocated inside `returnDocument` at line 70 is named `Loan2`, and the one allocated inside `isHolding` at line 78 is named `Loan3`. The OFG portion that propagates these objects is shown in Fig. 4.10, where allocated objects are contained in *gen* sets. No node has a *gen* set containing `Loan3`, since this object is not propagated any further inside user classes. It is just used to check the presence of a `Loan` object referencing a given `User` and `Document` in the `Collection loans` of class `Library` (line 78). This requires a direct invocation of method `contains`, implemented by a standard library (not a user) class. In Fig. 4.10, *out* sets are shown only for locations representing class attributes. They are exploited for object diagram construction.

4.5.2 Object Diagram Recovery

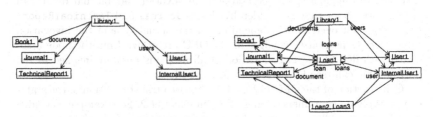

Fig. 4.11. Object diagrams for the *eLib* program. On the left, the diagram recovered from the driver class alone. On the right the complete diagram.

Fig. 4.11 depicts the object diagrams that are derived from the *out* information associated with nodes that represent class attributes. Specifically, the diagram on the left was obtained by considering only the allocation points in the driver class (Main), that is, using the results of flow propagation on the OFG of Fig. 4.9 only. Attributes users and documents of class Library have been found to reference objects User1, InternalUser1 and Book1, TechnicalReport1, Journal1 respectively. Since one object of type Library is allocated in the driver class (Library1), the object diagram contains such an object with outgoing edges toward User1, InternalUser1 labeled users, and toward Book1, TechnicalReport1, Journal1 labeled documents.

When the core classes of *eLib* are also analyzed (OFG in Fig. 4.10), the objects Loan1, Loan2, Loan3 are added to the object diagram. Objects Loan2 and Loan3 do not reach any class attribute in the OFG after flow propagation. This means that they cannot be stored inside any class attribute. Actually, they are temporary objects used respectively to remove a Loan from the library loans (line 71) and to check if a Loan with given User and Document exists in the library list of the loans (line 78). In the first case, the method removeLoan (line 48) is executed. It removes the given Loan from the list of the loans of the library, and it updates User and Document linked to the Loan object consistently. However, the two temporary objects Loan2 and Loan3 are no longer accessible after the completion of the returnDocument and isHolding operations.

According to the result of flow propagation in the OFG of Fig. 4.10, the object Loan1 is referenced by the attributes loan of Document, loans of Library, and loans of User. This is reflected in the object diagram by new associations outgoing from all objects of type Document, Library and User, and of any subtype. The attributes user and document of class Loan are found to contain the objects User1, InternalUser1 and Book1, TechnicalReport1, Journal1 respectively (see *out* sets in Fig. 4.9). Thus, all objects of type Loan will have an association with User1, InternalUser1 named user and with Book1,

TechnicalReport1, Journal1 named document. The final object diagram is shown in Fig. 4.11, on the right.

4.5.3 Discussion

By contrasting the class diagram recovered in Chapter 3 (Section 3.4) for the *eLib* program and the object diagram in Fig. 4.11 (right), the different nature of the information they convey becomes apparent. In the object diagram, only classes of actually allocated objects are present. Thus, no node of type Document is in the object diagram, since only objects of subclasses are allocated in the program. On the contrary, in the class diagram, the class Document is represented. Moreover, in this diagram the inheritance hierarchy is visible, while it is flattened in the object diagram, where emphasis is on the actual allocation type, instead of the declared type. Correspondingly, the relationships in the class diagram are replicated in the object diagram for all objects descending from a given class. For example, the link from Document to Loan is replicated for Book1, TechnicalReport1 and Journal1 in the object diagram. However, the target of the link is Loan1, but not Loan2 or Loan3. In other words, a link in the class diagram has disappeared in the object diagram, since the related class instances are never associated with each other by such a link. This occurs, in our example, for all incoming edges of class Loan in the class diagram, which disappear when the instances Loan2 and Loan3 are considered. Differently from Loan1, these two instances of class Loan do not participate in the associations from classes Document and User, and in the association from class Library depicted in the class diagram. Such kinds of information are not available from the class diagram, which generically indicates a set of associations for class Loan. Only when allocations of objects of class Loan are analyzed in detail, does it become clear that the object allocated inside borrowDocument is the one participating in the associations, while the other two do not.

Another interesting information that can be derived from the object diagram, but which is missing in the class diagram, is related to the outgoing links of objects Loan2 and Loan3. The document and the user that are referenced by these two temporary objects are those allocated inside the Main driver, and extracted from Library.documents and Library.users respectively (see also the OFG in Fig. 4.9). Actually, when a document is returned (temporary object Loan2) or when the presence of a loan is checked (temporary object Loan3), the involved document is obtained from the library by documentCode (docId in the command issued to the Main driver), resp. at lines 448 and 482. The user is either accessed by userCode (line 481), or it is obtained as the user who borrows a given document (method getBorrower, line 450). In all these cases, User and Document objects are extracted from those stored in the library, as depicted in the object diagram (Fig. 4.11, right).

4.5.4 Dynamic analysis

Let us consider a program execution in which the following commands are prompted:

```
addIntUser J. Smith, 5th ave., 214343, cs203
addIntUser D. White, 4th street, 212989, cs455
addBook Introduction to Java, B. Black, 213455213455
addBook A Guide to UML, R. Red, 455455455455
addJournal Computer Science Journal
borrowDoc 0, 2
returnDoc 2
isHolding 0, 2
exit
```

The related execution trace (over time) is given in Fig 4.12. During the static initialization of classes, the object Library1 is created and is assigned to the attribute lib of class Main (time 0). Creation of two internal users at times 1, 2 results in two new objects, InternalUser1 and InternalUser2, which are inserted into the attribute users of the object Library1. Similarly, the addition of two books (objects Book1, Book2) and of a journal (object Journal1) to the library changes the attribute documents of Library1, which eventually stores these three objects (time points 3, 4, 5). At time 6, a document is borrowed by a user. This requires the creation of a new object of type Loan, Loan1, which is inserted into Library1.loans. The attributes user and document of Loan1 are found to reference the objects InternalUser1 and Journal1 respectively. In turn, Journal1.loan is a reference to Loan1, which is the only object inside InternalUser1.loans. Returning the document Journal1 at time 7 determines the removal of Loan1 from Library1.loans, InternalUser1.loans and Journal1.loan. To achieve this, a temporary Loan object (Loan2) is created which references InternalUser1 and Journal1 through its attributes user and document. It is compared with the objects in Library1.loans to identify which Loan object to remove (resulting in Loan1). Execution of the command isHolding causes the creation of another temporary object of type Loan, Loan3, which also references InternalUser1 and Journal1. The presence of an identical object inside Library1.loans is checked during the execution of the requested operation.

Fig. 4.13 shows the object diagram that can be derived from the execution trace in Fig. 4.12. Arcs in this diagram are decorated with an indication of the time interval in which the related associations exist (from creation to deletion). Thus, Library1 is associated with its documents (Book1, Book2 and Journal1) and to its users (InternalUser1 and InternalUser2) for the whole duration of the program (until time 8), starting from the creation time of each object (3, 4, 5 for the documents and 1, 2 for the users). The command borrowDoc, issued at time 6, gives rise to the creation of Loan1, connected to InternalUser1 and Journal1, and inserted into the container loans of Library1. Since at the next time point (7) such a loan is deleted,

Time	Command	Allocations	Object attributes
0	\<static init\>	Library1	
1	addIntUser	InternalUser1	Library1.users={InternalUser1}
2	addIntUser	InternalUser2	Library1.users={InternalUser1, InternalUser2}
3	addBook	Book1	Library1.users={InternalUser1, InternalUser2}
			Library1.documents={Book1}
4	addBook	Book2	Library1.users={InternalUser1, InternalUser2}
			Library1.documents={Book1, Book2}
5	addJournal	Journal1	Library1.users={InternalUser1, InternalUser2}
			Library1.documents={Book1, Book2, Journal1}
6	borrowDoc	Loan1	Library1.users={InternalUser1, InternalUser2}
			Library1.documents={Book1, Book2, Journal1}
			Library1.loans={Loan1}
			Loan1.user=InternalUser1
			Loan1.document=Journal1
			InternalUser1.loans={Loan1}
			Journal1.loan=Loan1
7	returnDoc	Loan2	Library1.users={InternalUser1, InternalUser2}
			Library1.documents={Book1, Book2, Journal1}
			Library1.loans={}
			InternalUser1.loans={}
			Journal1.loan=null
			Loan2.user=InternalUser1
			Loan2.document=Journal1
8	isHolding	Loan3	Library1.users={InternalUser1, InternalUser2}
			Library1.documents={Book1, Book2, Journal1}
			Library1.loans={}
			InternalUser1.loans={}
			Journal1.loan=null
			Loan3.user=InternalUser1
			Loan3.document=Journal1

Fig. 4.12. Execution trace obtained by running the *eLib* program.

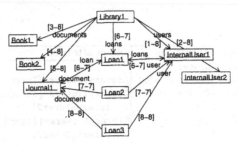

Fig. 4.13. Dynamic object diagram obtained from the execution trace of the *eLib* program.

the links connected to Loan1 cease to exist at time 7, their life interval being [6-7]. At time 7, the temporary object Loan2 is created to achieve the deletion of the previous loan. Such an object is connected to InternalUser1 and Journal1, but the related associations do not exist any longer when the object is dismissed. Thus, their life span is limited to the execution of the command returnDoc ([7-7]). Similarly, the object Loan3 is created at time 8 to verify the presence of a loan among those in the library. Being a temporary object, its life ends with the termination of the command. Correspondingly, the associations outgoing from Loan3 have a time interval [8-8].

A comparison of the static object diagram (Fig. 4.11, right) with the dynamic object diagram (Fig. 4.13) reveals the complementary nature of the information they convey. The static diagram represents all possible associations and all possible objects that may be created at run time conservatively. On the contrary, the dynamic diagram is partial and represents only the objects and the associations created during a particular program execution. Thus, since class TechnicalReport is never instantiated in the chosen execution, the dynamic diagram does not contain any object for it, while the possibility of creating TechnicalReport objects is accounted for in the static diagram. The dynamic diagram provides more information about object multiplicity. Class Book is instantiated twice in the execution being considered, and correspondingly, two objects are in the dynamic diagram (Book1, Book2). On the other side, the number of times a given allocation is executed at run time is unknown during a static analysis, so that no multiplicity information is included in the static diagram. Moreover, the dynamic diagram provides the time intervals for the associations depicted in it. This allows distinguishing, for example, more stable relationships, such as those between Library1 and its documents or users, from temporary relationships, such as those between Loan2, Loan3 and the referenced document/user. In general, in the static diagram, times of creation and removal of relationships and objects are not apparent, in that all possible relationships at any possible execution time are shown. On the contrary, the dynamic diagram shows the exact time at which relationships (objects) are created, changed, or deleted. On the other hand, this is known only for specific program executions.

4.6 Related Work

Information about class instances is collected at run-time by research prototypes, such as those described in [42, 62, 67, 97]. In these works, creation of objects and inter-object message exchange are captured by tracing the execution of a program under given scenarios. A novel approach for the dynamic analysis of object creation and of the inter-object relationships is described in [29]. It exploits the notion of *aspect*, introduced by Aspect Oriented Programming [40], and its ability to intercept a well defined execution point (join point), at which information about objects can be accessed and traced.

The OFG propagation exploited for static object diagram construction is based on the type inference technique for points to analysis [3]. More details on this and other related works are provided in Chapter 2, in the context of OFG construction and flow propagation. A major difference with the works in the type inference literature consists of the object sensitive variant (see Fig. 4.4), which requires an incremental OFG construction. Edges in the OFG depend on the objects referenced by program locations (object sensitivity), which are in turn the outcome of flow propagation on the OFG. OFG construction followed by flow propagation are repeatedly performed to produce the final, object sensitive, OFG of the program. Similar problems are faced in [57], where an object sensitive variant of [3] is investigated.

Experimental results obtained by applying the presented approach to a case study are provided in [89], where the information conveyed by class diagrams, static object diagrams and dynamic object diagrams is considered. Results indicate that the object diagram provides additional information with respect to the class diagram, being focused on the way a program actually uses the objects that instantiate the declared classes. Moreover, static and dynamic views of the objects capture complementary information. The former covers all statically admissible inter-object relationships, while the latter provides accurate multiplicity data for specific scenarios. Two novel object-oriented testing criteria, *Object coverage* and *Inter-object relationship coverage* are derived in [89] from the comparison of the static object diagram and of the diagrams associated to the execution of test cases. The number of test cases should be enough as to cover all object creations or inter-object relationships displayed in the static object diagram.

5

Interaction Diagrams

This chapter is focused on the extraction of a representation of the interactions that occur among the objects that compose an Object Oriented system. A static analysis of the source code provides a conservative superset of all possible interactions, while a dynamic analysis can be used to trace the behavior of the program during a given execution.

In Object Oriented programming, the overall functionality of an application emerges from the interactions among the communicating objects it instantiates. There is no single place where the instructions for a given system's functionality are concentrated. On the contrary, each object gives a small contribution to a larger picture, possibly delegating part of the computation to other objects. Thus, understanding the behavior emerging from the message exchange implemented in an Object Oriented system can be a difficult task. Interaction diagrams help programmers in such a task by offering a visual language for the display of the control transfers among objects.

Interaction diagrams can be obtained from the source code by augmenting the object diagram with information about method invocations. The sequence of method dispatches is considered and their ordering is represented in the two forms of the interaction diagrams: either in *collaboration diagrams*, which emphasize the message flows over the structural organization of the objects, or in *sequence diagrams*, which emphasize the temporal ordering. Recovery of these diagrams from the source code can be achieved by defining a proper analysis on the OFG and exploiting its outcome to statically resolve the method invocations. Dynamic recovery of the interaction diagrams can be obtained by running an instrumented version of the program and collecting the dynamic interactions among the objects from the execution trace.

For statically determined diagrams, a numbering algorithm, aimed at ordering events temporally, is also described in this chapter. It is used to attach time stamps to method calls, thus making the diagrams more informative. In order for the approach to scale to large systems, it is complemented by an extension of the interaction diagram recovery algorithm to handle incomplete systems, and by a focusing technique that can be used to locate and visualize only the interactions of interest. Correspondingly, focused numbering of the temporal events is also considered.

The chapter is organized as follows: Section 5.1 gives an overview on the interaction diagrams. Section 5.2 presents the specialization of the general flow propagation algorithm that is used for the reverse engineering of the interaction diagrams and some related problems, the first of which deals with the recovery of useful interaction diagrams in the presence of incomplete systems. Moreover, the usability problems of the resulting diagrams are also discussed. To make diagrams fit the cognitive abilities of humans, proper visualization techniques must be adopted. In particular, the possibility to focus on a computation of interest is described in detail, together with a related numbering algorithm, for the temporal ordering of the involved events. Interaction diagrams can be recovered at run time, for specific program's executions, as described in Section 5.3. Examples of interaction diagrams obtained for the *eLib* system are provided in Section 5.4, while a discussion of the related works ends the chapter.

5.1 Interaction Diagrams

Interaction diagrams are used to model the dynamic aspects of an Object Oriented system [7]. While class diagrams are used to represent the static structure of the system, in terms of its classes and of the relationships among classes, interaction diagrams are focused on class instances (objects), working together to carry out some task. Their behavior (instead of their static structure) is represented as a sequence of messages that are exchanged among objects. The evolution over time of the method dispatches characterizes the overall behavior.

As in the object diagram, the elements represented in the interaction diagrams are the objects created by a program. The main difference between object diagram and interaction diagrams is that the former represents the structure of the object system, in terms of inter-object relationships, while the latter deals with the behavior of communicating objects, expressed in terms of the method invocations issued among the objects in the system.

The interactions among objects can be modeled in two ways: by emphasizing the time ordering of the messages (*sequence diagrams*), or by emphasizing the sequencing of the messages in the context of the structural organization of the objects (*collaboration diagrams*). In the first case, a vertical time line is displayed and events are positioned on it to indicate their temporal ordering. In the latter case, the Dewey numbering system (incremented integer numbers separated by dots) is used to indicate that a given message triggers the exchange of a set of other nested messages. Thus, if 1 is the sequence number of the first message, 1.1 and 1.2 are respectively used for the first and second nested messages. Method calls prefixed by Dewey numbers label the inter-object relationships shown in a collaboration diagram.

Reverse engineering of the interaction diagrams from the code can be conducted either dynamically or statically. Dynamic extraction of the interactions among objects requires the availability of a full, executable system, which is run with some predefined input data. The statements issuing calls to methods are traced during the execution, with information for the unique identification of the source and target objects. The main disadvantages of this approach are that it does not apply to incomplete systems, but only to whole, executable ones, and that the resulting diagrams describe the system for a single execution with given input values. A static, conservative analysis of the code for the reverse engineering of the interaction diagrams addresses both problems. However, it may overestimate the set of admissible behaviors. This is why these two kinds of diagrams complement each other and it is desirable to have both of them during reverse engineering of a given Object Oriented system.

5.2 Interaction Diagram Recovery

The static recovery of the interactions among objects is done in two steps: first, the objects created by the program and accessible through program variables are inferred from the code. Then, each call to a method is resolved in terms of the possible source and target objects involved in the message exchange.

$$
\begin{array}{llll}
(1) & P & ::= & D^* S^* \\
(2) & D & ::= & a \\
(3) & & | & m(f_1, ..., f_k) \\
(4) & & | & cs(f_1, ..., f_k) \\
(5) & S & ::= & x = \text{new } c(a_1, ..., a_k); \quad gen[x] = \{c_i\} \\
(6) & & | & x = y; \\
(7) & & | & [x =] \, y.m(a_1, ..., a_k);
\end{array}
$$

where in (5) c_i is the object identifier associated with this allocation site.
$gen[n] = \emptyset$ for all locations different from the left hand side x in (5)
$kill[n] = \emptyset$ for all locations

Fig. 5.1. Flow propagation specialization to determine the set of objects allocated in the program that are (possibly) referenced by each program location.

A static approximation of the objects created by a program and of their mutual relationships can be obtained by performing a flow propagation inside the OFG, as described in more detail in Chapter 4. For the reader's convenience, the rules for the generation of the related flow information are reported also in Fig. 5.1. Each object allocation point in the program gives rise to an object identifier c_i, where c is the object's class name. Propagation of such object identifiers along the program's data flows (i.e., in the OFG) allows associating each variable with the set of statically determined objects it may reference.

The set of objects c_i extracted from a program approximates the set of objects the program may create at run time. The main source of approximation consists of their multiplicity: since it is impossible to determine statically the number of times a statement is executed, the actual multiplicity of each object c_i is unknown.

During interaction diagram construction, source and target of method invocations are resolved into a set of statically determined objects c_i. An alternative would be associating them with the respective classes, instead of their instances. However, the first choice provides a better approximation than just using the class of the objects that are invocation sources or targets. In fact, in the resulting interaction diagrams, objects of a same class allocated at different program points are distinguished in the first case, while they are represented as a single element in the second case. Moreover, objects belonging to a subclass of the declared class are assigned the exact type, as obtained from the allocation statement, while the analysis of method invocations at the class level does not allow distinguishing instances of the given class from instances of the subclasses.

```
resolveCall(expr: 'p.g()'): CallPairs
1    A ← class(scope(expr))
2    f ← method(scope(expr))
3    sources ← out[A.f.this]
4    if p is a class attribute
5        targets ← out[A.p]
6    else
7        targets ← out[A.f.p]
8    end if
9    return (sources, targets)
```

Fig. 5.2. Algorithm for the static resolution of a method call.

Once the objects referenced by program locations are obtained by the flow analysis on the OFG, method calls can be resolved by means of the algorithm shown in Fig. 5.2. Given a statement containing a call expression of the form `p.g()` inside a method `f` of class `A`, the source objects and the target objects of the call are respectively those referenced by the `this` pointer of the current method ($out[A.f.this]$) and by the location `p` ($out[A.f.p]$ or $out[A.p]$ in case `p` is a class attribute).

More complex Java expressions involving method calls can be easily reduced to the case reported in Fig. 5.2. For example, if a chain of attribute accesses precedes the method call, as in `p.q.g()`, the invocation targets are obtained from the last involved attribute: $out[B.q]$, where `B` is the class of the attribute `q` accessed through `p`. When another method call precedes the one to be solved, as in p.f().g(), the related **return** location can be used to determine the targets of the call: *out*[B.f.return], where B is the class of the method f accessed through p.

The procedure *resolveCall* given in Fig. 5.2 returns a pair of sets, *sources* and *targets*, containing the object identifiers that are statically determined as respectively possible source or target objects of the given invocation. The source and target objects returned by the procedure *resolveCall* will be connected by a *call* relationship in the interaction diagrams.

_____ *eLib* example _____

Let us consider the method addLoan from class Library (line 40). It contains four method calls (lines 42, 43, 45, 46) that must be resolved before constructing the interaction diagrams.

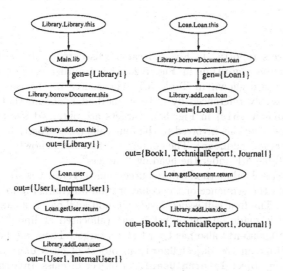

Fig. 5.3. Portion of OFG used for call resolution.

Fig. 5.3 shows the portion of OFG that contains the information required for the resolution of the four calls inside method addLoan. The object Library1, allocated at line 348 and assigned to the static attribute lib of class Main, is the object referenced by this inside addLoan. The object Loan1, allocated inside borrowDocument at line 60, is passed as the parameter loan to addLoan. The attribute user of class Loan is returned by the method getUser of class Loan and is assigned to the variable user (line 42), a local variable of method addLoan. The set of objects possibly referenced by the attribute user of class Loan was determined in the previous chapter (see

Fig. 4.9). In Fig. 5.3 it is represented as the *out* set of node Loan.user. By propagating such values in the OFG, the *out* set of Library.addLoan.user is computed. Similarly, the OFG edges that lead to Library.addLoan.doc (the local variable doc inside method addLoan) indicate that it references the objects stored inside the attribute document of class Loan. These were also determined in the previous chapter (see Fig. 4.9) and are reported as the *out* set of node Loan.document in Fig. 5.3.

Line	Call	Sources	Targets
42	loan.getUser()	Library1	Loan1
43	loan.getDocument()	Library1	Loan1
45	user.addLoan(loan)	Library1	User1, InternalUser1
46	doc.addLoan(loan)	Library1	Book1, TechnicalReport1, Journal1

Table 5.1. Source and target objects in method calls issued inside method addLoan in class Library.

The *out* sets reported in Fig. 5.3 can be used to resolve method calls, according to the algorithm in Fig. 5.2. The resulting sets of source and target objects are shown in Table 5.1. The source of the calls is the set of objects possibly referenced by this in method addLoan, that is, the set *out*[Loan.addLoan.this] in Fig. 5.3. Targets are obtained similarly, as the *out* sets of the locations involved in the four calls (resp. loan, loan, user, doc inside method addLoan). The content of these sets, shown in Fig. 5.3, is reported in Table 5.1 under the heading "Targets".

Given the resolved method calls (sources and targets), it is straightforward to either build the sequence or the collaboration diagram. Figure 5.4 depicts both of them. The first call issued inside method addLoan is a call to method getUser and is made on the object Loan1 (allocated at line 60). The second call (getDocument) also has Loan1 as its target. Then, method addLoan is invoked either on the object User1, an object of class User allocated at line 382, or on object InternalUser1, an object of class InternalUser allocated at line 390. The last call (still addLoan) has three possible target objects: Book1, TechnicalReport1, Journal1 (resp. allocated at lines 406, 414, 422). The source object of all these calls is Library1.

In Fig. 5.4, the associations between objects shown in the collaboration diagram at the bottom are those recovered during reverse engineering of the object diagram, as described in Chapter 4.

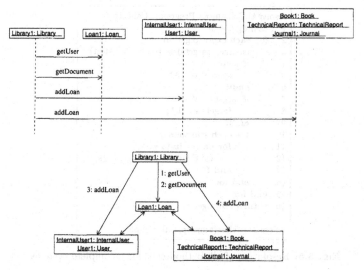

Fig. 5.4. Sequence (top) and collaboration (bottom) diagram built after call resolution for method addLoan in class Library.

5.2.1 Incomplete Systems

In order to produce complete interaction diagrams, the algorithm described in the previous section requires that all allocation points are in the code under analysis. This means that the system under analysis comprises all the driver modules necessary to build all of the needed objects. However, in Object Oriented programming it is very common to build only an incomplete system, consisting of a cohesive set of interacting classes that perform a given, well defined task, and are expected to be reused in different contexts. In these cases it would be desirable to be able to derive the interaction diagrams even if not all object creations are in the code, to understand the behavior of the incomplete subsystem in isolation, independently of its usages in a given application. To achieve this, all method invocations are taken into consideration and when the source or the target of a call are not associated with any recovered object, although their classes are part of the system under analysis, a generic object is introduced. The result is an interaction diagram in which placeholders (marked with an asterisk) for generic objects are present for objects not allocated inside the analyzed code.

Resolution of method calls for incomplete systems is shown in Fig. 5.5. All calls in the program are considered in sequence. Results of flow analysis are

```
resolveAllCalls(prog: Program): CallEdges
1    callEdges ← ∅
2    for each expr: 'p.g()' in prog
3        (sources, targets) ← resolveCall(stmt)
4        if sources = ∅
5            sources ← {A*}
6        endif
7        if targets = ∅
8            targets ← {B*}
9        endif
10       for each s in sources
11           for each t in targets
12               callEdges ← callEdges ∪ (s, t)_g
13           end for
14       end for
15   end for
16   return callEdges

where A = class(scope(p)), B = type(p)
```

Fig. 5.5. Resolution of all method calls for incomplete systems.

used to determine the source and target objects (invocation of procedure *resolveCall*). If one or both of the two sets are empty, a generic object associated to the declared class or interface is used instead (A* indicates a generic object of class/interface A or any derived/implementing class). In this way call edges are generated even when the object analysis algorithm fails to determine the object issuing or receiving a message.

When an object A_i allocated in the program portion under analysis is the source or target of a call, it cannot be excluded that another externally allocated object be an alternative source or target of the same call. Thus, A* must be always assumed implicitly as an alternative source or target, unless further information is available about the excluded code. Moreover, if the excluded code introduces data flows that alter the OFG, it is necessary to take them into account, in order for the result to remain conservative. An example of this situation is the presence of external container classes, discussed in detail in Chapter 2. The presence of a label A* indicates that no allocation point for the given object was found in the code, while A_i indicates that at least one allocation point was found, although other external allocations may also exist.

When, in the presence of subclassing, the allocation point is part of the analyzed code, the allocated object is assigned the exact type (e.g., if A1 inherits from A and the allocation expression is new A1() the object will be identified accurately as $A1_i$). On the contrary, when a generic object is introduced because the allocation point is missing, the actual type may be any derived class, and the recovered information is less precise than for objects allocated in the code (A* is used for the external allocation of objects of any subclass of A, including A itself).

_____ *eLib* example _____

Let us consider the code of just the core classes of the *eLib* program (Appendix A), excluding the driver class Main reported in Appendix B. When method addLoan (line 40) from class Library is analyzed, the source object of the four calls it contains (lines 42, 43, 45, 46) is not known. Actually, no allocation of objects belonging to class Library is performed inside the code in Appendix A. While for the first two calls it is possible to determine the target object, which is Loan1, the Loan object allocated at line 60, this is not possible for the last two calls. No object of either classes User and Document is ever allocated in the code under analysis. Correspondingly, the set *targets* returned by the procedure *resolveCall* is empty for the calls at lines 45, 46.

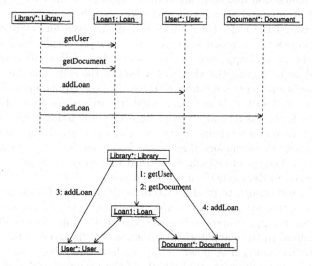

Fig. 5.6. Sequence (top) and collaboration (bottom) diagram for method addLoan in class Library. The analyzed code excludes the driver class Main.

Application of the rules in Fig. 5.5 leads to the introduction of a generic object Library* as the source of all four calls. Moreover, the generic objects User* and Document* are introduced for the calls at lines 45, 46. The resulting sequence and collaboration diagrams are shown in Fig. 5.6. By contrasting them with those in Fig. 5.4, the approximations introduced by generic objects become apparent. Only superclasses (e.g., User and Document) of actually allocated classes are specified with the generic objects, and no reference to specific allocation statements can be given (e.g., in Fig. 5.4 User1 is the object allocated at line 382, while in Fig. 5.6 allocation of User* is external and unknown).

5.2.2 Focusing

The interaction diagrams in Fig. 5.4 and 5.6 represent the message exchange among objects triggered by the execution of the method addLoan inside the class Library. In other words, the view focuses on the interactions occurring when a particular computation (i.e., method of interest, such as Library.addLoan) is performed. This corresponds to the natural approach of drawing the interaction diagrams in forward engineering. In fact, it usually makes no sense to draw just one huge diagram for the whole functioning of the system. It is preferable to split it up according to the most important subcomputations (i.e., the most important methods for the selected functionality). This is the key to handling the complexity of large systems.

When interaction diagrams are reverse engineered, the overall plot containing all objects and all message exchanges may be unusable, because its size may exceed the cognitive abilities of humans even for relatively small systems. However, it is possible to focus the view on specific methods, thus following the natural approach to the construction of these diagrams. This is achieved by restricting the view to a subset of the calls issued in the program: those belonging to a method of choice. The corresponding modification of the recovery algorithm is as follows. First, the procedure *resolveAllCalls* in Fig 5.5, which returns all call edges in the whole interaction diagram, is run. Then, only the nodes reachable in the *call graph* (the graph representing the call relationship between pairs of methods) from a method of choice are taken into account. The set of call edges returned by procedure *resolveAllCalls* is thus restricted to the methods in a selected portion of the call graph.

If this is not enough to produce interaction diagrams of manageable size, the second option available to the user is cutting a part of the system and analyzing an incomplete system, in such a way that it still includes all the key classes involved in the computation of interest. As discussed in the previous section, the introduction of generic objects allows analyzing incomplete systems as well. To summarize, applicability of the proposed approach to large systems can be achieved by filtering the relevant information in two ways:

1. Only the calls issued directly or indirectly from a method of interest are resolved.
2. An incomplete system, including only the interesting classes, is analyzed.

Method calls in a focused collaboration diagram are numbered according to the Dewey notation. Such numbering is exploited also to draw the sequence diagrams, in that the temporal (vertical) ordering is induced by them. It is possible to obtain the proper numbering of method calls by means of the numbering algorithms shown in Fig. 5.7, 5.8.

The first step, described in Fig. 5.7, consists of numbering each call statement in the program. The first time the procedure *numberCalls* is invoked, it has a method body (block of statements) as first and 1 as the second parameter. An incremental number is associated to each call statement (line 3)

```
numberCalls(stmtBlock: Statements, num: Integer): Integer
1   for each stmt in stmtBlock
2       if stmt = 'p.g()'
3           callNum[stmt] ← num
4           num ← num + 1
5       endif
6       if stmt = 'if (expr) bk1 else bk2'
7           n1 ← numberCalls(bk1, num)
8           n2 ← numberCalls(bk2, num)
9           num ← max(n1, n2)
10      endif
11      if stmt = 'while (expr) bk'
12          num ← numberCalls(bk, num)
13      endif
14  endfor
15  return num
```

Fig. 5.7. Numbering of method calls.

and each nested block of statements is handled similarly to the main block, by recurring inside it (at line 11 only the case of a while loop containing a nested block is represented for simplicity). Statements with more than one nested block of statements, such as an if statement with both then and else part, require a special treatment, in that the value of the number to use for the first statement following the if must be the maximum between the values generated inside the two nested blocks of statements (then and else part of the if).

———————————————— example ————————————————

```
class A {
    void f() {
        ...
        if (c) {
            o1.m1();            5    A.f → B1.m1
            o2.m2();            6    A.f → B2.m2
        } else {               5    A.f → B3.m3
            o3.m3();            7    A.f → B4.m4
        }
        o4.m4();
    }
}
```

Assuming *num* equal to 5 when the if statement above (inside method f of class A) is encountered, the absolute numbers attached to the calls to B1.m1 and B2.m2 are respectively 5 and 6, the absolute number attached to B3.m3 is 5, and the next value of *num*, used for B4.m4, is 7 (assuming that variables o1, o2, o3, o4 belong respectively to classes B1, B2, B3, B4). The alternative between the two branches of the if is indicated by giving them a same initial numbering (5, for both A.f → B1.m1 and A.f → B3.m3).

```
numberFocusedCalls(stmtBlock: Statements,
                   curNum: DeweyNumber)
1    for each stmt in stmtBlock
2        if stmt = 'p.g()'
3            deweyNum ← curNum.callNum[stmt]
4            printNumberedCall(deweyNum, stmt)
5            if g is not on the callStack
6                push(g, callStack)
7                numberFocusedCalls(body[g], deweyNum)
8                pop(g, callStack)
9            endif
10       endif
11       if stmt = 'if (expr) bk1 else bk2'
12           numberFocusedCalls(bk1, curNum)
13           numberFocusedCalls(bk2, curNum)
14       endif
15       if stmt = 'while (expr) bk'
16           numberFocusedCalls(bk, curNum)
17       endif
18   endfor
```

Fig. 5.8. Numbering of method calls focused on a method.

The second step in the generation of the Dewey numbers for the collaboration diagram, summarized in Fig. 5.8, is run under the assumption that the view is focused on some method. Correspondingly, *numberFocusedCalls* is invoked with the body of the selected method as the first parameter, and an empty Dewey number as the second parameter. When a call is encountered, the related Dewey number is obtained by concatenating the current Dewey number and the number of the call, separating them with a dot (line 3). The new Dewey number generated for the call is passed to a recursive invocation of *numberFocusedCalls*, executed on the body of the called method (line 7). Computation of the Dewey numbers inside the called method is not activated in case recursion is detected (check at line 5). For the other statements (lines 11 through 17), the procedure just enters each nested block of statements, where it is reapplied.

When multiple objects, belonging to different classes, are determined as the targets of a call (e.g., InternalUser1 and User1 for the call to addLoan in Fig. 5.4), the content of the invoked method may differ from object to object (method overriding). The procedure to compute the Dewey numbers (*numberFocusedCalls* in Fig. 5.8) is recursively called (line 7) for each different implementation (body) of the overridden method, thus including all of the possibile alternatives.

———————————————— *eLib* example ————————————————

Let us consider the direct and indirect method calls issued from inside the body of method `returnDocument`, class `Library`, line 66, shown in Table 5.2. The first called method, `isOut`, in turn invokes method `isAvailable` from class `Document`. Method `getBorrower` (second call in `returnDocument`) invokes `getUser` from class `Loan`. Finally, `Library.removeLoan`, the last invocation inside `returnDocument`, triggers the execution of four methods, reported at the bottom-right of Table 5.2. These do not perform any further method invocation.

Document.isOut:		
Line	Num	Called method
180	1	Document.isAvailable

Document.getBorrower:		
Line	Num	Called method
187	1	Loan.getUser

Library.returnDocument:		
Line	Num	Called method
68	1	Document.isOut
69	2	Document.getBorrower
71	3	Library.removeLoan

Library.removeLoan:		
Line	Num	Called method
50	1	Loan.getUser
51	2	Loan.getDocument
53	3	User.removeLoan
54	4	Document.removeLoan

Table 5.2. Transitive method calls issued from method `returnDocument` in class `Library`. Column *Num* reports their numbering.

Method calls are numbered in Table 5.2 (column *Num*) according to the rules given in Fig. 5.7. Let us consider a collaboration diagram focused on method `Library.returnDocument`. Computation of the Dewey numbers (see Fig. 5.8) starts with the body of method `Library.returnDocument` and an empty Dewey value. The three calls issued inside this method are thus numbered 1, 2, 3. Procedure *numberFocusedCalls* is then reapplied to the body of `Document.isOut`, with a current Dewey value equal to 1. The call to `isAvailable` issued inside `Document.isOut` is correspondingly numbered 1.1. Similarly, the call to `Loan.getUser` inside `Document.getBorrower` is numbered 2.1. Another call to the same method, issued from method `Library.removeLoan`, receives a different Dewey number: 3.1. The final Dewey numbers produced for the collaboration diagram focused on `returnDocument` are displayed in Fig. 5.9.

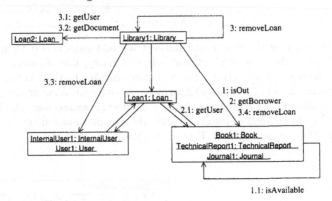

Fig. 5.9. Collaboration diagram focused on method **returnDocument** of class **Library**.

5.3 Dynamic Analysis

A second approach to the construction of the interaction diagrams for a given application relies on dynamic analysis, i.e., on the analysis of the run-time behavior. Interaction diagrams can be produced out of the execution traces obtained by executing the application on a set of test cases. The basic information that must be available from the execution traces to support the construction of the interaction diagrams consists of an identifier of the current object and of the object on which each method call is issued. More specifically, in order to instrument a program for interaction diagram construction, the following additions are required:

- Classes are augmented with an object identifier, computed within the execution of the class constructors.
- Upon method call, the identifier of the current and of the target object are added to the execution trace. Moreover, the name of the current method is also traced.
- Time stamps associated with method calls are produced and traced.

At this point, a straightforward postprocessing of the execution trace provides an interaction diagram for each test case executed. Each time a method call is found in the trace, a call relationship is drawn in the interaction diagram between the objects uniquely identified in the trace. Knowledge of the current method issuing the call is used to determine the current activation in the sequence diagram (see below). The ordering of the call events is induced by the time stamps.

Differently from the static analysis, the dynamic analysis produces a set of interaction diagrams, one for each test case. Even if each diagram usually represents a different interaction pattern, it is not ensured that all possible interactions are considered. This depends on the quality of the test cases. On the contrary, all possible behaviors are represented in the statically recovered diagrams.

——————————————— *eLib* example ———————————————

Let us consider two test cases for the *eLib* program[1]:

TC1 A book previously borrowed by a normal (not an internal) user of the library is returned, and the loan is closed.

TC2 An attempt is made to return a book which is already available for loan.

Both test cases result in the execution of the method `returnDocument` (line 66) from class `Library`, with a different parameter (resp., a borrowed and an available book).

Time	Cur. obj	Cur. method	Target obj	Called method
1	Library1	returnDocument	Book1	isOut
2	Book1	isOut	Book1	isAvailable
3	Library1	returnDocument	Book1	getBorrower
4	Book1	getBorrower	Loan1	getUser
5	Library1	returnDocument	Library1	removeLoan
6	Library1	removeLoan	Loan2	getUser
7	Library1	removeLoan	Loan2	getDocument
8	Library1	removeLoan	User1	removeLoan
9	Library1	removeLoan	Book1	removeLoan
Time	Cur. obj	Cur. method	Target obj	Called method
1	Library1	returnDocument	Book1	isOut
2	Book1	isOut	Book1	isAvailable

Table 5.3. Execution traces for test cases TC1 (top) and TC2 (bottom).

The related execution traces are shown in Table 5.3. Fig. 5.10 displays the sequence diagrams that are obtained from the execution traces. Method activations are shown on the vertical time lines as blank vertical boxes. Such information can be easily derived from the execution traces, since the name of the current method is also traced when a call is issued. Thus, at time 5 (TC1) a new method activation is started on the time line of the object `Library1` because of the call to `removeLoan`, which has a target object equal

---

[1] Ad hoc drivers must be defined for them. In particular, the driver class `Main` in Appendix B is not compatible with TC2.

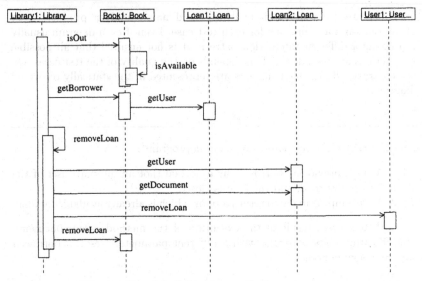

TC1: returnDocument called on a borrowed book

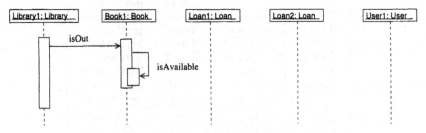

TC2: returnDocument called on an available book

Fig. 5.10. Sequence diagrams for method `Library.returnDocument` obtained by dynamic analysis, with test cases TC1 (top) and TC2 (bottom).

to the current object. Since successive calls are made with `Library1` as the current object and `removeLoan` as the current method, they depart from the nested activation in the time line of `Library1`. Similarly, a nested activation is created for the execution of `isAvailable` inside `isOut` at time 2 on object `Book1`.

The same method invocations are represented in the dynamic sequence diagram in Fig. 5.10 (top) and in the static collaboration diagram in Fig. 5.9. However, the partial nature of the dynamic analysis is apparent from the comparison of the sequence diagram at the bottom of Fig. 5.10 and the static collaboration diagram in Fig. 5.9. In fact, only two of all possible interactions are exercised in test case TC2, while all of them are conservatively shown in Fig. 5.9.

Another aspect of the partial information provided by the dynamic diagrams is the type of the objects issuing or receiving a call. In Fig. 5.10 it seems that the class of the object receiving the calls issued at times 1, 2, 3, 9 is Book and the class of the object receiving the call issued at time 8 is User. On the contrary, inspection of the statically recovered collaboration diagram in Fig. 5.9, which accounts for all statically possible objects involved in each call, reveals that other object types can be the targets of these calls (resp. TechnicalReport and Journal for the calls issued at 1, 2, 3, 9, and InternalUser for the call issued at 8). Additional test cases would be necessary to cover also these possibilities, while a static analysis conservatively reports all of them.

Where dynamic interaction diagrams are more precise than static diagrams is in object identification. In Fig. 5.10, the target of the calls isOut, getBorrower, removeLoan is a same object, Book1, of class Book. This means that exactly the same object receives these three calls. On the contrary, identity of the target of these three calls, numbered 1, 2 and 3.4 in Fig. 5.9, is not precisely defined in the case of a statically recovered diagram. The allocation point for the three alternative target objects is known exactly (line 406 for Book1, line 414 for TechnicalReport1, line 422 for Journal1). However, such allocation points may be executed repeatedly (actually, they are, since they belong to methods indirectly called inside the loop at line 521 in the main). Since it is not possible to distinguish two instances made during different loop iterations by means of a static analysis, the source and target objects in static diagrams such as that in Fig. 5.9 account for all objects allocated by the same allocation statement. On the contrary, a dynamic analysis allows distinguishing among them, and in a dynamic diagram two call relationships have the same source or the same target object if and only if exactly the same object issues or receives the calls. In the presence of dynamic binding, the knowledge of the exact object identity obtained through the dynamic analysis allows for a smaller, though possibly incomplete, set of potentially invoked polymorphic variants of the same method.

5.3.1 Discussion

As with the object diagram, static and dynamic extraction of the interaction diagrams provide different and complementary information. In static interaction diagrams, all possible method calls among all possible objects created in the program are represented. Actually, some of them may never occur in any program execution, due to the presence of infeasible paths that cannot (in general) be identified statically. However, the result is conservative. There does not exist any interaction among objects that is not represented in a statically recovered interaction diagram. Moreover, objects involved in the interactions are necessarily of one of the classes reported in the static diagrams, and cannot be of any other class.

The main limitation of the statically recovered interaction diagrams is related to the identity of the objects represented in the diagrams. When two arcs depart from a same object or enter a same object in a static interaction diagram, it cannot be ensured that the same object will actually issue or receive the calls associated with such arcs. In fact, object identity is given by the allocation statement in the program, but such a statement can be in general executed multiple times, giving rise to different objects that are represented as a single element in a static interaction diagram. On the contrary, the identity of the objects represented in dynamic interaction diagrams is based on a unique identifier that is generated and traced at run time for each newly created object. Thus, a precise object identification is possible, and correspondingly the presence of call arcs departing from or entering into the same object indicates that exactly this object is involved in the interaction.

On the other side, the main limitation of the dynamic diagrams is related to the quality of the test cases used to produce them. It may happen that not all possible interactions are exercised by the available test cases, or that not all possible type combinations are tried. In order to increase the amount of information carried by the dynamic views, it is possible to measure the level of coverage achieved with respect to the corresponding static diagram. Thus, a test case selection criterion may be defined as follows: if all object types and all possible interactions in the static diagram are covered by the available test cases, the set of dynamic diagrams obtained from the execution traces can be considered satisfactory.

From the point of view of the usability of the diagrams, static and dynamic views have contrasting properties. A static diagram concentrates all the information about the behavior of a method in a single place, the interaction diagram focused on the given method, while several dynamic diagrams may be necessary to cover all relevant interactions associated to a given method. This indicates a higher usability of the static diagrams, since just one diagram per method must be inspected. On the other side, static diagrams tend to be larger than dynamic diagrams, in that the latter account for a specific, limited execution scenario, while the former represent all possibilities.

5.4 The *eLib* Program

The full, static interaction diagram for the *eLib* program (Appendix A and B), obtained by considering all interactions among objects possibly triggered by the main control loop (line 527), contains a number of nodes, arcs and labels largely beyond the cognitive capabilities of a human being, mainly because of the high number of edges and of the very high number of labels (more than 200) on the edges (each edge label represents a method call). It should be recognized that this happens for a relatively small application such as *eLib*. In larger, more realistic, programs the problem is exacerbated. Consequently, usage of the focusing technique described in Section 5.2.2 appears to be mandatory for any program under analysis.

When focused interaction diagrams are taken into consideration, their size is largely reduced. If focused diagrams are produced for the *eLib* program, the typical number of edges is between 5 and 10, while labels are typically in the range 5-20. Thus, focusing seems to be a very effective technique to make the information reverse engineered from the code useful and usable. Interaction diagrams focused on selected methods restrict the scope of the program comprehension effort to a given computation and provide an amount of data that can be managed by a human being. Overall, they represent a good trade-off between providing detailed information and considering a single functionality at a time.

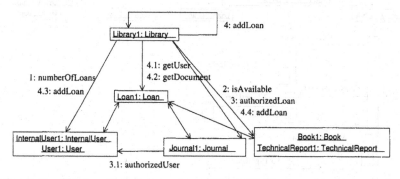

Fig. 5.11. Collaboration diagram focused on method `borrowDocument` of class `Library`.

Fig. 5.11 shows the collaboration diagram obtained by focusing on the method `borrowDocument` of class `Library`. The interactions occurring among the objects to realize the library functionality of document loan are pretty clear from the diagram. First, the number of loans held by the user who intends to borrow a document is checked (call to `numberOfLoans`), and if it exceeds a given threshold the loan is negated. Then, availability of the selected document is verified (call to `isAvailable`). A third check is about the authorization to borrow the chosen document. The method `authorizedLoan` is called on the given document, which may belong to class `Book`, `TechnicalReport` or `Journal`. In the first two cases, method `authorizedLoan` return a fixed value (resp. `true` and `false`). In the last case, authorization depends on the user category. Thus, the value returned by `authorizedLoan` is obtained by invoking the method `authorizedUser` on the borrowing user. This method returns **true** for internal users, who have more privileges than the normal user, while it returns **false** for the other users. In the diagram, it can be observed that **authorizedLoan** is numbered 3 and **authorizedUser** is numbered 3.1. The latter is a nested invocation occurring only when the target object of **authorizedLoan** is of type **Journal**.

If all checks give positive answers, the document can be borrowed. This is achieved by calling the method **addLoan** (call number 4), after creating a new **Loan** object (**Loan1**). In turn, this call triggers the execution of four nested methods. First of all, user and document are accessed from the **Loan** object **Loan1** (calls 4.1 and 4.2). Then, method **addLoan** is invoked on these two objects of type **User** and **Document** (calls 4.3 and 4.4). In this way, a bidirectional association is created between **Loan** object and **User** object, and between **Loan** object and **Document** object.

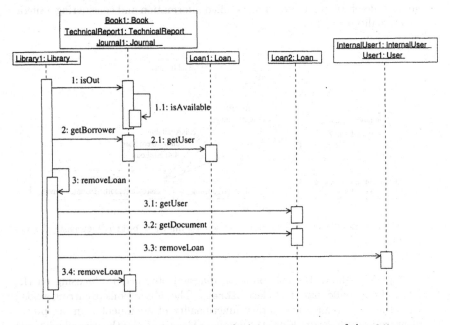

Fig. 5.12. Sequence diagram focused on method **returnDocument** of class **Library**.

Fig. 5.12 shows the sequence diagram focused on the method **returnDocument** of class **Library**. It clarifies the message exchange that occurs when a document is returned to the library. First of all, a check is made to see if the document is actually out (call number 1, **isOut**). If this is not the case, nothing has to be done. A nested method execution is triggered by **isOut**, which resorts to **isAvailable** to produce the answer. If the document is out, its current borrower is obtained by requesting it via the document (call to

getBorrower, number 2). In turn, the Document object redirects the request of
the borrower to the Loan object associated to it (call 2.1, getUser). It should
be noted that the involved Loan object is Loan1, i.e., the instance allocated at
line 60. A new, temporary Loan object (Loan2, allocated at line 70), is then
created and passed to removeLoan (call number 3) as a parameter. Inside
removeLoan (nested activation in Fig. 5.12) user and document associated
with the temporary Loan object are obtained (calls 3.1 and 3.2), and a call to
method removeLoan on both of them (calls number 3.3 and 3.4) deletes the
associations of these two objects toward the Loan object being removed. In
this way, not only the Loan object is removed from the list of current loans
held by the Library, but the inverse associations from User and Document to
Loan are also updated. The resulting state of the library is thus consistent.

Class Library provides methods to print information about stored data.
Two examples of methods that can be invoked for such a purpose are
printAllLoans and printUserInfo. Their interaction diagrams are displayed
in Fig. 5.13 and 5.14.

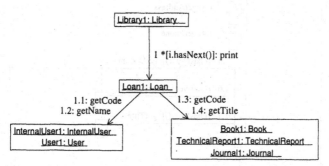

Fig. 5.13. Collaboration diagram focused on method printAllLoans of class
Library.

The first and only method execution invoked inside method printAll-
Loans (from class Library) is on object Loan1. Such an invocation, numbered
1 in Fig. 5.13, is iterated as long as the condition reported in square brackets
before the method name (print) is true. This condition requires that method
hasNext, called on the iterator i running over all loans in the library, returns
true. Thus, printAllLoans delegates the print functionality to the Loan objects stored in the library inside an iteration. In turn, each Loan object can
print complete loan information by requesting some of the data to the User
and Document objects associated with it. This is the reason for the nested
calls 1.1, 1.2 (toward objects InternalUser1 or User1) and 1.3, 1.4 (toward
objects Book1, TechnicalReport1, Journal1).

This example highlights the usefulness of showing conditions in square
brackets. The existence of an iteration over all loans in the library can be

grasped immediately from the collaboration diagram, due to the indication of a loop (asterisk before the call to **print**) and of the loop condition (in square brackets). While for larger diagrams the explicit indication of all conditions in square brackets may make them unreadable, because of an excessive label size, for small or medium size diagrams it may be extremely useful to include them in the arc labels. They provide important hints on the behavior of the method under analysis.

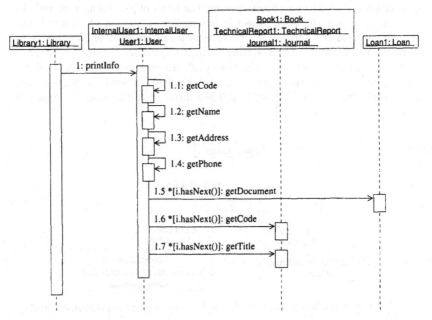

Fig. 5.14. Sequence diagram focused on method **printUserInfo(User user)** of class **Library**.

The method **printUserInfo** from class **Library** (see Fig. 5.14) has a parameter of type **User**, referencing a **User** object. The printing of information about this library user is completely delegated to the **User** object. Thus, **printUserInfo** contains just a method call, numbered 1, that transfers the control of the execution to method **printInfo** of class **User**. Inside this method, several data are obtained on the current object, by activating nested method invocations (numbered 1.1, 1.2, 1.3, 1.4). Then, the sequence of loans held by the given user are considered iteratively. For each of them, the borrowed document is requested (call to **getDocument**, number 1.5). The identifier and title of such a document are then accessed, by means of methods **getCode** (number 1.6) and **getTitle** (number 1.7). These further calls are still inside the same iteration. Retrieved information about the borrowed documents is printed to the standard output.

The sequence diagram depicted in Fig. 5.14 exploits the following results of flow propagation in the OFG:

- $out[\text{User.loans}] = \{\text{Loan1}\}$
- $out[\text{Loan.document}] = \{\text{Book1, TechnicalReport1, Journal1}\}$

Such results are conservative, but inaccurate in two respects: different loans should be associated with different kinds of users and no document of kind TechnicalReport should be ever present in a loan. In fact, documents of type Journal can be borrowed only by internal users (see check at line 59). Consequently, one would expect that User.loans and InternalUser.loans reference two different sets of objects, where only the second contains loans of Journals. On the contrary, only one node, User.loans, is in the OFG, and InternalUser just inherits the value of attribute loans from its superclass. On the other side, the authorization of a given User to borrow a document depends on the outcome of the call at line 59, to method authorizedLoan. A static analysis of the source code can hardly distinguish among the possible outcomes of this call, depending on the actual type of the target object and of the parameter. Similarly, the impossibility of creating a new loan when the given document is of type TechnicalReport is also hard to determine from a static analysis. In fact, it still depends on the outcome of the call to authorizedLoan at line 59.

The inaccuracies of the static analysis used to approximate the objects referenced by the attribute loans of class User and by the attribute document of class Loan have the following consequences for the sequence diagram in Fig. 5.14. The two calls to getCode and getTitle (numbered 1.6 and 1.7 resp.) have two objects as possible sources (namely, User1 and InternalUser1), and three objects as possible targets (namely, Book1, TechnicalReport1 and Journal1). However, object TechnicalReport1 can never be the target of the two calls, since technical reports are never authorized for loan and consequently cannot be referenced by the attribute document of Loan1. Object Journal1 can be the target of the two calls only when the source is InternalUser1, while it can never be returned by getDocument when the source is User1, since normal users are not allowed to borrow journals. The static analysis conducted to determine the objects possibly referenced by class attributes cannot detect such infeasible situations, implied by the behavior of authorizedLoan. In general, static analyses have only limited capabilities of dealing with the detection of infeasible conditions. On the other side, the results shown in Fig. 5.14 are conservative, in that they account for all possible run time behaviors. No interaction among objects can occur, when printUserInfo is called, that is not represented in the statically recovered diagram.

It would also be possible to recover the sequence diagram for the print-UserInfo method of class Library by means of a dynamic analysis. The related test cases would include a sequence of operations that change the state of the library, by adding users and documents, as well as Loan objects associated to users borrowing documents. The method printUserInfo should be invoked with the library in different states. The resulting sequence diagrams would resemble that obtained statically and represented in Fig. 5.14, with a few important differences. Only instances of classes Book and Journal would be present in the diagram, since there is no way to make a TechnicalReport object participate in a loan. Moreover, when the source of the calls number 1.6 and 1.7 is of type User, the target is always of type Book, in that there is no way to make a Journal object participate in a loan, when the associated user is not an InternalUser.

The example above highlights the different and complementary nature of statically and dynamically recovered interaction diagrams. The former represent all possible interactions in a single diagram, but may include interactions that can never occur due to infeasible conditions that cannot be detected statically. The latter show only interactions that are ensured to be possible, since they are obtained by an actual program execution. However, their results are scattered in a set of diagrams (one for each test case), none of which usually represents all possible interactions in a conservative way.

5.5 Related Work

Information about class instances collected at run-time is dealt with by several research prototypes [42, 62, 67, 97]. In these research projects, creation of objects and inter-object message exchange are captured by tracing the execution of the program in a given set of scenarios. In [67] static information limited to method invocations (call graph) can be combined with execution traces, thanks to a common representation of both data in a single database of logic facts, from which views are created through queries. In [41] the call graph is animated by highlighting the currently executing methods. Construction of call graphs for Object Oriented programs and their accuracy are considered in [28, 83].

Sequence diagrams are constructed by means of a dynamic analysis in [29]. The proposed approach exploits Aspect Oriented Programming [40] to intercept the execution of method calls in a non invasive way. The original source code is weaved with an external aspect that defines which run time events to capture and which data to record. The original code does not need be instrumented at all. Aspects are used to instrument Java code also in [8], where a mapping is defined between a metamodel of the execution traces and a metamodel of the scenario diagrams, adapted from the UML sequence diagram metamodel. Such a mapping is given as a set of consistency rules expressed in the Object Constraint Language (OCL) [98]. They account for the message exchanges that occur in non-distributed as well as in distributed systems and they are used to reverse engineer UML sequence diagrams from execution traces. In distributed systems, the order of execution of the methods is determined without resorting to a global clock, by matching each sequence of remote calls with the corresponding sequence of remote method executions.

In [20], points-to analysis is exploited to statically recover all possible execution traces for a given object, represented in a so-called Object Process Graph. Sequences of relevant instructions, including invocation instructions, are represented in the resulting graphs. Among the devised applications, these graphs can be used for protocol validation.

Experimental results on the application of the method described in this chapter to a large C++ system are presented in [90]. The static technique for the reverse engineering of the interaction diagrams has been applied to about half million lines of C++ code. To generate diagrams of manageable size, both partial analysis (with sub-systems being considered separately) and focusing (on each single method) have been exploited. Combined together, they have been fundamental to produce usable diagrams. The resulting views have been evaluated by the author of the related code, who judged them extremely informative and able to summarize information spread across the code. The lesson we learned is that the interactions among objects are a great help in support of program comprehension, but at the same time they require proper interactive facilities and reduction methods to scale to large software systems.

6

State Diagrams

State diagrams can be used to describe the behavior exhibited by objects of a given class. They show the possible states an object can be in and the transitions from state to state, as triggered by the messages issued to the object.

The effect of a method invocation on a target object depends on the state the object is in before the call. Thus, a description of an Object Oriented system in terms of message exchange only (see previous chapter, *Interaction diagrams*) does not reveal the state-dependent nature of the class behavior. This is where state diagrams can give a useful contribution.

Reverse engineering of the state diagrams from the code is a difficult task, that cannot be fully automated. The states of the objects in the system under analysis are defined by the values assumed by their fields. However, it is not possible to describe each n-tuple of field values as a distinct state, because of their intractable growth, and equivalence classes of field values must be introduced. The definition of such equivalence classes requires a manual intervention, while recovery of the state transitions can be automated, by means of an *abstract interpretation* of the program. Thus, given an abstract description of the field values and of the primitive operations on the abstract field values, it is possible to automatically derive a state diagram for the class, where the possible combinations of abstract values define the states, while the effects of method invocations are associated with the state transitions.

This chapter is organized as follows: the first section summarizes the main features represented in state diagrams and discusses the possibility of reverse engineering them from an existing program. Section 6.2 provides a summary of the main concepts behind abstract interpretation. A thorough treatment of abstract interpretation would occupy a much longer book portion. The presentation given in this chapter aims at providing the basic background knowledge necessary to understand the technique involved in state diagram recovery, which is described in detail in Section 6.3, from an operational point of view. The application of the presented method to the *eLib* program is discussed in Section 6.4, while related works are commented in Section 6.5.

6.1 State Diagrams

The behavior of the objects that belong to a given class can be described by means of state diagrams [1, 7, 31]. States represent conditions that characterize the lifetime of an object, so that objects remain in a given state for a time interval, until some action occurs that makes the state condition invalid and triggers a state transition. Given the fields of a class, the combinations of all possible values define the most detailed decomposition of the class behavior into states. However, such a decomposition is typically impractical, for the huge number of states, and not very meaningful, for the high number of equivalent states. Thus, field values are aggregated into equivalence classes that partition the set of all field value combinations. Each equivalence class is represented as a state and an object is in such a state as long as its field values are in the related equivalence class.

An object may change its state in response to a message it receives. Thus, state transitions are associated to method calls, and the dynamics of an object is abstracted into the state changes induced by method calls.

Available notations for the state diagrams [1, 7, 69] allow for a richer set of properties that can be incorporated into them. For example, each state can be characterized by entry and exit actions, ongoing activity and the inclusion of *submachines* (contained sub-state diagrams). Moreover, transitions can be guarded by conditions and temporized events can be added to the events of the kind method call. However, for the purposes of this chapter, the basic elements of the state diagrams described above are sufficient. They consist of:

- **States,** identified as equivalence classes of field values.
- **Transitions,** triggered by method calls.

———————————————— *coffee machine* example ————————————————

Fig. 6.1 shows the state diagram for a hypothetical class that manages the main functions of an automatic coffee machine. The coffee machine accepts quarters of dollars in input (up to two quarters), and requires an amount equal to half of a dollar to prepare a coffee. The user can, at any time, insert a quarter, request the return of the quarters inserted so far or request the preparation of the coffee. Of course, the coffee will be prepared only if two quarters have previously been inserted.

The behavior of the coffee machine class, described informally above, is explicitly represented in Fig. 6.1. Let us assume that the class field q records the number of quarters inserted so far, and that the boolean flag r represents the possibility to request the preparation of the coffee. According to the diagram in Fig. 6.1, the initial state of the objects of this class after creation is S_0, with $q = 0$ and $r = F$ (F represents the boolean value *false*, while T represents *true*). Graphically, S_0 is identified as the creation state because it

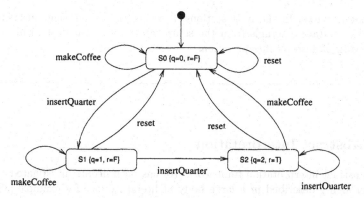

Fig. 6.1. Example of state diagram describing an automatic coffee machine.

is directly reached from the small solid filled circle, which represents the entry state of the diagram.

Requests to prepare a coffee (*makeCoffee*) or return money (*reset*) issued in S_0 have no effect (self transitions outgoing from S_0), while the insertion of a quarter (*insertQuarter*) triggers the transition from S_0 to S_1. In the latter state, the number of quarters inserted so far is 1 and coffee cannot yet be prepared ($q = 1, r = F$).

A request to prepare a coffee issued in S_1 has no effect (self transition), while a request to return the inserted quarter has the effect of triggering a transition back to the initial state, as well as the "visible" effect of actually returning a quarter to the user. Insertion of a further quarter originates a transition to S_2, where $q = 2$ and $r = T$.

In S_2 coffee can be prepared ($r = T$). Thus, an invocation of *makeCoffee* has the "visible" effect of delivering the beverage to the user, and has the "internal" effect of restoring the initial state S_0. A request to return money (*reset*) can also be issued in S_2, resulting in 2 quarters being returned to the user, and the system moving to the initial state S_0. When the coffee machine is in S_2, additional quarters cannot be accepted. Correspondingly, their insertion (call to *insertQuarter*) does not change the internal state (self transition) and has the effect of immediately returning the inserted coin.

Usefulness of the state diagrams is pretty clear from the example above. The same method call can have very different effects, according to the state of the target object. For example, a call to *insertQuarter* results in an increment of q in S_0 and S_1, but not in S_2, and changes the value of the flag r only in S_1. While interaction diagrams are focused on the message exchange that occurs among a set of collaborating objects, state diagrams are focused on the internal changes that occur within a single object of a given class. The kind of information they provide is thus complementary, and a complete description of the system's behavior can be achieved by properly combining these two alternative views. In the next sections, a technique for the semi-automatic recovery of state diagrams from the source code will be defined within the framework of *abstract interpretation*.

6.2 Abstract Interpretation

The abstract interpretation framework [16] has been deeply investigated and is thoroughly described in a large body of literature (see for example [38]). Abstract interpretation is presented in this section from an operational perspective, with the purpose of providing a survey of the algorithmic details necessary for its usage in reverse engineering of the state diagrams. Some of the theoretical and formal aspects are deliberately skipped.

The aim of abstract interpretation is determining the outcome of any program execution, with any possible input, by approximating the actual program behavior with an abstract behavior. Actual variable values are replaced by abstract values and the effect of each program statement on the variable values is abstracted into the effect it has on the corresponding abstract values. Abstract values represent equivalence classes of actual values, so that the problem of determining all values that all variables may have at each program point and in any execution becomes tractable.

In order to perform an abstract interpretation of a given program, the following entities must be defined:

- A domain of abstract values (*abstract domain*).
- A mapping from concrete to abstract values (*abstraction*).
- The abstract semantics of all primitive operations in the given program (*abstract interpretation*).

The main constraint on the abstract domain is that it must define a complete semi-lattice (with ordering "$\leq$"), i.e., its elements must be partially ordered and for each two elements a unique least upper bound must exist. The main constraint on the abstract interpretations of primitive operations is that they must be order-preserving.

Let us indicate with D the abstract domain, and with Int_s the abstract interpretation of statement s. The requirement on Int_s is the following:

$$\forall v \in D, \forall w \in D, v \leq w \Rightarrow Int_s(v) \leq Int_s(w)$$

Usually, concrete variable values are replaced by symbolic values which encode entire equivalence classes of values, and the abstract domain is the powerset of the set of symbolic values. The powerset can be partially ordered by set inclusion, and such an ordering defines a complete lattice, thus satisfying the constraint on the abstract domain.

Abstract operations are typically defined for individual symbolic values, the extension to sets of values (i.e., elements of the abstract domain) being straightforward.

The choice of the appropriate abstract domain is crucial, to obtain results that address the original motivation for performing an abstract interpretation of the program. While a too fine-grained domain makes abstract interpretation computationally intractable, a too high-level domain might produce over-conservative results, that are not useful to answer the initial questions on the program. In fact, the output of abstract interpretation is *safe*, i.e. the values produced in any actual execution are always a "concretization" of the abstract values. However, the latter might be over-conservative, i.e., the abstract values produced by the abstract interpretation might entail concrete values that can never occur in a real execution.

Once abstract domain and abstract operations are defined, the abstract interpretation of the program consists of computing the fixpoint of the abstract values collected at each statement from the predecessors and transformed by the abstract interpretation function associated with such a statement.

─────────── *coffee machine* example ───────────

The two state variables in the automatic coffee machine example are q, holding the number of quarters inserted so far, and r, which is *true* when coffee can be obtained from the machine. Different abstract domains can be chosen when performing an abstract interpretation of this program. For example, the following symbolic values can be used for variables q and r:

Concrete values	Abs value (1)
$q = 0$	$q{:}0$
$q = 1$	$q{:}1$
$q = 2$	$q{:}2$
$q > 2$	$q{:}gt2$
$r = true$	$r{:}T$
$r = false$	$r{:}F$

Another possible abstraction might collapse all values of q greater than zero into a single symbolic value:

Concrete values	Abs value (2)
$q = 0$	$q{:}Z$
$q > 0$	$q{:}GZ$
$r = true$	$r{:}T$
$r = false$	$r{:}F$

Abstract semantics must then be defined for the operations in the program. Since only constant values are assigned to the variables q and r, the following simplified abstract interpretation table can be defined for the assignment operator:

Operation	Abs sem (1)	Abs sem (2)
q = 0	$\{q{:}{*}\} \rightarrow \{q{:}0\}$	$\{q{:}{*}\} \rightarrow \{q{:}Z\}$
q = 1	$\{q{:}{*}\} \rightarrow \{q{:}1\}$	$\{q{:}{*}\} \rightarrow \{q{:}GZ\}$
q = 2	$\{q{:}{*}\} \rightarrow \{q{:}2\}$	$\{q{:}{*}\} \rightarrow \{q{:}GZ\}$
r = true	$\{r{:}{*}\} \rightarrow \{r{:}T\}$	$\{r{:}{*}\} \rightarrow \{r{:}T\}$
r = false	$\{r{:}{*}\} \rightarrow \{r{:}F\}$	$\{r{:}{*}\} \rightarrow \{r{:}F\}$

where $\{q{:}{*}\}$ and $\{r{:}{*}\}$ indicate any symbolic value prefixed respectively by "$q{:}$" or "$r{:}$". The abstract semantics of the increment operator is straightforward:

Operation	Abs sem (1)
q++	$\{q{:}0\} \rightarrow \{q{:}1\}$
	$\{q{:}1\} \rightarrow \{q{:}2\}$
	$\{q{:}2\} \rightarrow \{q{:}gt2\}$
	$\{q{:}gt2\} \rightarrow \{q{:}gt2\}$

Operation	Abs sem (2)
q++	$\{q{:}Z\} \rightarrow \{q{:}GZ\}$
	$\{q{:}GZ\} \rightarrow \{q{:}GZ\}$

The other operators used in the coffee machine program are relational operators, such as the equality comparison. Since variables are compared only to constant values in this program, the following simplified abstract semantics of the equality comparison can be used:

Operation	Abs sem (1)
q == 2	*true* for the abstract value $q{:}2$
	false for the abstract values $q{:}0$, $q{:}1$, $q{:}gt2$

Operation	Abs sem (2)
q == 2	*unknown* for the abstract value $q{:}GZ$
	false for the abstract value $q{:}Z$

If the abstract value of q is q:GZ, the result of the evaluation of q == 2 is unknown, and conservatively one has to assume that both possibilities might occur. When the relational expression q == 2 is part of a conditional statement (e.g., if (q == 2) r = true;), the result of its abstract interpretation determines the way abstract values are propagated forward. If the result is *true*, the abstract value is propagated only along the *then* branch of the conditional statement. If the result is *false*, only the *else* branch is followed. If the result is unknown, both branches are taken.

The abstract semantics above have been given for individual abstract values, but the generalization to sets of abstract values is easy to achieve. For example, the increment applied to the set $\{q$:0, q:$gt2$, r:$T\}$ gives $\{q$:1, q:$gt2$, r:$T\}$, i.e., the increment is applied separately to individual values and the result is the union of the results. Of course, when it is applied to r:T it behaves like the identity. Another example is the equality comparison. Abstract evaluation of q == 2 for $\{q$:1, q:$gt2$, r:$T\}$ gives *false* for the first two values and is *undefined* on the third abstract value. If the condition q == 2 is part of an *if* statement, all values will be propagated only along the false branch (including r:T), since no abstract value reaching the *if* statement can ever make the related condition true. If the set of abstract values reaching the *if* statement is $\{q$:1, q:2, r:$T\}$, the condition can be both true and false. Correspondingly, $\{q$:2, r:$T\}$ is propagated along the *then* branch, while $\{q$:1, r:$T\}$ is propagated along the *else* branch. In order to decide if the abstract value r:T should be propagated only along the *then* branch (with q:2) or the *else* branch (with q:1), a more refined abstract domain would be necessary, in which q and r are represented jointly (e.g., using the abstract values $<q$:$1,r$:$T>$, $<q$:$2,r$:$T>$, ..., $<q$:$gt2,r$:$F>$). In the second abstract domain, if $\{q$:GZ, r:$T\}$ reaches the same *if* statement, both values must be propagated along both branches of the conditional statement, in that the value of the related condition is unknown.

	Abs dom (1)	Abs dom (1)	Abs dom (2)
	Initial values		
	$\{q$:0, r:F$\}$	$\{q$:1, r:F$\}$	$\{q$:Z, r:F$\}$
public int insertQuarter() {	$\{q$:0, r:F$\}$	$\{q$:1, r:F$\}$	$\{q$:Z, r:F$\}$
if (q == 2)			
return 1;	{}	{}	{}
q++;	$\{q$:1, r:F$\}$	$\{q$:2, r:F$\}$	$\{q$:GZ, r:F$\}$
if (q == 2)			
r = true;	{}	$\{q$:2, r:T$\}$	$\{q$:GZ, r:T$\}$
return 0;	$\{q$:1, r:F$\}$	$\{q$:2, r:T$\}$	$\{q$:GZ, r:T, r:F$\}$
}	$\{q$:1, r:F$\}$	$\{q$:2, r:T$\}$	$\{q$:GZ, r:T, r:F$\}$

Fig. 6.2. Example of abstract interpretation under different initial conditions and for different abstract domains.

Fig. 6.2 shows three abstract interpretations of the method `insertQuarter`. The first two refer to the abstract domain (1) with 4 symbolic values for q, while the last one refers to the smaller domain (2) with only 2 symbolic values for q. Two different initial conditions are considered in the first two interpretations.

In the first abstract interpretation, conditions in both *if* statements evaluate to false, since $q:2$ is not among the propagated values. Correspondingly, the output of the two associated *then* branches is the empty set. In the second abstract interpretation, the first condition q == 2 evaluates to false, while the second evaluates to true, due to the incremented value assigned to q. Thus, only the *else* branch is taken in the first *if*, while the *then* branch is taken in the second *if* statement. As a result, in the second interpretation the final abstract value of r is $r:T$, indicating that the coffee machine is ready to prepare a coffee.

In the last abstract interpretation, the result of incrementing $q:Z$ is $q:GZ$. Such a value does not allow deciding on the truth value of the condition in the second *if* statement. Correspondingly, both branches are taken, and the final result contains both values $r:T$ and $r:F$, associated to variable r. The only "true" value is $r:F$, because when the starting value of q is zero ($q:Z$), the *then* branch of the *if* statement cannot be taken and $r:T$ cannot be assigned to r. However, the low granularity of the abstract domain chosen does not allow distinguishing $q = 1$ from $q = 2$ and correspondingly the actual execution path cannot be obtained. It should be noticed however that the paths followed during abstract interpretation are a superset of the "true" paths (safe interpretation), and that the final results contain those that actually occur (conservative output).

The higher accuracy obtained using the first abstract domain, with respect to the second one, indicates the importance of choosing the right abstraction. Such a choice depends on the problem being solved by abstract interpretation. In some cases, the gross grain abstraction (2) may suffice. In the next section, application of abstract interpretation to the recovery of the state diagrams will be described and the problem of choosing the right abstraction will be reconsidered in such a context.

6.3 State Diagram Recovery

The first step in the recovery of a state diagram for a given class consists of defining an appropriate abstract domain for its attributes and (possibly) for the variables involved in attribute computations. Correspondingly, the abstract semantics of each operation in the class methods must be also provided.

Then, abstract interpretation of the class methods gives the transitions from state to state to be represented in the state diagram. The algorithm for this final step is described in detail below.

In a state diagram, the effects of method invocation on the attribute values are abstracted by considering only "meaningful" equivalence classes of such values. The decision on which equivalence classes should be considered is a non trivial one, and deeply affects the characteristics of the resulting state diagram. Thus, the role of the programmer in this recovery process consists of establishing proper groupings of attribute values that correspond to the different states in which the class can be, and that give rise to different behaviors, in response to method invocations. Such a choice can by no means be automated. Usually, indicators of the boundary values that separate the equivalence classes are available from the constant values used in conditional expressions (if any). Since different execution paths are taken when values are below or above these boundaries, it is likely that these characterize meaningful equivalence classes of values. However, human intervention is unavoidable to determine the proper granularity of the abstraction. Moreover, it is often the case that accurate results can be obtained from abstract interpretation only if some groups of attributes/variables are described jointly, since they are mutually influenced by the values of the each other. If no joint description is adopted, the result of abstract interpretation is over-conservative and produces a state diagram where abstract values that can never occur in any execution are present in some states. A possible solution is an iterative state diagram recovery process, where the output of an initial guess on a possible abstract domain is refined if it appears that the resulting state diagram contains lots of non admissible attribute values.

```
1   initStates = {}, pendStates = {}, allStates = {}
2   for each class constructor c
3       s = interpret(c, {})
4       initStates = initStates ∪ {s}
5       pendStates = pendStates ∪ {s}
6       allStates = allStates ∪ {s}
7   end for
8   while | pendStates | > 0
9       r = remove(pendStates)
10      for each class method m
11          s = interpret(m, r)
12          if s ∉ allStates
13              pendStates = pendStates ∪ {s}
14              allStates = allStates ∪ {s}
15          end if
16      end for
17  end while
```

Fig. 6.3. Algorithm for the recovery of the state diagram.

Fig. 6.3 shows the pseudocode of the recovery algorithm. It assumes that an abstract domain for the class variables has already been properly defined.

First of all, the algorithm determines the initial states in which any object of the given class can be. This is obtained by executing an abstract interpretation of each class constructor starting from an initially empty state (see line 3). The state obtained at the exit of each constructor after abstract interpretation is one of the possible initial states for the objects of this class (line 4). Such a state is also a possible starting point for a further method invocation, so that it must be inserted into a set of pending states (*pendStates*) that will be considered later by abstract interpretation (line 5). Each available class method will be applied to them. Moreover, the state reached after constructor execution is one of the states to be included in the resulting state diagram. Correspondingly, it is inserted into the set of all the states in the diagram (*allStates*, line 6). All the edges in the state diagram that end at the initial states, recovered in this phase, depart from the entry state of the diagram, which is conventionally indicated as a small solid filled circle.

Then, the recovery algorithm repeatedly executes an abstract interpretation of the class methods as long as there are pending states to be considered (loop at line 8). Each pending state is removed from *pendStates* (line 9), and each class method is interpreted using the removed pending state as the initial state (line 11). When the final state obtained by the abstract interpretation has not yet been encountered, it is added both to the set of still pending states (line 13) and to the set of diagram states (line 14).

Recovery of the edges in the state diagram is not explicitly indicated in Fig. 6.3. However, the related rules are quite simple. As described above, the initial states (*initStates*) are the targets of edges outgoing from the entry state. As regards the other states, when the abstract interpretation of method m is conducted (line 11), the starting state used by the interpretation is r, and the final state it produces is s. Thus, an edge labeled m is added in the state diagram from r to s.

_____ *coffee machine* example _____

Let us consider the application of the algorithm in Fig. 6.3 to a hypothetical class `CoffeeMachine`, implementing the *coffee machine* example, using the first abstract domain (1) defined in Section 6.2. Let us assume that this class has only one constructor, which resets the behavior of the machine by assigning 0 to q and false to r. Correspondingly, only one initial state is recovered by performing the abstract interpretation of the constructor starting from the empty set: $\{q{:}0,\ r{:}F\}$ (see Fig. 6.4, method `CoffeeMachine`).

The class `CoffeeMachine` may define three methods, `reset`, `insertQuarter` and `makeCoffee`, which, following the steps in Fig. 6.3, are interpreted from the only pending state produced so far, the initial state $\{q{:}0,\ r{:}F\}$. While `reset` and `makeCoffee` give a final state equal to the initial state (see Fig. 6.4), so that no other pending state is generated, method `insertQuarter` produces

Method	Initial state	Final state
CoffeeMachine	{}	{q:0, r:F}
reset	{q:0, r:F}	{q:0, r:F}
	{q:1, r:F}	{q:0, r:F}
	{q:2, r:T}	{q:0, r:F}
insertQuarter	{q:0, r:F}	{q:1, r:F}
	{q:1, r:F}	{q:2, r:T}
	{q:2, r:T}	{q:2, r:T}
makeCoffee	{q:0, r:F}	{q:0, r:F}
	{q:1, r:F}	{q:1, r:F}
	{q:2, r:T}	{q:0, r:F}

Fig. 6.4. Results of the abstract interpretation of the methods in the CoffeeMachine class under all possible initial states.

a final state never encountered so far, $\{q:1,\ r:F\}$. This is added to the set of pending states and is examined in the next iteration of the algorithm. The detailed steps performed in the abstract interpretation of insertQuarter from the initial state $\{q:0,\ r:F\}$ have already been described (see Fig. 6.2).

Then, the next pending state, $\{q:1,\ r:F\}$, is considered. The abstract interpretation of makeCoffee produces a final state equal to the initial one, while reset gives a final state equal to the already encountered state $\{q:0,\ r:F\}$. Interpretation of insertQuarter (see Fig. 6.2) generates a new state, $\{q:2, r:T\}$. Interpretation of reset, insertQuarter and makeCoffee from such a state completes the execution of the state diagram recovery algorithm. A graphical display of the resulting diagram has been provided previously, in Fig. 6.1.

6.4 The *eLib* Program

Let us consider the class Document from the *eLib* program (see line 159 in Appendix A). Among its attributes, the one which mostly characterizes its state is loan. The set of all possible values that can be assigned to loan can be abstracted into *loan:null*, representing the case where loan references no object (the document is not borrowed), and *loan:Loan1*, representing the case where loan references an object of type Loan (the document is borrowed). The abstract domain to use in the construction of the state diagram for this class is thus:

$$\wp(\{loan{:}null,\ loan{:}Loan1\})$$

where $\wp$ indicates the powerset.

The class methods that may change the state (restricted to the attribute loan) of a Document object are: addLoan (defined at line 202) and removeLoan (defined at line 205). In order to perform their abstract interpretation, the specification of the abstract semantics is required for the two following assignment statements (taken from lines 203 and 206):

Statement	Abstract semantics
loan = ln	$\{loan:\!*\} \rightarrow \{loan:Loan1\}$
loan = null	$\{loan:\!*\} \rightarrow \{loan:null\}$

The underlying hypothesis is that the method addLoan has a precondition, requiring that it is invoked only with a non null parameter. Such a check is not performed by the method itself, being considered the caller's responsibility. Under this hypothesis, the first assignment, where the right hand side is the parameter ln of addLoan, does not need to include *loan:null* in the result set of its abstract semantics.

Here is the result of the abstract interpretation of the constructor Document (line 166), of the methods addLoan (line 202) and removeLoan (line 205) from all possible starting states:

Method	Initial state	Final state
Document	{}	{loan:null}
addLoan	{loan:null}	{loan:Loan1}
	{loan:Loan1}	{loan:Loan1}
removeLoan	{loan:null}	{loan:null}
	{loan:Loan1}	{loan:null}

We can assume that addLoan is called only if the Document is available (see check at line 59), i.e., from state $\{loan:null\}$, and that removeLoan is called only when the document is out (see check at line 68). This prunes two self-transitions from the state diagram: that from $\{loan:Loan1\}$ to $\{loan:Loan1\}$, due to the call of addLoan, and that from $\{loan:null\}$ to $\{loan:null\}$, due to removeLoan. The resulting state diagram is shown in Fig. 6.5.

As a second example, let us consider the class User (see line 281) and its attribute loans, which can be regarded as the one that defines the state of the objects belonging to this class. Since loans is of type Collection, its values can be abstracted by the number of elements it contains. We can distinguish the case of no element inserted (abstract value *loans:empty*), from the case of one element inserted (abstract value *loans:one*), from the case of more than one element inserted (abstract value *loans:many*).

The methods that possibly modify the content of the Collection loans are: addLoan (line 314) and removeLoan (line 320). Correspondingly, the abstract semantics of the following operations is required:

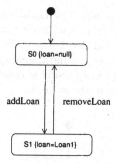

Fig. 6.5. State diagram for class Document.

Statement	Abstract semantics
loans.add(loan)	$\{loans:empty\} \rightarrow \{loans:one\}$
	$\{loans:one\} \rightarrow \{loans:many\}$
	$\{loans:many\} \rightarrow \{loans:many\}$
loans.remove(loan)	$\{loans:empty\} \rightarrow \{loans:empty\}$
	$\{loans:one\} \rightarrow \{loans:empty, loans:one\}$
	$\{loans:many\} \rightarrow \{loans:one, loans:many\}$

Removal of an element from a Collection containing just one element may give an empty collection, if the removed element is contained in the Collection, or an unchanged Collection, if the element is different from the contained one. Removal of an element from a Collection with more than one (*many*) elements may still give a Collection with more than one element, or may give a Collection with exactly one element, if it previously contained two elements, among which one is equal to that being removed.

Assuming that the precondition of the method removeLoan is the presence of its parameter loan in the Collection loans (this is ensured in its invocation inside class Library at line 53, as apparent from the body of method returnDocument, lines 66–75), the abstract semantics given above can be simplified into:

Statement	Abstract semantics
loans.add(loan)	$\{loans:empty\} \rightarrow \{loans:one\}$
	$\{loans:one\} \rightarrow \{loans:many\}$
	$\{loans:many\} \rightarrow \{loans:many\}$
loans.remove(loan)	$\{loans:empty\} \rightarrow \{loans:empty\}$
	$\{loans:one\} \rightarrow \{loans:empty\}$
	$\{loans:many\} \rightarrow \{loans:one, loans:many\}$

The abstract interpretation of methods User (line 288), addLoan (line 314) and removeLoan (line 320) using the abstract semantics above, produces the state diagram depicted in Fig. 6.6. The transition from state *{loans:many}* to *{loans:one, loans:many}* due to the invocation of `removeLoan` is represented as a non deterministic choice between the target states *{loans:one}* and *{loans:many}*. Moreover, the precondition of `removeLoan` discussed above ensures that it is never called when *loans* is *empty*. Thus, no self-transition labeled `removeLoan` is present in the state S_0.

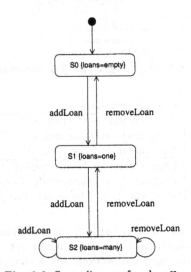

Fig. 6.6. State diagram for class `User`.

Let us consider the class `Library` (see line 3). Its three attributes `documents`, `users`, and `loans` define the state of its objects. It is possible to consider these three attributes separately, building a distinct state diagram for each of them. The result is a set of so-called *projected* state diagrams. The overall state of the class, described by the joint values of all its state variables, is projected onto a single state variable, by considering the values it can assume and ignoring the values assumed by the other variables.

Since the three attributes `documents`, `users`, and `loans` are containers of other objects, it is possible to abstract their values into the symbolic values *empty* and *some*, indicating respectively that no object is contained or that some (i.e., at least one) objects are contained. Abstract interpretation of the methods that modify these containers is similar to the abstract interpretation of the methods of class `User` described above, with the only difference being that the values of container `loans` from class `User` have been modeled by three abstract values (*empty*, *one*, and *many*), while for class `Library` no distinction is made between *one* and *many*, both of which are abstracted as *some*.

The three projected state diagrams resulting from the abstract interpretation of methods `addDocument` (line 24), `removeDocument` (line 31), `addUser` (line 8), `removeUser` (line 15), `addLoan` (line 40), `removeLoan` (line 48) are depicted in Fig. 6.7. The removal methods `removeDocument` and `removeUser` have no effect if applied in the state S_0 (*empty*) of the diagrams for the attributes `documents` and `users`. On the contrary, the removal method `removeLoan` can never be invoked in the state S_0 of the diagram for `loans`, because of the check performed by the calling method `returnDocument` (see line 68, where `isOut` returns *true* only if the document references a non null `Loan` object, stored inside the attribute `loans` of class `Library`).

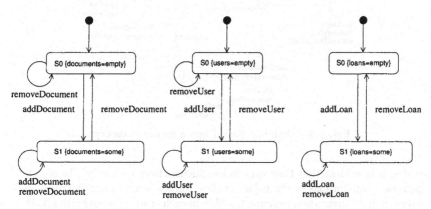

Fig. 6.7. Projected state diagrams for class `Library`.

If the attributes of a class vary independently from each other, the combined state diagram can be obtained as the Cartesian product of the projected state diagrams, with a number of states that grows as the product of the number of states in the separate diagrams. Transitions are obtained by all combinations of transitions in the substates.

If we consider the combined state diagram for class `Library`, the total number of states it contains is not 8 ($2 \times 2 \times 2$), as it would occur in case of independent projections. The combined state diagram, shown in Fig. 6.8, contains 5 states, because some combinations in the Cartesian product are prohibited by preconditions that are checked before calling some of the methods in this class.

Let us represent the three abstract values that have been defined for the three state attributes (`document`, `users`, `loans`) of this class as a triple, with the symbolic values e indicating the abstract value *empty* and s indicating *some*. The triple $< e, s, e >$ is thus the abstract value for a combined state of class `Library`, with the following joint values of the state variables: *documents=empty, users=some, loans=empty*.

Fig. 6.8 shows the combined state diagram, as obtained by applying some constraints (explained below) on the invocation of the involved methods. As regards the first two variables represented in the triples that characterize the

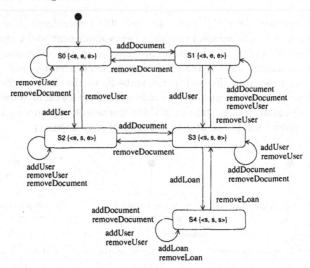

Fig. 6.8. Combined state diagram for class `Library`.

states, it is evident that they vary independently from each other. In fact, all possible combinations of the values of these variables are in the diagram, and every method invocation remains possible in each state. Correspondingly, the upper part of the diagram in Fig. 6.8 contains exactly 4 (i.e., 2×2) states (S_0, S_1, S_2, S_3) and 20 related transitions.

The invocation of method `addLoan` can only be made in state S_3, where *documents=some* and *users=some*, i.e., only in the presence of registered users and documents in the library. In fact, the method `borrowDocument` checks (see line 57) that both of its parameters (`user` of type `User` and `doc` of type `Document`) are not null. Since such parameters are obtained from class `Library`, which in turn exploits its attributes `users` and `documents` to retrieve them, the execution of `borrowDocument` proceeds until the invocation of `addLoan` only if at least one user (referenced by parameter `user`) and one document (referenced by `doc`) are in the library. The result of calling `addLoan` in S_3 is a transition to S_4, where all state variables are equal to *some*, i.e., there are registered users and documents, and there are active loans.

Since method `removeLoan` is never called with `loans` empty, as discussed above, the only state that has outgoing transitions labeled by `removeLoan` is S_4, where *loans=some*. The deletion of a loan can either lead to a state in which some loans are still active (self transition in S_4), or it can lead to a state where no loan is active in the library (S_3). This is the reason for the non deterministic transition triggered by `removeLoan`, with two possible target states.

In state S_4, removal of documents (method `removeDocument`) or users (method `removeUser`) can never result in a state of the library with an empty set of documents and some loans still active ($< e, s, s >$), or with an empty set of users and some loans still active ($< s, e, s >$). In fact, it is not possible to remove a user who is borrowing some documents (see check performed at line 17), and it is not possible to remove a document that is borrowed by a user (see check performed at line 33). Consequently, when one or more loans are active (*loans:some*), the associated users and documents cannot be removed from the library, thus making the states $< e, s, s >$ and $< s, e, s >$ unreachable.

6.5 Related Work

Recovering a finite state model of a program has been investigated in the context of model checking [15, 19]. One of the major obstacles that has been encountered in the extension of model checking from hardware to software verification is the problem of constructing a finite state model that approximates the executable behavior of a program in a reliable way. Manual construction of such models is expensive and error prone. For complex systems it is out of the question. The possibility of using abstract interpretation for this purpose has been investigated in [15, 19]. Automated support for the abstraction of the source code into a finite state model is provided by the tool Bandera, which allows for the integration of abstraction definitions into the source code of the program under analysis. Moreover, customization of the abstraction to check a particular property is also possible.

Another tool that employs abstraction to produce a tractable model of an input software system is Java Path Finder [95]. Program annotations consisting of user-defined predicates are used to generate another Java program in which concrete statements are replaced by the abstracted ones. Model checking is conducted on the abstracted version of the program, which exhibits a tractable, finite state, behavior. The model checker explores the state space by performing a symbolic execution of the program. The state being propagated in the symbolic execution includes a heap configuration, a path condition on primitive fields, and thread scheduling. Whenever the path condition is updated, it is checked for satisfiability using an external decision procedure. If it cannot be satisfied, the model checker backtracks. In this way, infeasible portions of the state space are not explored. Java Path Finder has been used for test case generation [96], with the test criterion (e.g., reaching every control flow branch) encoded as a property. When the model checker can determine a path along which such a property is true, associated with a satisfiable path condition, it is possible to find a *witness*, that is, a set of concrete values that make the path condition true and respect the constraints on the heap configuration (i.e., on the object fields referencing other objects). This is easily converted into a test case for the given program.

Besides program understanding, one of the most important applications of the state diagrams, possibly recovered from the code, is state-based testing [6,

92]. According to this testing methodology, the class under test is modeled by its state diagram and a set of test cases is considered adequate for the unit test of the class when the states and the transitions in the state diagram are covered up to a level specified in the objective coverage criterion. The most widely used coverage criterion in state-based testing is transition coverage. It requires that all transitions from state to state be exercised at least once by some test case. This ensures that a class is not delivered with untested states or state transitions. As a support to defect finding, it forces programmers to test their code by exercising all the states and all the possible state changes triggered by messages received by the object under test.

7

Package Diagram

The complexity involved in the management and description of large software systems can be faced by partitioning the overall collection of the composing entities into smaller, more manageable, units. Packages offer a general grouping mechanism that can be used to decompose a given system into sub-systems and to provide a separate description for each of them.

Packages represented in the package diagram show the decomposition of a given system into cohesive units that are loosely coupled with each other. Each package can in turn be decomposed into sub-packages or it can contain the final, atomic entities, typically consisting of the classes and of their mutual relationships.

The dependency relationships shown in a package diagram represent the usage of resources available from other packages. For example, if a method of a class contained in a package calls a method of a class that belongs to a different package, a dependency relationship exists between the two packages.

Most Object Oriented programming languages provide an explicit construct to define packages. Thus, their recovery from the source code is just a matter of performing a pretty simple syntactic analysis. Dependencies among packages are also quite easy to retrieve, since they correspond to references to resources possessed by other packages (method calls, usage of types, etc.).

A more interesting and challenging situation is one in which no package structure was defined for a given software system, while its evolution over time has made it necessary (for example, because of an increased system's size). Code analysis techniques can be employed to determine appropriate groupings of entities to be inserted in a same package. In this scenario, packages are recovered from a system that does not possess any package structure at all. Another similar scenario consists of restructuring an existing package organization. If there are reasons to believe that the current decomposition of the system into packages is not satisfactory, code analysis can be used to determine an alternative decomposition, with more cohesive and less coupled packages. Migration to the new package structure can thus be supported by the recovery of an alternative package organization from the code, ignoring the existing one. The exercise of recovering a package structure from the code can be useful also to assess the validity of the current decomposition into packages, by contrasting that recovered with the existing one.

The scenarios in which package diagram recovery applies are clarified in Section 7.1. Among the techniques available for the identification of cohesive groups of classes, clustering is considered in detail in Section 7.2, while concept analysis is presented in Section 7.3. Application of these two methods to the *eLib* program is described in Section 7.4. A discussion of the related works concludes the chapter.

7.1 Package Diagram Recovery

The complexity of large software systems can be managed by decomposing the overall system into smaller units, called *packages*, that are internally highly cohesive and that exhibit a low coupling with the other packages in the decomposition. In turn, each package can be decomposed into sub-packages, when its complexity requires a finer grain subdivision. The atomic elements eventually included in the lower level packages are usually the classes used in each subsystem. Although the decomposition into packages is a general mechanism that can be used also with entities different from classes (e.g., states in state diagrams), in the following we will focus on the most frequently occurring case, in which packages contain groups of classes (or other sub-packages).

Since modern Object Oriented programming languages, such as Java, provide an explicit mechanism for package definition, recovery of the organization of the classes into packages and of the decomposition of packages into subpackages is straightforward and requires just the ability to parse the source code. The dependency relationship between packages is also easy to retrieve. In fact, once the kinds of relevant dependencies are defined (e.g., method calls between classes in different packages; declaration of variables whose type is defined in another package), their identification in the source code is typically just a matter of performing some simple syntactic or semantic (construction of symbol table with type information) analysis.

Software systems tend to evolve over time in a manner that is difficult to predict in advance, so that their periodic reorganization is often necessary to preserve the original quality of the design. In this context, recovery of the package diagram from the source code cannot be based on the declared packages, since these may reflect the initial decomposition of the system, which does not correspond any longer its actual structure. Techniques for the reverse engineering of highly cohesive and lowly coupled groups of classes play an important role in this situation.

Three possible scenarios in which package diagram recovery should be based on the actual code organization, instead of the declared package structure, are depicted in Fig. 7.1. When classes are not grouped into packages

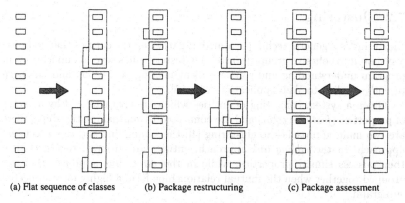

(a) Flat sequence of classes   (b) Package restructuring   (c) Package assessment

Fig. 7.1. Scenarios of package diagram recovery from code properties.

(see Fig. 7.1, (a)) or when the existing package structure is considered inappropriate (see Fig. 7.1, (b)), recovery of the package diagram from the code may provide useful indications on how to (re-)organize classes into packages. In these two cases, either no package structure exists, or the available package structure is ignored. A third situation may occur, in which the existing package structure is evaluated to identify opportunities of improvement (see Fig. 7.1, (c)). In such a scenario, the recovered package diagram is expected to have a large overlap with the existing package organization, and interesting information is provided by the differences (if any). Classes that are assigned to different packages in the two package diagrams (the actual and the recovered one) should be carefully inspected to assess the opportunity of reassigning them. The resulting organization of the system, in all three cases sketched above, will be characterized by more cohesive packages with fewer dependencies between each other. This is expected to affect positively the activities of program understanding and code evolution.

Recovery of the package diagram in the three scenarios of Fig. 7.1 is based on proper code properties. Classes that exhibit commonalities in such properties are grouped in a same package. Several algorithms can be employed to identify such commonalities and to group classes together. The code properties to consider in the recovery process vary accordingly, and may be customized based on the available knowledge about the system. Typical examples of such properties are the types of class attributes and of method variables and parameters, and the invocations of methods that belong to other classes. The fact that a group of classes operate on the same types or depend one on the other due to method invocations hint that they should be grouped into a same package. In the next two sections more details are provided on which properties to consider and how to infer packages (i.e., highly cohesive and loosely coupled groupings of classes) from such properties.

7.2 Clustering

Clustering is a general technique aimed at gathering the entities that compose a system into cohesive groups (*clusters*). Clustering has several applications in program understanding and software reengineering [4, 54, 99], and has been recently applied to Web applications [52, 65].

Given a system consisting of entities which are characterized by a vector of properties (*feature vector*) and are connected by mutual relationships, there are two main approaches to clustering [4]: the sibling link and the direct link approach. In the *sibling link* approach, entities are grouped together when they possess similar properties, while in the *direct link* approach they are grouped together when the mutual relationships form a highly interconnected sub-graph.

Main issues in the application of the sibling link approach are the choice of the features to consider in the feature vectors, the definition of an appropriate similarity measure based on such features and the steps for the computation of the clusters, given the similarity measures. The following section, *Feature Vectors*, examines such issues in detail.

In the direct link approach, clustering is reduced to a combinatorial optimization problem. Given the relationships that connect entities with each other, the goal of clustering is to determine a partition of the set of entities which concurrently minimizes the connections that cross the boundaries of the clusters and maximizes the connections among entities belonging to a same cluster. Details for the application of this approach are provided in the following section, *Modularity Optimization*.

7.2.1 Feature Vectors

A *feature vector* is a multidimensional vector of integer values, where each dimension in the vector corresponds to one of the features selected to describe the entities, while the coordinate value represents the number of references to such a feature found in the entity being described. Selection of the appropriate features to use with a given system is critical for the quality of the resulting clusters, and may be guided by pre-existing knowledge about the software.

In the literature, several different features have been used to characterize procedural programs, with the aim of remodularizing them [4, 54, 99]. Some of such features apply to Object Oriented software as well, and can be used to derive a package diagram from the source code of the classes in the system under analysis. Examples of such features are the following:

User-def types: Declaration of attributes, variables or method parameters whose type is a user defined type.
Method calls: Invocation of methods that belong to other classes.

The rationale behind the two kinds of features above is that classes operating on the same data types or using the same computations (method calls) are likely to be functionally close to each other, so that clustering is expected to group them together.

In addition to the syntactic features considered above, informal descriptive features can be exploited for clustering as well. For example, the words used in the identifiers defined in each class under analysis or in the comments are informal descriptive features that may give a useful contribution to clustering. The main limitations of informal features are that they depend on the ability of the code to be self-documenting and that they may be not up to date, if they have not been evolved along with the code. On the other side, they are more abstract than the syntactic features, being closer to a human understanding of the system.

Once the features to be considered in the feature vectors have been selected, a proper similarity measure has to be defined. It will be used by the clustering algorithm to compare the vectors. The entities with the most similar feature vectors are inserted in a same cluster. In alternative to the similarity measure, it is possible to define a distance measure and to group vectors at minimum distance. Usually, similarity measures are favored over distance measures, because they have a better behavior in presence of empty or quasi-empty descriptions. In fact, if most (all) of the entries in two feature vectors are zero, any distance measure will have a very low value, thus suggesting that the two entities should be clustered together. However, it may be the case that the two entities are very dissimilar and that the low distance is just a side effect of the quasi-empty description. Consequently, it is preferable to use similarity, instead of distance, measures, in presence of quasi-empty descriptions.

Among the various ways in which similarity between two vectors can be defined, the metrics most widely used in software clustering are the normalized product (cosine similarity) and the association coefficients.

Normalized product: Normalized vector product of the feature vectors:
$$sim(X, Y) = X^T Y / (\|X\|\|Y\|)$$

Association coefficients: Derived metrics are based on the following coefficients:

$a = \|X \cap Y\|$
$b = \|X \setminus Y\|$
$c = \|Y \setminus X\|$
$d = \|\mathcal{F} \setminus (X \cup Y)\|$

Jaccard: $sim(X, Y) = a/(a + b + c)$
Simple Matching: $sim(X, Y) = (a + d)/(a + b + c + d)$
Sørensen-Dice: $sim(X, Y) = 2a/(2a + b + c)$

The normalized product gives the scalar product between two vectors, reduced to unitary norm. Thus, it measures the cosine of the angle between the vectors. The normalized product is maximum (+1) when the two vectors are co-linear and have the same direction, i.e., the ratio between the respective components is a positive constant: $X = \alpha Y$, with $\alpha > 0$. In the general case, the normalized product is minimum (-1) when the two vectors are co-linear, but have opposed directions: $X = \alpha Y$, with $\alpha < 0$. However, since feature vectors associated with software components count the number of references to each feature in each component, the coordinate values are always non negative and the normalized product is correspondingly always greater than or equal to zero. Thus, the minimum value of the normalized product is not -1 for the feature vectors we are interested in. Such a minimum, equal to 0 under the hypothesis of non negative coordinates, is obtained when the two vectors are orthogonal with each other, that is, when non-zero values occur always at different coordinates. In other words, two vectors with non negative coordinates have zero normalized product if the first has zeros in the positions where the second has positive values, and vice-versa.

Association coefficients are used to compute various different similarity metrics, among which the Jaccard, the Simple Matching, and the Sørensen-Dice similarities. These coefficients are based on a view of the feature vectors as the characteristic function of sets (of features). Thus, the first coefficient, a, measures the number of features that are common to the two vectors X and Y, i.e., the intersection between the sets of features represented in the two feature vectors. Coefficients b and c measure the number of features in the first (second) set but not in the second (first). Coefficient d measures the number of features that are neither in X nor in Y ($\mathcal{F}$ is the set of all features).

Given the four association coefficients, several similarity metrics can be defined, based on them. For example, the Jaccard similarity metric counts the number of common features a over the total number of features in the two vectors $(a + b + c)$. It is 1 when X and Y have exactly the same features, while it is 0 when they have no common feature. The Simple Matching similarity metric gives equal weight to the common (a) and to the missing (d) features. This metric is equal to 1 when two vectors have the same common and missing features, i.e., coefficients b and c are zero. In other words, no feature exists which belong to one vector but not to the other. The Simple Matching metric is zero when each feature belongs exclusively to the first or to the second vector (no common and no commonly missing feature). Finally, the Sørensen-Dice similarity metric is a variant of the Jaccard metric, in which the common features are counted twice, because they are present in both vectors.

In the literature, several different clustering algorithms have been investigated [99], with different properties. Among them, hierarchical algorithms are the most widely used in software clustering. Hierarchical algorithms do not produce a single partition of the system. Their output is rather a tree, with the root consisting of one cluster enclosing all entities, and the leaves consisting of singleton clusters. At each intermediate level, a partition of the system is available, with the number of clusters increasing while moving downward in the tree.

Hierarchical algorithms can be divided into two families: divisive and agglomerative algorithms. Divisive algorithms start from the whole system at the tree root, and then divide it into smaller clusters, attached as children of each tree node. On the contrary, agglomerative algorithms start from singleton clusters and join them together incrementally.

```
1   create N singleton clusters, one per feature vector
2   while there are > 1 clusters do
3       compute the similarity between each pair of clusters
4       find the clusters with highest similarity
5       merge these clusters into a new cluster
6   end while
```

Fig. 7.2. Agglomerative clustering algorithm.

Fig. 7.2 shows the main steps of the agglomerative clustering algorithm. After creating a singleton cluster for each feature vector, the algorithm merges the most similar clusters together, until one single cluster is produced. It will be the root of the resulting clustering hierarchy.

A critical decision in the implementation of this algorithm is associated to step 3. While it is obvious how similarity between singleton clusters is measured, since it just accounts for applying the metric chosen among those presented above, the similarity between clusters that contain more than one entity can be computed in different, alternative ways. Given two clusters C_1 and C_2, containing respectively n and m entities, their similarity is computed from the similarities $(s_{1,1}, ..., s_{i,j}, ..., s_{n,m})$ between each pair of contained entities, according to so-called *linkage rules*. Among the linkage rules reported in the literature, the most widely used in software clustering are the single linkage and the complete linkage:

Single linkage (or closest neighbor):

$$s = \max_{i,j} (s_{i,j})$$

Complete linkage (or furthest neighbor):

$$s = \min_{i,j} (s_{i,j})$$

Single linkage is known to give less coupled clusters, while complete linkage gives more cohesive clusters (with *cohesion* measuring the average similarity between any two entities clustered together, and *coupling* measuring the average similarity between any two entities belonging to different clusters).

Since feature vectors tend to be sparse, coupling naturally tends to be low. As a consequence, more importance is typically given to cohesion, so that the complete linkage is the typical rule of choice.

An alternative approach to computing the similarity between clusters is offered by the *combined clustering algorithm* [70]. In this approach, clusters are also associated with feature vectors that describe them. Initially, singleton clusters have a feature vector that is coincident with that of the enclosed entity. Then, when a cluster contains n feature vectors, $X_1, ..., X_n$, its own feature vector is given by their sum: $X_1 + ... + X_n$. Thus, a cluster is associated to a feature vector with each coordinate given by the sum of the values of the same coordinate in all contained vectors.

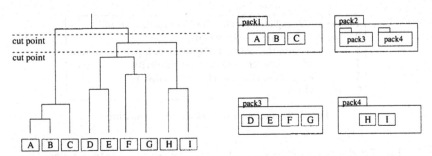

Fig. 7.3. Clustering hierarchy (left), with two cut points selected, and associated package diagram (right).

When hierarchical clustering is applied for package diagram recovery, a partition of the classes can be obtained by cutting the hierarchy at an appropriate height (see Fig. 7.3). Successive cuts at different heights can be generated and assessed. Higher level cuts followed by lower level cuts indicate the cases where packages contain sub-packages. Lower level cuts eventually define packages that contain only classes.

With reference to Fig. 7.3, two cut points have been selected in the clustering hierarchy. The topmost cut defines a package containing two other packages, and a package containing 3 classes. The lower level cut in turn defines the content of the two packages that are merged at the higher level cut.

Problems that may occur when clustering is applied to software components, such as the classes, are the generation of a *black hole*, in which one cluster absorbs everything incrementally, while moving upward in the hierarchy, or, at the other extreme, the generation of a *gas cloud*, in which all singleton clusters tend to remain almost unchanged until the final grouping into a single final cluster [4]. Careful selection of the features to use, of the similarity measure between vectors and of the clustering algorithm to apply allow avoiding such problems.

7.2.2 Modularity Optimization

The approach to clustering based on modularity optimization [54] focuses on the relationships that hold among the entities to be clustered, rather than their features. In this setting, the goal of clustering is optimizing the level of modularity, so that the resulting grouping of the entities concurrently minimizes *coupling* (i.e., the connections between components of distinct clusters) while maximizing *cohesion* (i.e., the connections between components in a same cluster).

When this approach is applied to package diagram recovery, the relationships that hold among the classes have to be taken into account. The alternative choices span across those represented in the class diagram:

- Inheritance.
- Association.
- Aggregation.
- Composition.
- Dependency.

All or a subset of them can be used for clustering. As discussed below, it may be important to be able to give different relationships different weights.

Given a set of entities (classes, in case of package diagram recover) and of relationships (inter-class relationships), cohesion and coupling can be formally defined as follows:

Cohesion: $A_i = \frac{\mu_i}{N_i^2}$

Coupling: $E_{i,j} = \frac{\epsilon_{i,j}}{2N_i N_j}$

where μ_i is the number of relationships internal to cluster C_i, $\epsilon_{i,j}$ is the number of relationships between clusters C_i and C_j, and N_i is the number of entities inside cluster C_i. If auto-loops cannot occur in the relationships being considered, the denominator of A_i becomes $N_i(N_i - 1)$.

A_i and $E_{i,j}$ range between 0 and 1. A_i is 1 when the entities in cluster C_i are fully connected with each other ($\mu_i = N_i^2$ with auto-loops, $\mu_i = N_i(N_i - 1)$ without auto-loops), while it is 0 when they are completely disconnected. $E_{i,j}$ is equal to 1 when each entity of cluster C_i is connected to each entity of cluster C_j and vice-versa. $E_{i,j}$ is 0 when the entities in C_i and C_j have no connection with each other.

A joint measure of the modularization quality, MQ, can be obtained as the difference between the normalized total cohesion and the normalized total coupling:

$$MQ = \frac{1}{k} \sum_{i=1}^{k} A_i - \frac{1}{\frac{k(k-1)}{2}} \sum_{i=1}^{k-1} \sum_{j=i+1}^{k} E_{i,j}$$

where k is the number of clusters. Since A_i is between 0 and 1, the sum over all clusters will be between 0 and k, hence the normalizing denominator of the first term in MQ. As regards the sum of $E_{i,j}$ over all pairs of different clusters, the maximum will be $k(k - 1)/2$, i.e., equal to the number of such pairs. This number is used to normalize the second term in MQ, so as to make it range between 0 and 1.

As a consequence of the normalization of the sums, MQ is bounded between -1 (no cohesion, maximum coupling) and 1 (no coupling, maximum cohesion). The latter situation is of course the most desirable one. Thus, the clustering algorithm based on the modularity metric MQ aims at determining the partition of the entities into clusters that maximizes MQ.

The problem of clustering has been turned into a combinatorial optimization problem. Consequently, the heuristics available from the field of combinatorial optimization can be used to approximate the optimal solution. The exact optimal solution is in general non computable, since the number of possible partitions for which MQ should be determined grows exponentially with the number of entities to be clustered.

```
1    S ← {e₁,...,eₙ}
2    P ← GenerateRandomPartition(S)
3    repeat
4        BNP ← BetterNeighboringPartitions(P)
5        if BNP ≠ ∅
6            P ← SelectRandomly(BNP)
7        end if
8    until P does not change
9    P_opt ← P

where e₁,...,eₙ are the entities to be clustered.
```

Fig. 7.4. Hill-climbing clustering algorithm.

In the literature, several algorithms have been investigated to determine the clusters that maximize MQ [32, 54]. Fig. 7.4 shows a simple algorithm, based on the *hill-climbing* technique. It exploits the notion of neighbor partition. A partition NP is a *neighbor* of a partition P if it is the same as P except for a single element that belongs to different clusters in the two partitions. Initially, a random partition P is produced out of the set S of the entities to be clustered (line 2, Fig. 7.4). Then, an optimization loop is entered, which ends when the chosen strategy is unable to further improve the current partition of the entities. At line 4, a subset of all neighboring partitions, consisting of those with a higher MQ than P, is determined and assigned to BNP. If at least one better neighbor partition actually exists, P is reassigned (line 6). When more than one improvement directions are possible, one is chosen randomly. In the end, a (sub-)optimal partitioning of the entities is produced which can be interpreted as the package diagram being recovered from the inter-class relationships.

The main limitation of the algorithm in Fig. 7.4 is that its result is quite sensitive to the initial, random partition, from which optimization is started. This can be (partially) mitigated by executing it several times, starting from different initial partitions. More sophisticated methods (e.g., based on genetic algorithms) to cope with this problem can be found in the literature.

When a large software system is analyzed, the number of clusters in the (sub-)optimal partition may be big. In this case, it makes sense to cluster the clusters, thus creating a hierarchy of packages. The first step consists of applying the modularization algorithm to the set of all the entities, which are assigned to different clusters. A new higher-level graph is then built by treating each cluster as a single entity. Given two nodes in this higher-level graph, if there exists at least one edge between any two enclosed entities, then there is an edge between the higher-level nodes in the new graph. The clustering algorithm is re-applied to the new graph, in order to discover the next higher-level graph, and so on, until all components have coalesced into a single cluster.

Symmetrically, when the clusters obtained by the optimization of MQ contain a large number of entities, it makes sense to re-apply the clustering algorithm inside each higher-level cluster, until groupings of entities of manageable size are produced. The hierarchy of the packages is obtained as an effect of clustering re-computation within previously determined clusters.

The algorithm described above needs be improved in cases where not only the existence of a relationships is important, but also the number of instances of the relationship and the kind of relationship matter. This is especially true with Object Oriented systems. For example, the presence of an inheritance relationship between two classes may be a stronger indicator of the fact that the two related classes should belong to a same package, than the existence of a dependency due to a method call. Thus, inheritance should be weighted more than dependency. Moreover, the fact that a high number of method calls exists between two classes should result in a stronger relationship than in the case of a small number of calls.

Therefore, the technique described above has to account for the so-called *interconnection strength* of the relationships: a proper weighting mechanism must be defined for the inter-class relationships, according to the number of instances and/or the kind of relationships being considered.

7.3 Concept Analysis

Concept analysis [25] is a branch of lattice theory that permits grouping *objects* that have common *attributes*. Concept analysis has been successfully applied to code restructuring and modularization [24, 50, 71, 75, 88, 94], with functions as the objects, and properly selected function properties as the attributes (e.g., accesses to global variables, accesses to dynamic locations and presence of user-defined structured types in the signature, including the return types). A few survey papers [78, 79, 82] account for the applications of concept analysis to software engineering in general.

The possibility to use concept analysis for package diagram recovery descends from its ability to determine maximal groupings of objects sharing maximal subsets of common attributes. In this application of concept analysis, the objects to be considered are the classes of the program, while the attributes are selected among the class properties. The choice of which properties to include in the analysis is quite important and may lead to different results. Examples of class properties that are highly related to the cohesion that packages are expected to exhibit are the following:

- User defined types used in the declarations of class attributes, method parameters, return values, and/or local variables.
- Method calls.
- Relationships a class has with other classes (aggregation, inheritance, etc.).

- Informal properties such as words in method identifiers, comments, etc.

The output of concept analysis represents a candidate package diagram for the given program, in that classes are grouped together when they share maximal sets of properties. For example, classes operating on the same, user defined types, calling the same methods, related to the same classes, or including the same descriptive information, are likely to be a cohesive group that can be possibly interpreted as a package of the system.

The starting point for concept analysis is a *context* (O, A, R), consisting of a set of objects O, a set of attributes A and a binary relation R between objects and attributes, stating which attributes are possessed by each object.

Let $X \subseteq O$ and $Y \subseteq A$. The mappings $\sigma(X) = \{a \in A | \forall o \in X : (o,a) \in R\}$ (the common attributes of X) and $\tau(Y) = \{o \in O | \forall a \in Y : (o,a) \in R\}$ (the common objects of Y) form a *Galois connection*, that is, these two mappings are antimonotone and extensive.

A *concept* is a maximal collection of objects that possess common attributes, i.e., it is a grouping of all the objects that share a common set of attributes. More formally a concept is a pair of sets (X, Y) such that:

$$X = \{o \in O | \forall a \in Y : (o,a) \in R\} = \tau(Y)$$
$$Y = \{a \in A | \forall o \in X : (o,a) \in R\} = \sigma(X)$$

X is said to be the *extent* of the concept and Y is said to be the *intent*.

The definition given above is mutually recursive (X is defined in terms of Y and vice-versa), thus it cannot be used in a constructive way (it just helps deciding if a pair (X, Y) is or is not a concept). However, several algorithms for computing the concepts from a given context are available (see below).

A concept $c_0 = (X_0, Y_0)$ is a *subconcept* of concept $c_1 = (X_1, Y_1)$ ($c_0 \le c_1$) if $X_0 \subseteq X_1$ (or, equivalently, $Y_1 \subseteq Y_0$). The subconcept relation forms a complete partial order (the *concept lattice*) over the set of concepts [25].

The fundamental theorem for concept lattices [25] relates subconcepts and superconcepts as follows:

$$\bigsqcup_{i \in I}(X_i, Y_i) = (\tau(\bigcap_{i \in I} Y_i), \bigcap_{i \in I} Y_i)$$

The least upper bound (*supremum*) of a set of concepts (join operation) can be computed by intersecting their intents and finding the common objects of the resulting intersection. Dually, the largest lower bound (*infimum*) can be computed as follows:

$$\sqcap_{i \in I}(X_i, Y_i) = (\bigcap_{i \in I} X_i, \sigma(\bigcap_{i \in I} X_i))$$

The steps of a simple bottom-up concept construction algorithm (see [75]) are the following:

1. Compute the bottom element of the concept lattice: $(\tau(\sigma(\emptyset)), \sigma(\emptyset))$, with $\sigma(\emptyset) = A$.
2. Compute the *atomic* concepts – smallest concepts with extent obtained by treating each object as a singleton: $(\tau(\sigma(\{o\})), \sigma(\{o\})), o \in O$
3. Close the set of atomic concepts under join (**AtomicConceptClosure**).

The procedure **AtomicConceptClosure**, which computes the transitive closure of the atomic concepts under the least upper bound (join) relationship, is given in Fig 7.5.

```
AtomicConceptClosure
1     worklist ← {(c′, c)|c ≰ c′ ∧ c′ ≰ c}
2     while worklist ≠ ∅
3          (c₀, c₁) ← RemoveFirst(worklist)
4          c″ = c₀ ⊔ c₁
5          if c″ is yet to be discovered
6               for each pairs of concepts (c″, c)
7                    if c ≰ c″ ∧ c″ ≰ c
8                         Add(worklist, (c″, c))
9                    end if
10              end for
11         end if
12    end while
```

Fig. 7.5. Bottom-up concept formation algorithm. Procedure **AtomicConcept-Closure**.

A worklist is initialized with all pairs of concepts that are not sub concepts of each other (line 1). Then, the formation of superconcepts is tried, as long as there are pairs of concepts to consider in the worklist. Each such pair gives raise to a unique supremum, computed at line 4. If such a concept has not yet been discovered, it is added to the list of known concepts (not shown) and it is compared with all concepts produced so far. For each concept that is unrelated with the new one (line 7), a pair is generated and added to the worklist. In the end, the transitive construction of all superconcepts, starting from the atomic concepts, gives the final set of all the concepts, organized into the concept lattice.

The key observation for using concept analysis in package diagram recovery is that a package corresponds to a formal concept. Let us consider, for example, the method calls issued inside the code of the classes under analysis. A concept consists of a set of classes performing a set of same method calls, which are not simultaneously made by the code of any other class outside the concept.

	m_1	m_2	m_3
A_1	×	×	
A_2	×	×	
A_3	×		×

Table 7.1. Example of context: the objects are the classes A_1, A_2, A_3 and the attributes are the calls to methods m_1, m_2, m_3.

An example of such kind of context is given in Table 7.1. The set of objects consists of the three classes A_1, A_2, A_3, and the attributes are the calls to methods m_1, m_2, m_3. Table 7.1 indicates which class invokes which method. After applying concept analysis to this example, the following concepts are identified:

- $c_1 = (\{A_1, A_2, A_3\}, \{m_1\})$
- $c_2 = (\{A_1, A_2\}, \{m_1, m_2\})$
- $c_3 = (\{A_3\}, \{m_1, m_3\})$
- $c_4 = (\{\}, \{m_1, m_2, m_3\})$

Concept c_1 indicates that all the three classes call method m_1. Concept c_2 states that both A_1 and A_2 call both m_1 and m_2. A_3 is the only class calling both m_1 and m_3 (concept c_3), while no class has the property of calling all three methods (c_4).

The concept lattice associated with the concepts $c_1, ..., c_4$ above is depicted in Fig. 7.6 (nodes have the shape used in package diagrams). Edges indicate the subconcept relationships and are upward directed. Inside each concept (package), the names of the classes that have been grouped together are shown, while the related attributes are not indicated.

Concepts are good candidates for the organization of classes into packages. In fact, each concept is, by definition, characterized by a high cohesion of its objects around the chosen attributes. However, concepts may have extents

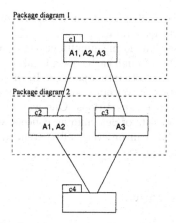

Fig. 7.6. Example of concept lattice, showing the candidate packages.

with non-empty intersections. Correspondingly, not every collection of concepts represents a potential package diagram. To address this problem, the notion of concept partition was introduced (see for example [75]). A *concept partition* consists of a set of concepts whose extents are a partition of the object set O. $CP = \{(X_1, Y_1), \ldots, (X_n, Y_n)\}$ is a concept partition *iff*:

$$\bigcup_{i=1}^{n} X_i = O \text{ and } \forall i \neq j, X_i \cap X_j = \emptyset$$

A concept partition allows assigning every class in the considered context to exactly one package. In the example discussed above, the two following concept partitions can be determined (see dashed boxes in Fig. 7.6):

- $CP_1 = \{c_1\}$
- $CP_2 = \{c_2, c_3\}$

The first partition contains just one concept, c_1, and corresponds to a package diagram with all three classes A_1, A_2, A_3 in the same package, on the basis of their shared call to m_1. The second partition generates a proposal of package organization in which A_1 and A_2 are inside a package, since they call both m_1 and m_2, while A_3 is put inside a second package for its calls to m_1 and m_3. It should be noted that the second package organization permits a violation of encapsulation, since classes of different packages have a shared method call, namely to m_1. It ensures that no class outside c_2 invokes *both* m_1 and m_2, while m_1 alone can be invoked outside c_2. This example gives a deeper insight into the modularization associated with a concept partition: even in cases in which the only package diagram that does not violate encapsulation is the trivial one, with all the classes in one package, concept analysis can extract alternative organizations of the packages into cohesive units, that occasionally are allowed to violate encapsulation.

It might be the case that no meaningful concept partition is determined out of the initial context, although each concept, taken in isolation, represents a meaningful grouping of classes into a package. In this situation, the package organization indicated by the concepts can be taken into account by relaxing the constraint on the concept partitions. One way to achieve this result is described in [88], and consists of determining concept sub-partitions, instead of concept partitions, that can be eventually extended to a full partition of the set of classes under analysis.

7.4 The *eLib* Program

The *eLib* program is a small application consisting of just 8 classes. Thus, it makes no sense to organize them into packages. However, the exercise of applying the package diagram recovery techniques to the *eLib* program may be useful to understand how the different techniques work in practice and how their output can be interpreted.

Algorithm	Feat./rel.	Partition
Agglom.	Types	{Book} {InternalUser} {Journal, TechnicalReport} {User, Document, Library, Loan}
Agglom.	Calls	{InternalUser} {Book, Journal, TechnicalReport} {User, Document, Library, Loan}
Mod. opt.	Cl. diag.	{Book} {InternalUser} {Journal} {TechnicalReport} {User, Document, Loan} {Library}
Mod. opt.	Calls	{Book} {InternalUser} {Journal} {TechnicalReport} {User, Document, Library, Loan}
Concept	Types	{Book} {InternalUser} {Journal, TechnicalReport} {User, Document, Library, Loan}

Table 7.2. Class partitioning produced by different package diagram recovery algorithms.

Table 7.2 summarizes the results obtained by the agglomerative clustering method (first two lines, labeled *Agglom.*), by the modularity optimization method (lines 3 and 4, labeled *Mod. opt.*), and by concept analysis (last line, labeled *Concept*). The second column contains the kind of features or relationships that have been taken into account (a detailed explanation follows). The last column gives the resulting package diagram, expressed as a partition of the set of classes in the program.

In the application of the agglomerative clustering algorithm, two kinds of feature vectors have been used. In the first case, each entry in the feature

Class	Feature vector
Library	<0, 5, 12, 0, 0, 0, 10, 0>
Loan	<0, 1, 3, 0, 0, 0, 3, 0>
Document	<0, 2, 1, 0, 0, 0, 3, 0>
Book	<0, 0, 0, 0, 0, 0, 0, 0>
Journal	<0, 0, 0, 0, 0, 0, 1, 0>
TechnicalReport	<0, 0, 0, 0, 0, 0, 1, 0>
User	<0, 3, 1, 0, 0, 0, 1, 0>
InternalUser	<0, 0, 0, 0, 0, 0, 0, 0>

Table 7.3. Feature vectors based on declared variable types.

vector represents any of the user defined types (i.e., each of the 8 classes in the program). The associated value counts the number of references to such a type in the declarations of class attributes, method parameters, local variables or return values. Table 7.3 shows the feature vectors based on the type information. The types in each position of the vectors read as follows:

```
<Library, Loan, Document, Book, Journal, TechnicalReport, User,
InternalUser>
```

It should be noted that the feature vectors for classes `Book` and `Internal-User` are empty. This indicates that the chosen features do not characterize these two classes at all, and consequently they do not permit grouping these two classes with any cluster.

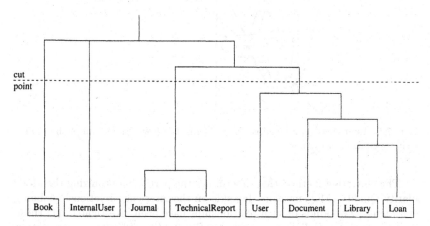

Fig. 7.7. Clustering hierarchy for the *eLib* program (clustering method *Agglom-Types*).

Fig. 7.7 shows the clustering hierarchy produced by the agglomerative algorithm applied to the feature vectors in Table 7.3. The (manually) selected cut point is indicated by a dashed line. The results shown in the first line of Table 7.2 correspond to this cut point. Classes `User`, `Document`, `Library`, `Loan` are clustered together. So are `Journal`, `TechnicalReport`, while `Book` and `InternalUser` remain isolated, due to their empty description.

The agglomerative clustering algorithm was re-executed on the *eLib* program, with different feature vectors. The number of invocations of each method is stored in the respective entry of the new feature vectors. Thus, for example, the first component of the feature vectors, associated with method `User.getCode`, holds value 1 for classes `Document`, `Library`, `Loan`, in that they contain one invocation of such a method (resp. at lines 220, 10, 152), while such an entry contains a zero in the feature vectors for all the other classes, which do not call method `getCode` of class `User`.

The class partition obtained by cutting the clustering hierarchy associated with these feature vectors is reported in the second line of Table 7.2. Now the two classes `Book` and `InternalUser` have a non empty description, so that they can be properly clustered. The resulting package diagram is the same that was produced with the feature vectors based on the declared variable types, except for class `Book`, which is aggregated with {`Journal`, `TechnicalReport`}.

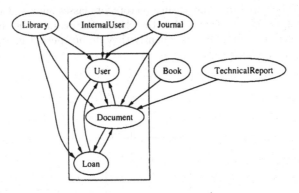

Fig. 7.8. Inter-class relationships considered in the first application of the modularity optimization method.

The clustering method that determines the partition optimizing the Modularity Quality (MQ) measure depends on the inter-class relationships being considered. Two kinds of such relationships have been investigated: (1) those depicted in the class diagram reported in Fig. 3.9 (i.e., inheritance, association and dependency); (2) the method calls.

Fig 7.8 shows the inter-class relationships considered in the first case. Given the low number of classes involved, an exhaustive search was conducted to determine the partition which maximizes MQ. The result is the partition in the third line of Table 7.2 (see also the box in Fig 7.8). It corresponds to a value of MQ equal to 0.91 and it was obtained by giving the same weight to all kinds of relationships. Actually, giving different weights to different kinds of relationships does not change the result, as long as the ratios between the weights remains small enough (less than 5). Big ratios between the weights lead to an optimal MQ reached when all classes are in just one cluster.

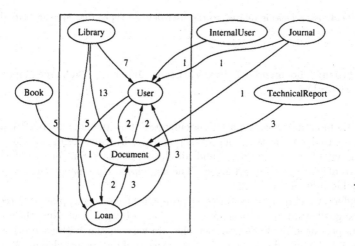

Fig. 7.9. Call relationships considered in the second application of the modularity optimization method.

In the second case (call relationships), the optimal partition is associated with MQ = 0.87, and it differs from the previous one only for the position of class Library, which is merged with {User, Document, Loan} (see Table 7.2). Call relationships considered in this second clustering based on MQ are weighted by the number of calls issued within each class. Thus, the call relationship between Loan and User is weighted 3 because there are three invocations of methods belonging to class User, issued from methods of class Loan (resp. at lines 148, 152, 153). Fig. 7.9 shows the weighted call relationships considered in this second application of the modularity optimization method (the only non-singleton cluster is surrounded by a box).

Finally, concept analysis was applied to the context that relates the classes to the declared type of attributes, method parameters and local variables (see Table 7.4). Classes Book and InternalUser have been excluded, since they do not declare any variable of a user-defined type (see discussion of the feature vectors in Table 7.3 given above). Two concepts are determined from such a context:

$c_1 = (\{$User, Document, Library, Loan$\}, \{$User, Document, Loan$\})$

Class	Type		
	Loan	Document	User
Library	×	×	×
Loan	×	×	×
Document	×	×	×
Journal			×
TechnicalReport			×
User	×	×	×

Table 7.4. Each class is related to the user-defined types that appear in its declarations.

$c_2 = (\{\text{User, Document, Library, Loan, Journal, TechnicalReport}\},$
$\quad \{\text{User}\})$

Although no concept partition emerges, it is possible to partition the classes based on the two concepts c_1 and c_2, by considering all classes in the extent of c_1 as one group, and all classes in the extent of c_2 but not in the extent of c_1 as a second group. The associated class partition is reported in the last line of Table 7.2.

Different techniques and different properties have been exploited to recover a package diagram from the source code of the *eLib* program. Nonetheless, the results produced in the various settings are very similar with each other (see Table 7.2). They differ at most for the position of one or two classes. A strong cohesion among the classes User, Document, Loan was revealed by all of the considered techniques. Actually, these three classes are related to the overall functionality of this application that deals with *loan management*. Even if different points of view are adopted (the relationships among classes, the declared types, etc.), such a grouping emerges anyway. The *eLib* program is a small program that does not need be organized into multiple packages. However, if a package structure is to be superimposed, the package diagram recovery methods considered above indicate that a package about *loan management* containing the classes User, Document, Loan could be introduced. The class diagram of the *eLib* program (taken from Fig. 1.1) with such a package structure superimposed is depicted in Fig. 7.10.

7.5 Related Work

The problem of gathering cohesive groups of entities from a software system has been extensively studied in the context of the identification of abstract data types (objects), program understanding, and module restructuring, with reference to procedural code. Some of these works [13, 51, 102] have already

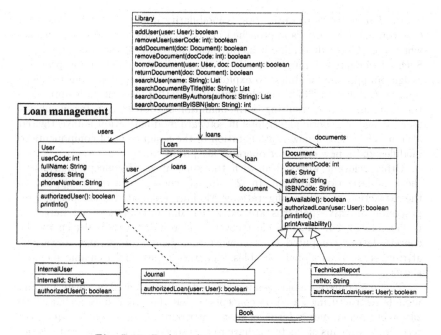

Fig. 7.10. Package diagram for the *eLib* program.

been discussed in Chapter 3. Others [4, 52, 54, 91, 99] are based on variants of the clustering method described above.

Atomic components can be detected and organized into a hierarchy of modules by following the method described in [26]. Three kinds of atomic components are considered: abstract state encapsulations, grouping global variables and accessing procedures, abstract data types, grouping user defined types and procedures with such types in their signature, and strongly connected components of mutually recursive procedures. Dominance analysis is used to hierarchically organize the retrieved components into subsystems.

Some of the approaches to the extraction of software components with high internal cohesion and low external coupling exploit the computation of software metrics. The ARCH tool [73] is one of the first examples embedding the principle of information hiding, turned into a measure of similarity between procedures, within a semi-automatic clustering framework. Such a method incorporates a weight tuning algorithm to learn from the design decisions in disagreement with the proposed modularization. In [11, 22] the purpose of retrieving modular objects is reuse, while in [61] metrics are used to refine the decomposition resulting from the application of formal and heuristic modularization principles. Another different application is presented in [46], where cohesion and coupling measures are used to determine clusters of processes. The problem of optimizing a modularity quality measure, based on cohesion and coupling, is approached in [54] by means of genetic algorithms, which are able to determine a hierarchical clustering of the input modules. Such a technique is improved in [55] by the possibility to detect and properly assign omnipresent modules, to exploit user provided clusters, and to adopt *orphan* modules. In [53] a complementary clustering mechanism is applied to the interconnections, resulting in the definition of tube edges between subsystems. Usage of genetic algorithms in software modularization is investigated also in [32], where a new representation of the assignment of components to modules and a new crossover operator are proposed.

Other relevant works deal with the application of concept analysis to the modularization problem. In [24, 45, 77] concept analysis is applied to the extraction of code configurations. Modules associated with specific preprocessor directive patterns are extracted and interferences are detected. In [50, 71, 75, 84, 94], module recovery and restructuring is driven by the concept lattice computed on a context that relates procedures to various attributes, such as global variables, signature types, and dynamic memory access.

The main difference between module restructuring based on clustering and module restructuring based on concepts is that the latter gives a characterization of the modules in terms of shared attributes. On the contrary, modules recovered by means of clustering have to be inspected to trace similarity values back to their commonalities.

Module restructuring methods based on concepts suffer from the difficulty of determining partitions, i.e., non overlapping and complete groupings of program entities. In fact, concept analysis does not assure that the candidate modules (concepts) it determines are disjoint and cover the whole entity set. In the approach proposed in [88], such a problem is overcome by using concept subpartitions, instead of concept partitions, and by providing extension rules to obtain a coverage of all of the entities to be modularized.

8

Conclusions

This chapter deals with the practical issues related to the adoption of reverse engineering techniques within an Object Oriented software development process. Tool support and integration is one of the main concerns. This chapter contains some considerations on a general architecture for tools that implement the techniques presented in the previous chapters. A survey of the existing support and of the current practice in reverse engineering is also provided.

Once an automated infrastructure for reverse engineering is in place, the process of software evolution has to be adapted so as to smoothly integrate the newly offered functionalities. This accounts for revising the main activities in the micro-process of software maintenance. The kind of support offered to *program understanding* has been already described in detail (see Chapter 1, *eLib* example). The way other activities are affected by the integration of a reverse engineering tool in the development process are described in this chapter, by reconsidering the *eLib* program and the change requests sketched in Chapter 1. Location of the changes in the source code, change implementation and assessment of the ripple effects are conducted on the *eLib* program, using, whenever possible, the information reverse engineered from the code.

A vision of the software development process that could be realized by exploiting the potential of reverse engineering concludes the chapter. The opportunities offered by new programming languages and paradigms for reverse engineering are outlined, as well as the possibility of integration with emerging development processes.

This chapter is organized as follows: Section 8.1 describes the main modules to be developed in a reverse engineering tool for Object Oriented code. Reverse engineered diagrams can be exploited for change location and implementation, as well as for change impact analysis. Their usage with the *eLib program* is presented in Section 8.2. The authors' perspectives on potential improvements of the current practices are given in Section 8.3, with reference to new programming languages and development processes. Finally, related works are commented in the last section of the chapter.

8.1 Tool Architecture

Implementation of the algorithms described in the previous chapters is affected by practical concerns, such as the target programming language, the available libraries, the graphical format of the resulting diagrams, etc. However, it is possible to devise a general architecture to be instantiated in each specific case. In this architecture, functionalities are assigned to different modules, so as to achieve a decomposition of the main task into manageable, well-defined sub-tasks. In turn, each module requires a specialization that depends on the specific setting in which the actual implementation is being built.

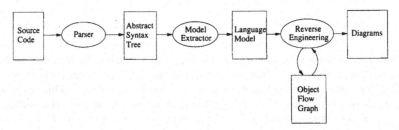

Fig. 8.1. General architecture of a reverse engineering tool.

Fig. 8.1 shows the main processing steps performed by the modules composing a reverse engineering tool. The first module, *Parser*, is responsible for handling the syntax of the source programming language. It contains the grammar that defines the language under analysis. It parses the source code and builds the derivation tree associated with the grammar productions. A higher-level view of the derivation tree is preferable, in order to decouple successive modules from the specific choices made in the definition of the grammar for the target language. Specifically, the intermediate non-terminals used in each grammar production are quite variable, being strongly dependent on the way the parser handles ambiguity (e.g., bottom-up and top-down parsers require very different organizations of the non-terminals). For this reason, it is convenient to transform the derivation tree into a more abstract tree representation of the program, called the Abstract Syntax Tree (AST). In this program representation, chains of intermediate non-terminals are collapsed, and only the main syntactic categories of the language are represented [2].

The AST is a program representation that reflects the syntactic structure of the code. However, reverse engineering tools are based on a somewhat different view of the source code. In the remainder of this chapter, this view is referenced as the *language model* assumed by a reverse engineering tool. In a language model, several syntactic details can be safely ignored. For example, the tokens delimiting blocks of statements (curly braces, **begin, end,** etc.) are irrelevant, while the information of interest is the actual presence of a sequence of statements. Thus, in the language model, tokens such as delimiters of statement blocks and parameters, separators in parameter lists and statement sequences, etc., are absent. On the other hand, information not explicitly represented in the AST is made directly available in the language model. For example, each variable involved in an expression is linked to its declaration. Each method call is resolved in terms of all the type-compatible definitions of the invoked method. Each class is associated with its superclass, as well as the interfaces it implements. Such cross-references are not obtained by means of plain identifiers, as in the AST, but are links toward the referenced elements in the language model. For example, if class A extends class B, the AST for class A contains just a child node for the *extends* clause, leading to the identifier B, while in the language model an association exists between the model element for class A and the model element for class B. An example of (simplified) language model for the Java language is described in detail below. The module responsible for building the language model out of the AST of an input program is the *Model Extractor* (see Fig. 8.1).

Based upon the language model of the input program, reverse engineering algorithms can be executed to recover alternative design views. The output is a set of diagrams to be displayed to the user. In some cases, a further abstraction of the language model that *Reverse Engineering* algorithms have in input is necessary. For example, most (but not all) of the techniques described in the previous chapters require that the data flows in the target Object Oriented program be abstracted into a data structure called the Object Flow Graph (OFG). Such a data structure is built internally into the *Reverse Engineering* module and is shared by all the algorithms that depend on it. Flow propagation of proper information inside the OFG leads to the recovery of the design views of interest. These are converted into a graphical format of choice, in order for the final user to be able to visualize them.

8.1.1 Language Model

Since reverse engineering techniques span over a wide spectrum, depending on the kind of high-level information being recovered, it is quite important to design a general language model that supports all of the alternative algorithms. In turn, each algorithm may have an internal representation of the source code, different from the language model itself. However, the main requirement on the language model is that all the information necessary for the reverse engineering algorithms to work and (possibly) build their own internal data structures must be available in the language model. Thus, the language model plays a critical, central role in the architecture described above and should be designed very carefully. An example of such a model is given in Fig. 8.2 for the Java language. Only the most important entities are shown (for space reasons), with no indication of their properties.

A Java source file contains the definition of classes within a name space called *package*. In turn, packages can be nested. Thus, the topmost entity

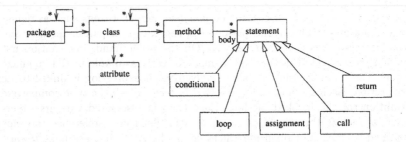

Fig. 8.2. Simplified Java language model. Containment and inheritance relationships are shown.

in the language model for Java (see Fig. 8.2, left) is the *package* and a self-containment relationship in the package entity represents nesting. Eventually, packages contain classes (containment from *package* to *class* in Fig. 8.2). The main property of the entity *package* (not shown in Fig. 8.2) is its *name*, that uniquely identifies it.

The properties of the entity *class* include the *name*, *visibility*, as well as its *superclass*, implemented *interfaces*, etc. The entities in turn contained inside classes are the class members. Thus, the entity *class* is connected to the entity *attribute* and to the entity *method*. Moreover, classes can be nested inside other classes. This is the reason for the self-containment outgoing from the entity *class*.

The entity *attribute* has properties such as *name, type, visibility, initializer*, etc. Similarly, the entity *method* has properties such as *name, formal parameters, return type, visibility*, etc. The body of each method is represented as a sequence of statements in the language model (containment from *method* to *statement* labeled *body* in Fig. 8.2).

Statements can be of different types. Some of them are enumerated in Fig. 8.2, connected to their abstraction *statement* by an inheritance relationship. Conditional statements are used for constructs such as `if` and `switch`. Among their properties, they hold a reference to the *expression* entity used in the tested condition (not shown in Fig. 8.2). The `if` *conditional* statement has a *then-part* and an *else-part*, which are in turn sequences of statements (similarly to the *body* of a method). The `switch` statement is associated with a sequence of `cases`, each containing the respective statements to execute.

Loop statements include `while`, `for` and `do-while` loops. Their main properties are the tested condition (an *expression* entity, not shown in Fig. 8.2) and the loop body (a sequence of *statements*). `For` loops have also an *initializer* and an *increment* part.

Assignment statements have two main components, the *left hand side* and the *right hand side*. While the latter is a generic *expression*, the former must eventually reference a location. This is achieved by constraining it to a *unary expression*, instead of a generic *expression*.

Call statements involve a dereference chain (*primary expression*), eventually leading to the object which is the target of the invocation. Other important properties are the *name* of the called method, the *actual parameter list* (a list of *expressions*), and links toward all type-compatible methods in the language model. In the case of an invocation of a library method, the call is marked as *library call.*

When the control flow inside a method is interrupted to return a value to the caller, a *return* statement is encountered. The main property of this entity is the *expression* that defines the returned value.

Among the entities and relationships not shown in Fig. 8.2 for space reasons, the most important one is the entity *expression*, accounting for all mathematical expressions supported by the language, possibly intermixed with method invocations. The sub-hierarchy of the *expression* entities closely resembles that available in most programming languages (either procedural or Object Oriented).

The information represented according to the model in Fig. 8.2 is sufficient to build the OFG for a given source code, as well as to conduct all other analyses that do not depend on the OFG and have been described in the previous chapters. Thus, it can be used as the basic representation exploited by all reverse engineering techniques implemented in the *Reverse Engineering* module.

8.2 The *eLib* Program

The change request for the *eLib* program, anticipated in Section 1.2, is reconsidered now that several design views have been recovered from the *eLib* code and are available for inspection.

In summary, the modification to be implemented involves the following issues:

- The program should support the reservation of books not available for loan (i.e., borrowed).
- A document can be reserved by a user if it is currently borrowed by another user and if no other user has already reserved it (one reservation per document only).
- Permission to reserve a document follows the same policy used for the loans: only users that are authorized to loan a given document can reserve it when it is out.
- When a reserved document is returned to the library, only the user who made the reservation can borrow it.
- Reservations can be cleared at any time (both before and after a document is returned).

The design diagrams extracted from the code in the previous chapters are used to locate the code portions to be changed and to define the approach to implement the change, at a high level. Then, design diagrams are recovered from the new system, to assess the portions of the system actually impacted by the change. These are expected to be the main target of the testing activity to be conducted before releasing the new version of the program.

8.2.1 Change Location

Let us consider the class diagram depicted in Fig. 1.1. The class Loan is used to instantiate an association between a user and a document, that comes into existence each time a document is borrowed by a user. Such an association is objectified into instances of class Loan, which are stored inside the attribute loans of class Library, thus remaining accessible to the library.

The role played by the class Loan in the class organization depicted in Fig. 1.1 is very similar to that required for the implementation of the reservation mechanism. In fact, a reservation is an association between a user and a document, that comes into existence each time a document is reserved by a user. Moreover, the class Library needs to maintain a persistent list of the currently active reservations. To achieve this, the user-document association representing a reservation can be objectified, by instantiating a new class, that we will call Reservation.

Similarly to class Loan, class Reservation has two stable references toward classes User and Document, which implement the association between a user and a document, where the former is reserving the latter. Moreover, an attribute of class Library, which we will call reservations, can be used to store the list of current reservations (objects of class Reservation).

From the short description given above, it is clear that the two classes Loan and Reservation are very similar. Thus, it might be the case that a common abstraction can be defined, implementing the shared functionalities of these two classes. Inheritance of such functionalities would avoid their duplication in the two classes Loan and Reservation.

The common mechanism shared by Loan and Reservation consists of the association between an object of class User and an object of class Document, implemented by means of two attributes referencing the two classes being associated and by means of a method to create such an association. Moreover, methods to access each participant in the association and to assess equality are expected to be also provided. We will call UserDocumentAssociation the class containing such common functionalities. Classes Loan and Reservation extends it and inherit these fuctionalities from it.

The other classes in Fig. 1.1 are expected to be not affected by the change to be implemented. However, additions and modifications of existing data members may be necessary. For example, class Library must provide interface methods to reserve a document (reserveDocument) and to clear a reservation (clearReservation). In turn, the implementation of these methods may be based on private methods addReservation and removeReservation, defined in classes Library, User and Document, with a role similar to that of addLoan and removeLoan. Another convenience method that should be added is isReserved in class Document, which, similarly to isAvailable, checks if a reservation was made for a given document (attribute reservation not null, similarly to attribute loan for isAvailable) A method isReserving could play a similar role as isHolding in class Library. Other useful methods are related to the printing and searching facilities (e.g., printReservation in class Document).

Let us consider the instances of the *eLib* classes, by looking at the static and dynamic object diagrams depicted in Fig. 1.2. Introduction of the reservation mechanism would result in a new object, Reservation1, representing all instances of class Reservation stored in the library, referenced through the attribute reservations.

Similarly to the objects Loan2 and Loan3, temporarily created by return-Document and isHolding, two temporary objects Reservation2 and Reservation3 may be necessary in the implementation of clearReservation and isReserving.

Let us consider the interactions occurring when a document is borrowed (see Fig. 1.3). Given the parallel behavior of reservations and loans, a similar diagram is expected to hold for method reserveDocument, with some slightly different checks (e.g., with isAvailable replaced by isReserved) and the same authorization controls. On the other side, the method borrowDocument itself is expected to be impacted by the change being implemented. In fact, if the document requested for loan is currently reserved, it can be borrowed only by the user who reserved it. In such a case, creation of the loan must include the deletion of the existing reservation.

The original interaction diagram for the method returnDocument from class Library is shown in Fig. 1.4. The sequence of messages exchanged among the involved objects has the overall effect of deleting a Loan object, which is removed from the list stored in the Library and which becomes no longer referenced by the User and Document it was previously associated with. Such an operation is not affected by the introduction of a reservation mechanism. In fact, a loan is closed in the same way, regardless of the fact that the related document is reserved or not. It becomes available anyway after the loan is dropped. Thus, we expect that the sequence diagram in Fig. 1.4 remains unchanged in the new version of the *eLib* program.

The state diagrams in Fig. 1.5, 1.6 are not affected by the change being implemented. In fact, the state of a User or a Document, in terms of the loan(s) they are associated with, continues to obey the dynamics represented in these diagrams. The same is true for the joint dynamics of the documents, users and loans referenced by a Library object (see Fig. 1.6). However, introduction of a new attribute, reservations, in class Library, and of backward links from User, Document to Reservation, creates a demand for additional views of the states of User, Document and Library. For the latter, a joint description of *loans* and *reservations* may be useful to characterize the transitions allowed in each combined state.

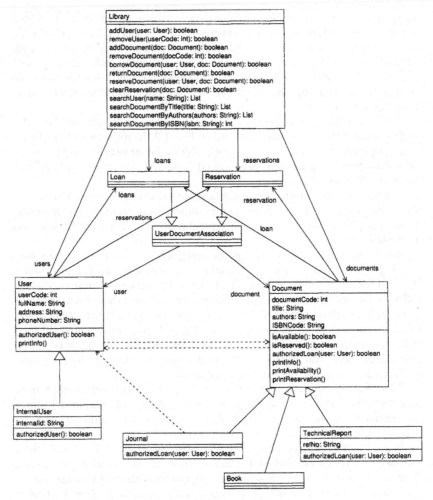

Fig. 8.3. New class diagram for the *eLib* program.

8.2.2 Impact of the Change

After implementing the change request described above, all diagrams presented in Chapter 1 have been recomputed. In the following text, they are commented, with the aim of identifying the main differences with respect to the original program. Such differences indicate which code portions have been affected by the change. This helps understanding the new organization of the application, but can also be useful in defining a test plan, where changed parts are exercised more extensively. Unexpected ripple effects may also come to light thanks to the assessment of the changes performed.

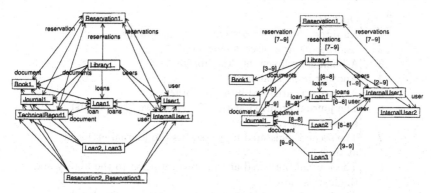

Fig. 8.4. Static (left) and dynamic (right) object diagram for the *eLib* program.

Fig. 8.3 shows the new class diagram obtained after change implementation. As anticipated in the previous section, a class (UserDocumentAssociation) has been introduced to factor out all operations involved in the creation of an association between a user and a document. Classes Loan and Reservation (the latter is a new class) represent specific cases of UserDocumentAssociation.

Class Library stores the list of the active reservations inside its attribute reservations. Hence, the link from Library to Reservation labeled reservations. User and document participating in a reservation possess a reference to the related Reservation object. In the class diagram, this is indicated by the association from User to Reservation (labeled reservations) and by the association from Document to Reservation (labeled reservation).

Among the methods listed in the lower compartment of class Library, some new members are apparent in Fig. 8.3. For example, the method reserveDocument has been added, offering the functionalities to create a reservation of a document by a user. The method clearReservation deletes the reservation associated with a given document doc (parameter of the method). Both of them return *true* upon successful completion of the operation.

In the class Document, among others, the method isReserved has been added, returning *true* when called onto reserved documents (i.e., documents with non-null reservation attribute). Information about any reservation possibly made on a document can be printed by calling the method printReservation from class Document.

Let us consider the relationships that hold among the objects instantiating the classes in Fig. 8.3. Fig. 8.4 shows the static and dynamic object diagrams recovered from the code of the modified application. The dynamic object diagram has been obtained from the execution of the following scenario:

Time	Operation
1	An internal user is registered into the library.
2	Another internal user is registered.
3	A book is archived into the library
4	Another book is archived.
5	A journal is archived into the library.
6	The journal archived at time 5 is borrowed by the first registered user.
7	The second registered user reserves the journal archived at time 5.
8	The journal borrowed at time 6 is returned to the library and the loan is closed.
9	The librarian verifies that the loan was actually closed.

The only difference with respect to the scenario described in Section 1.4 is the operation occurring at time 7, when a document not available for loan is reserved by an authorized user (only internal users can borrow journals).

In the static object diagram (Fig. 8.4, left), accounting for all possible inter-object relationships that may occur in any program execution, three new nodes are present, representing instances of class Reservation: Reservation1, Reservation2 and Reservation3. The object Reservation1 is created by the method reserveDocument, in class Library, each time a user makes a reservation on a document not available for loan. The object Library1 holds the list of such objects (link from Library1 to Reservation1). Moreover, the involved user and document also possess a reference to it (links from Book1, Journal1, TechnicalReport1 and from User1, InternalUser1).

The object Reservation2 is created inside method clearReservation in class Library. It is a temporary object referencing user and document (links toward User1, InternalUser1 and Book1, Journal1, TechnicalReport1) involved in the reservation to be canceled, but not referenced by them (no backward link, as shown in Fig. 8.4, left). This object is passed to method removeReservation from class Library, where the library operation remove on the Collection reservations is invoked with this object as a parameter. Implicitly, the method equals of class Reservation is called to check if Reservation2 is present inside reservations, and in case of positive answer, it is removed.

The object Reservation3 is another temporary object, created inside method isReserving in class Library. It is passed to the library operation contains, called on the Collection reservations to check if Reservation3 is present inside it. Method equals of class Reservation is once again invoked implicitly.

The dynamic object diagram shown on the right in Fig. 8.4 gives a partial view of the inter-object relationships, holding when the scenario described above is executed. Specifically, since the reservation requested at time 7 can be completed successfully, in that the related document is not available for loan, it is not already reserved by another user, and the given user is authorized to borrow it, an object representing the reservation (`Reservation1`) is created. It is accessible from `Library1` through the link `reservations`, and it has a bidirectional association with the two specific objects involved in the reservation: `Journal1` and `InternalUser2`.

It should be noted that, differently from the static object diagram, in the dynamic view objects participating in a relationship are uniquely identified, thus making the diagram easier to interpret. On the other hand, the main disadvantage of the dynamic view is that it holds only for the specific scenario for which it was built.

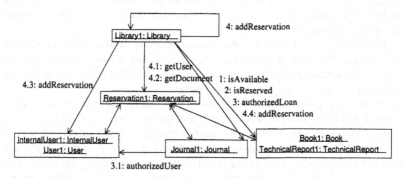

Fig. 8.5. Collaboration diagram focused on method `reserveDocument` of class `Library`.

Fig. 8.5 shows the collaboration diagram for the method `reserveDocument` of class `Library`. This is a completely new method, introduced in class `Library` to support the reservation mechanism.

The first three calls (`isAvailable`, `isReserved`, `authorizedLoan`) check whether the reservation can take place or not. A document can be reserved only if it is not available and not already reserved (calls number 1 and 2). Moreover, the reservation proceeds only if the given `user` (first method's parameter) has the permission to reserve the given document `doc` (second method's parameter). This is checked by the call number 3 (`authorizedLoan`), which requires a nested call to `authorizedUser` (numbered 3.1) when the document being reserved is a `Journal`, since only internal users can borrow journals.

If all checks above are positive, a reservation is created by means of the call number 4 (`addReservation`). Target of this call is `Library1`, i.e., the same object on which method `reserveDocument` was originally invoked.

The parameter passed to `addReservation` is a newly created object of class `Reservation`, indicated as `Reservation1` in Fig. 8.5. Such an object is the target of the invocations numbered 4.1 and 4.2, aimed at obtaining `User` and Document involved in the reservation. Then, method addReservation inserts the object Reservation1 into the Collection reservations of the library (i.e., of object Library1) and calls the method addReservation on the user and document participating in the reservation, in order to create backward links directed toward Reservation1. Possible sources of these links are InternalUser1, User1 and Book1, Journal1, TechnicalReport1 (the latter is an inaccuracy introduced by the static analysis method employed).

The collaboration diagram described above is extremely useful to understand the logics behind the reservation mechanism and its interactions with the loan authorization policy. The contribution to the reservation functionality of code fragments belonging to different classes is presented in a summary, compact form in Fig. 8.5. Recovering the same knowledge by code reading would require jumping from class to class, with the risk of missing relevant message exchanges.

The behavior of the method borrowDocument is substantially changed by the implementation of the reservation mechanism, while this is not the case for method returnDocument. A comparison of the interaction diagram in Fig. 8.6 with that in Fig. 1.3 reveals the differences.

In the message exchanges that precede the call to addLoan, we can notice a few differences. In addition to the checks performed by calling methods numberOfLoans, isAvailable and authorizedLoan (calls number 3, 4, 5 in Fig. 8.6), the method borrowDocument verifies that, if the document is already reserved (call number 1 to isReserved), the user who made the reservation is the same who is now requesting the loan (call number 2 to getReserver). If this is not the case, the method borrowDocument is aborted and returns *false*.

If all checks performed by calls 1 through 5 give a positive answer, borrowing can proceed and a new loan can be inserted into the library. The object representing such a new loan is indicated as Loan1 in Fig. 8.6. It is passed as a parameter to the next invoked method, addLoan (call number 6, issued on object Library1 itself).

The first four operations carried out inside the new version of method addLoan in class Library are the same as in the original method (compare calls 6.1, 6.2, 6.3, 6.4 in Fig. 8.6 with calls 4.1, 4.2, 4.3, 4.4 in Fig. 1.3). The next operations have been added to ensure a correct management of the reservations possibly made on the document being borrowed.

If the document being borrowed was previously reserved (call 6.5 to isReserved), the user who made the reservation is accessed (call 6.6 to getReserver) to verify that it is coincident with the one activating the loan. This is a safety, redundant check with respect to that performed through calls 1 and 2 in Fig. 8.6. It is made under the hypothesis that addLoan could be called also by methods other than borrowDocument.

Once such a check gives a positive answer, the reservation is canceled, by invoking method removeReservation of class Library (call number 6.7). The called method deletes its parameter, Reservation1, from the Collection

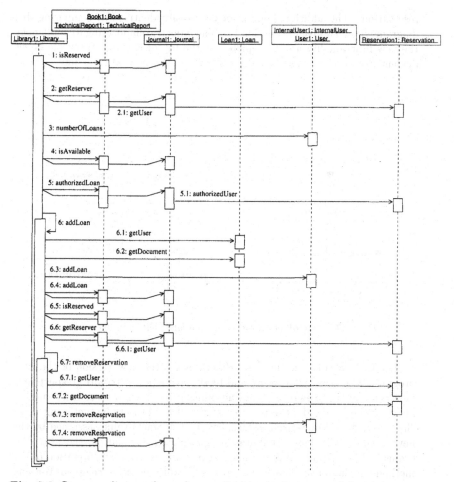

Fig. 8.6. Sequence diagram focused on method `borrowDocument` of class `Library`.

`reservations` of `Library1`. In order to also delete the backward links from `User` and `Document` involved in the reservation, the two associated objects are retrieved by respectively calling `getUser` and `getDocument` on `Reservation1` (calls number 6.7.1, 6.7.2). Then, invocation of `removeReservation` on the two retrieved objects (calls 6.7.3, 6.7.4) completes the execution of `remove-Reservation` inside class `Library`. In turn, the method `removeReservation` inside the class `Document` assigns a *null* value to the attribute `reservation`, while `removeReservation` inside class `User` deletes `Reservation1` from the attribute `reservations`, of type `Collection`.

The sequence diagram in Fig. 8.6 provides a centralized, compact view of the code changes introduced to handle document loans in the presence of reservations. The additional operations are easily identified by comparing this diagram with that given in Section 1.5. The objects collaborating to implement the new functionality are all depicted at the top of Fig. 8.6, their role being evident from the message exchanges shown on the vertical time lines.

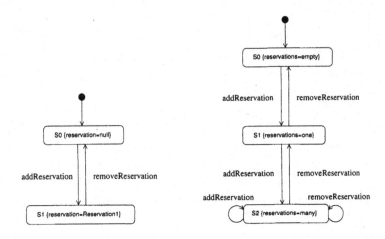

Fig. 8.7. State diagram for class Document (left) and User (right).

Let us now consider the state diagrams for the new version of the *eLib* program. The classes Document and User have a new attribute (respectively, reservation and reservations) accounting for the new reservation mechanism. Correspondingly, the possible states of the objects instantiating these classes can be characterized in terms of the (abstract) values assumed by the new attributes. If these attributes are considered in isolation, the state diagrams in Fig. 8.7 are obtained by executing an abstract interpretation of the methods in these two classes. The abstract values used for reservation and reservations parallel those used for loan (in class Document) and loans (in class User) in Section 1.6 (see Fig. 1.5). Specifically, the two abstract values *null* and *Reservation1* are used for Document.reservation, while *empty, one* and *many* are used for User.reservations.

As apparent from Fig. 8.7, the dynamics of the state changes associated with the two new attributes are similar to those already described for Document.loan and User.loans. This is a confirmation of the analog roles played by loans and reservations. The two related classes, Loan and Reservation, descend from a common super-class, UserDocumentAssociation, and inherit from it the associations with User and Document. Correspondingly, the state changes induced inside these latter classes are similar when attributes loans/reservations or loan/reservation are respectively considered.

Specifically, as regards the class User (see Fig. 8.7, right), in the initial state S_0, the only invocation that can occur is the invocation of method addReservation. This leads to state S_1, where a call to addReservation results in S_2 as the new state, while a call to removeReservation brings the class state back to S_0. In state S_2 addReservation leaves the current state unchanged, while removeReservation may leave it unchanged or lead to S_1, when one reservation remains in the Collection reservations.

The state diagram for class Document (see Fig. 8.7, left) indicates that addReservation is called only when the document is not currently reserved (*reservation=null*), while removeReservation is called only when the document is reserved (*reservation=Reservation1*).

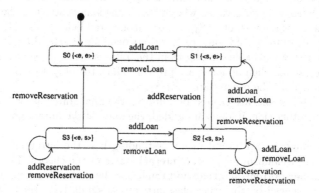

Fig. 8.8. State diagram for class Library.

Introduction of the reservation mechanism requires that a new attribute, reservations, of type Collection, be added inside the class Library. Since the values of this attribute interact with the values of attribute loans, because the logics behind reserving and borrowing a document are interleaved, it makes sense to describe the values of these two attributes jointly. The procedure is similar to that followed to produce the joint description given in Section 1.6, Fig. 1.6.

Let us indicate the joint values of loans and reservations (both of type Collection) as a pair, using the abstract value e for an empty Collection and s when some (i.e., at least one) elements are inside the given Collection. Thus, a pair $< s, e >$ indicates that the attribute loans hold some (more than zero) elements, while reservations is empty. In other words, there are active loans in the library, but there is no active reservation.

Fig. 8.8 shows the state diagram that results from the abstract interpretation of the methods of class Library with the abstract values described above. The initial state produced by the constructor of class Library (S_0) has both containers (loans and reservations) empty. An invocation of addLoan leads the library to state S_1 (non empty loans, empty reservations), while no invocation of `addReservation` (neither of the removal methods) can ever occur in S_0, due to the checks performed in the code issuing such invocations. Specifically, the only invocation to `addReservation` is inside method `reserveDocument` of class `Library`, where the call is issued only if the document being reserved is not available. This implies that at least one loan must exist ($loans=s$).

In state S_1, loans can be added and removed. In the latter case, the new state is S_0 when no loan remains inside the `Collection loans`. Moreover, in state S_1 reservations can be made, since not all documents are available. This leads to state S_2, $< s, s >$.

In state S_2, loans and reservations can be added and removed. If eventually no reservation remains, the new state is S_1, a state already described above. If method `removeLoan` is called when exactly one loan is active in the library, the new state is a fourth one (S_3), never encountered before, characterized by an empty set of loans and some reservations pending. It should be noted that this state is not reachable directly from the initial state S_0, since reservations cannot be added when no loans are present. Thus, the only way to reach it is to go through all the other states, S_0, S_1, S_2.

If all reservations are cleared in state S_3, the final state that is reached is S_0. On the other side, if loans are added, the state of the library goes back to S_2.

State diagrams are useful in understanding how the introduction of the reservation mechanism affects the internal states of the classes. The new attributes `reservations` and `reservation` inside the classes `User` and `Document` are not influenced by the other class attributes, similarly to the original attributes `loans` and `loan` in the same classes. On the contrary, in the class `Library`, `loans` and `reservations` are mutually related. Their joint description given in the state diagram of Fig. 8.8 highlights the permitted transitions in each state and the possible paths from one state to another one. This is potentially useful to support comprehension of the changed system and of the differences with respect to the original one. It will also help in the definition of test cases for the changed classes, particularly when the state-based testing approach is being used [6, 92]. In fact, this may turn out to be its primary use.

8.3 Perspectives

The authors' position is that *all the information about a program should be in the source code*. From a purely observational point of view, the well-known effects of software evolution, consisting of a progressive misalignment of source code and other sources of information about a program, entail that only the source code is reliable. So, de-facto, most information about a program *is* in the source code. On the prescriptive side, one could take as the extreme consequence the fact that everything *should* be part of the code (including design, documentation, etc.).

The first view gives a central role to reverse engineering in the future of software development. Although this discipline was born with the problems of legacy systems in mind, new software systems, developed according to modern programming paradigms such as the Object Oriented one, are not free from the problems related to program comprehension and modification. As described in this book, the comprehension problems involved in understanding Object Oriented systems are different from those arising with more traditional software, but remain the main concerns during the evolution phase. Reverse engineering has the potential to address them.

The view in which all relevant information about a program is centralized in a single source, the code, comes from the Extreme Programming (XP) development process [36]. In this methodology, limited effort is devoted to design and design documents are not maintained over time. They are considered a temporary support to communication and understanding, that is abandoned when software engineers move to the implementation. The absence of design information is mitigated by pair programming, by continuous execution of refactoring, and by the description of functionalities in terms of test cases. Reverse engineering can make an important contribution here [93]. In fact, understanding the organization of an application and of the interactions among its objects is a quite difficult task in the XP setting. As discussed in this book, there are several diagrams that can be extracted automatically from the source code and approximate quite well this kind of information.

Looking at the emerging programming languages and paradigms, we can hypothesize an increasing role of reverse engineering. Programming languages tend to evolve so as to maintain very precise information about the program's behavior in the source code. Modern compilers rely on this information to perform several checks, optimizations and transformations. Examples of this kind of information are type parameters (genericity) and metadata (e.g., annotations), that will be included in the next version (1.5) of the Java language. Aspect Oriented Programming [40] and introspection capabilities (e.g., Java reflection, OpenJava) are going in the same direction, in that they support a programmable interface to the internal units of a program.

All this has a twofold effect. On one hand, it simplifies reverse engineering, in that the source code becomes a richer information repository, that can be queried automatically by tools. On the other hand, it makes the design diagrams reverse engineered from the source code much more meaningful and useful, in that they are based on information directly encoded in the program (and checked by the compiler), instead of using information inferred by means of approximate static or dynamic analysis methods. Availability of accurate diagrams easily extracted from the code will make the reverse engineering option even more appealing, getting closer to the XP vision that everything is in the source code. In fact, maintaining and evolving multiple descriptions of a software system is much too expensive and error prone. Only by focusing on the source code as the single source of information, is it possible to keep costs low and to avoid communication errors resulting from inconsistent views.

8.4 Related Work

Reverse engineering tools have been mainly developed to support the analysis of existing procedural software, written in widely used programming languages such as C and Cobol [5, 12, 13, 14, 23, 26, 33, 34, 37, 43, 39, 59, 64, 66]. It is only in the last 10 years that the problem of reverse engineering design views from Object Oriented code has been considered [9, 20, 28, 29, 44, 42, 62, 67, 72, 74, 83, 85, 97, 101].

Some works [9, 44, 72, 74, 85, 101] are focused on the problem of identifying well-known, recurring architectural solutions, called *design patterns*, which are widely employed in the design of Object Oriented systems. Important information about the design rationale is recovered when such patterns are matched in the code.

In [29, 42, 62, 67, 97], the creation of objects and inter-object message exchange are captured by tracing the execution of a program on a given set of scenarios. This allows for a dynamic recovery of the interaction diagrams from a complete Object Oriented application.

Static analysis is employed in [20] to reverse engineer so-called Object Process Graphs, giving a finite description of all possible operation sequences, extracted for individual stack and heap-allocated objects.

The construction of call graphs for Object Oriented programs and their accuracy are considered in [28, 83].

8.4.1 Code Analysis at CERN

The material presented in this book is based on previous work conducted in the context of a collaboration with CERN, (Conseil Européen pour la Recherche Nucléaire), the research center performing high energy physics experiments in Geneva. The new experiments (currently under preparation at CERN) represent a major challenge in terms of the resources involved, including many software resources. Historic libraries developed in Fortran at CERN to support the execution of high energy physics experiments have since been ported to C++. Such a tremendous effort was conducted in a very heterogeneous and loosely controlled development environment, which involves lots of institutions distributed world-wide and many persons with a wide range of software engineering skills.

The collaboration of the authors with CERN aimed at studying methodologies and tools to control and improve the quality of the code developed at CERN. One of the planned deliverables in such a streamline was the reverse engineering tool *RevEng*, for extracting UML diagrams from C++ code.

The architecture of *RevEng* and its language model, described in more detail in [63], are similar to those given above for the Java language.

Among the diagrams that *RevEng* extracts from a program, are the class, object and interaction diagrams which have been described here. Their utility has been empirically assessed in [87, 89, 90].

The ROOT C++ library [10], which is widely employed in High Energy Physics computing, offers several containers and container operations for instances of subclasses of the top level class TObject. Such containers are declared without indicating the contained objects' type. Thus, they are prone to the problems discussed in Chapter 3, occurring when the class diagram is reverse engineered in presence of weakly typed containers. Experimental results obtained on CERN code indicate that there is a substantial difference between class diagrams produced with or without running the container analysis algorithm described in Chapter 3. A large fraction of inter-class relations is missed if container types are not determined. Moreover, the diagrams of improved quality are expected to be much closer to the mental model of the application under analysis. They can therefore be used more effectively for the high-level comprehension of the system and for its evolution.

The complementary roles of static and dynamic analysis of the source code in the extraction of the object diagram, discussed in Chapter 4, is investigated in [89], with reference to a case study in the C++ language. In [90], 27 C++ systems developed at CERN have been analyzed, with the purpose of extracting the related interaction diagrams. Empirical data indicate that diagrams of manageable size can be generated thanks to the possibility of performing a partial analysis and of focusing the view on each computation of interest (see Chapter 5 for a description of these two techniques). The resulting views have been evaluated by the authors of the related code, who judged them extremely informative. They were able to summarize information otherwise spread throughout the code.

A

Source Code of the *eLib* program

```
1    import java.util.*;
2    import java.io.*;

3    class Library {
4      Map documents = new HashMap();
5      Map users = new HashMap();
6      Collection loans = new LinkedList();
7      final int MAX_NUMBER_OF_LOANS = 20;

8      public boolean addUser(User user) {
9        if (!users.containsValue(user)) {
10         users.put(new Integer(user.getCode()), user);
11         return true;
12       }
13       return false;
14     }

15     public boolean removeUser(int userCode) {
16       User user = (User)users.get(new Integer(userCode));
17       if (user == null || user.numberOfLoans() > 0) return false;
18       users.remove(new Integer(userCode));
19       return true;
20     }

21     public User getUser(int userCode) {
22       return (User)users.get(new Integer(userCode));
23     }
```

```
24       public boolean addDocument(Document doc) {
25         if (!documents.containsValue(doc)) {
26           documents.put(new Integer(doc.getCode()), doc);
27           return true;
28         }
29         return false;
30       }

31       public boolean removeDocument(int docCode) {
32         Document doc = (Document)documents.get(new Integer(docCode));
33         if (doc == null || doc.isOut()) return false;
34         documents.remove(new Integer(docCode));
35         return true;
36       }

37       public Document getDocument(int docCode) {
38         return (Document)documents.get(new Integer(docCode));
39       }

40       private void addLoan(Loan loan) {
41         if (loan == null) return;
42         User user = loan.getUser();
43         Document doc = loan.getDocument();
44         loans.add(loan);
45         user.addLoan(loan);
46         doc.addLoan(loan);
47       }

48       private void removeLoan(Loan loan) {
49         if (loan == null) return;
50         User user = loan.getUser();
51         Document doc = loan.getDocument();
52         loans.remove(loan);
53         user.removeLoan(loan);
54         doc.removeLoan();
55       }

56       public boolean borrowDocument(User user, Document doc) {
57         if (user == null || doc == null) return false;
58         if (user.numberOfLoans() < MAX_NUMBER_OF_LOANS &&
59             doc.isAvailable() && doc.authorizedLoan(user)) {
60           Loan loan = new Loan(user, doc);
61           addLoan(loan);
62           return true;
63         }
64         return false;
65       }
```

```
66        public boolean returnDocument(Document doc) {
67          if (doc == null) return false;
68          if (doc.isOut()) {
69            User user = doc.getBorrower();
70            Loan loan = new Loan(user, doc);
71            removeLoan(loan);
72            return true;
73          }
74          return false;
75        }

76        public boolean isHolding(User user, Document doc) {
77          if (user == null || doc == null) return false;
78          return loans.contains(new Loan(user, doc));
79        }

80        public List searchUser(String name) {
81          List usersFound = new LinkedList();
82          Iterator i = users.values().iterator();
83          while (i.hasNext()) {
84            User user = (User)i.next();
85            if (user.getName().indexOf(name) != -1)
86              usersFound.add(user);
87          }
88          return usersFound;
89        }

90        public List searchDocumentByTitle(String title) {
91          List docsFound = new LinkedList();
92          Iterator i = documents.values().iterator();
93          while (i.hasNext()) {
94            Document doc = (Document)i.next();
95            if (doc.getTitle().indexOf(title) != -1)
96              docsFound.add(doc);
97          }
98          return docsFound;
99        }

100        public List searchDocumentByAuthors(String authors) {
101          List docsFound = new LinkedList();
102          Iterator i = documents.values().iterator();
103          while (i.hasNext()) {
104            Document doc = (Document)i.next();
105            if (doc.getAuthors().indexOf(authors) != -1)
106              docsFound.add(doc);
107          }
108          return docsFound;
109        }
```

```
110        public int searchDocumentByISBN(String isbn) {
111          Iterator i = documents.values().iterator();
112          while (i.hasNext()) {
113            Document doc = (Document)i.next();
114            if (isbn.equals(doc.getISBN()))
115              return doc.getCode();
116          }
117          return -1;
118        }

119        public void printAllLoans() {
120          Iterator i = loans.iterator();
121          while (i.hasNext()) {
122            Loan loan = (Loan)i.next();
123            loan.print();
124          }
125        }

126        public void printUserInfo(User user) {
127          user.printInfo();
128        }

129        public void printDocumentInfo(Document doc) {
130          doc.printInfo();
131        }

132      }
```

—————————————————————file Loan.java —————————————————————

```
133      class Loan {
134        User user;
135        Document document;

136        public Loan(User usr, Document doc) {
137          user = usr;
138          document = doc;
139        }

140        public User getUser() {
141          return user;
142        }
```

```
143      public Document getDocument() {
144         return document;
145      }

146      public boolean equals(Object obj) {
147         Loan loan = (Loan)obj;
148         return user.equals(loan.user) &&
149            document.equals(loan.document);
150      }

151      public void print() {
152         System.out.println("User: " + user.getCode() +
153            " - " + user.getName() +
154            " holds doc: " + document.getCode() +
155            " - " + document.getTitle());
156      }
157   }
```

———————————————file Document.java —————————————

```
158      import java.util.*;

159      class Document {
160         int documentCode;
161         String title;
162         String authors;
163         String ISBNCode;
164         Loan loan = null;
165         static int nextDocumentCodeAvailable = 0;

166         public Document(String tit) {
167            title = tit;
168            ISBNCode = "";
169            authors = "";
170            documentCode = Document.nextDocumentCodeAvailable++;
171         }

172         public boolean equals(Object obj) {
173            Document doc = (Document)obj;
174            return documentCode == doc.documentCode;
175         }

176         public boolean isAvailable() {
177            return loan == null;
178         }

179         public boolean isOut() {
180            return !isAvailable();
181         }
```

```
182        public boolean authorizedLoan(User user) {
183          return true;
184        }

185        public User getBorrower() {
186          if (loan != null)
187            return loan.getUser();
188          return null;
189        }

190        public int getCode() {
191          return documentCode;
192        }

193        public String getTitle() {
194          return title;
195        }

196        public String getAuthors() {
197          return authors;
198        }

199        public String getISBN() {
200          return ISBNCode;
201        }

202        public void addLoan(Loan ln) {
203          loan = ln;
204        }

205        public void removeLoan() {
206          loan = null;
207        }

208        protected void printAuthors() {
209          System.out.println("Author(s): " + getAuthors());
210        }

211        protected void printHeader() {
212          System.out.println("Document: " + getCode() +
213            " - " + getTitle());
214        }
```

```
215      protected void printAvailability() {
216        if (loan == null) {
217          System.out.println("Available.");
218        } else {
219          User user = loan.getUser();
220          System.out.println("Hold by " + user.getCode() +
221                             " - " + user.getName());
222        }
223      }

224      protected void printGeneralInfo() {
225        System.out.println("Title: " + getTitle());
226        if (!getISBN().equals(""))
227          System.out.println("ISBN: " + getISBN());
228      }

229      public void printInfo() {
230        printHeader();
231        printGeneralInfo();
232        printAvailability();
233      }
234    }
```

──────────────────────file Book.java ──────────────────────

```
235    class Book extends Document {
236      public Book(String tit, String auth, String isbn) {
237        super(tit);
238        ISBNCode = isbn;
239        authors = auth;
240      }
241
242      public void printInfo() {
243        printHeader();
244        printAuthors();
245        printGeneralInfo();
246        printAvailability();
247      }
248    }
```

──────────────────────file Journal.java ──────────────────────

```
249    class Journal extends Document {
250      public Journal(String tit) {
251        super(tit);
252      }
```

```
253        public boolean authorizedLoan(User user) {
254          return user.authorizedUser();
255        }

256    }
```

_____file TechnicalReport.java_____

```
257    class TechnicalReport extends Document {
258        String refNo;

259        public TechnicalReport(String tit, String ref, String auth) {
260          super(tit);
261          refNo = ref;
262          authors = auth;
263        }

264        public boolean authorizedLoan(User user) {
265          return false;
266        }

267        public String getRefNo() {
268          return refNo;
269        }

270        protected void printRefNo() {
271          System.out.println("Ref. No.: " + getRefNo());
272        }

273        public void printInfo() {
274          printHeader();
275          printAuthors();
276          printGeneralInfo();
277          printRefNo();
278        }
279    }
```

_____file User.java_____

```
280    import java.util.*;

281    class User {
282        int userCode;
283        String fullName;
284        String address;
```

```
285      String phoneNumber;
286      Collection loans = new LinkedList();
287      static int nextUserCodeAvailable = 0;

288      public User(String name, String addr, String phone) {
289         fullName = name;
290         address = addr;
291         phoneNumber = phone;
292         userCode = User.nextUserCodeAvailable++;
293      }
294
295      public boolean equals(Object obj) {
296         User user = (User)obj;
297         return userCode == user.userCode;
298      }

299      public boolean authorizedUser() {
300         return false;
301      }

302      public int getCode() {
303         return userCode;
304      }

305      public String getName() {
306         return fullName;
307      }

308      public String getAddress() {
309         return address;
310      }

311      public String getPhone() {
312         return phoneNumber;
313      }

314      public void addLoan(Loan loan) {
315         loans.add(loan);
316      }

317      public int numberOfLoans() {
318         return loans.size();
319      }

320      public void removeLoan(Loan loan) {
321         loans.remove(loan);
322      }
```

```
323      public void printInfo() {
324         System.out.println("User: " + getCode() + " - " + getName());
325         System.out.println("Address: " + getAddress());
326         System.out.println("Phone: " + getPhone());
327         System.out.println("Borrowed documents:");
328         Iterator i = loans.iterator();
329         while (i.hasNext()) {
330           Loan loan = (Loan)i.next();
331           Document doc = loan.getDocument();
332           System.out.println(doc.getCode() + " - " + doc.getTitle())
333         }
334      }
335    }
```

──────────────────────file InternalUser.java ──────────────────

```
336    class InternalUser extends User {
337      String internalId;

338      public InternalUser(String name, String addr,
339            String phone, String id) {
340        super(name, addr, phone);
341        internalId = id;
342      }

343      public boolean authorizedUser() {
344         return true;
345      }

346    }
```

B

Driver class for the *eLib* program

──────────── file Main.java ────────────

```
347    class Main {
348        static Library lib = new Library();

349        public static void printHeader() {
350            System.out.println("COMMANDS:");
351            System.out.println("addUser name, address, phone");
352            System.out.println("addIntUser name, address, phone, id");
353            System.out.println("rmUser userId");
354            System.out.println("addBook title, authors, ISBN");
355            System.out.println("addReport title, ref, authors");
356            System.out.println("addJournal title");
357            System.out.println("rmDoc docId");
358            System.out.println("borrowDoc userId, docId");
359            System.out.println("returnDoc docId");
360            System.out.println("searchUser name");
361            System.out.println("searchDoc title");
362            System.out.println("isHolding userId, docId");
363            System.out.println("printLoans");
364            System.out.println("printUser userId");
365            System.out.println("printDoc docId");
366            System.out.println("exit");
367        }
```

```
368        public static String[] getArgs(String cmd) {
369          String args[] = new String[0];
370          String s = cmd.trim();
371          if (s.indexOf(" ") != -1) {
372            s = s.substring(s.indexOf(" "));
373            args = s.trim().split(",");
374            for (int i = 0 ; i < args.length ; i++)
375              args[i] = args[i].trim();
376          }
377          return args;
378        }

379        public static void addUser(String cmd) {
380          String args[] = getArgs(cmd);
381          if (args.length < 3) return;
382          User user = new User(args[0], args[1], args[2]);
383          lib.addUser(user);
384          System.out.println("Added user: " + user.getCode() +
385          " - " + user.getName());
386        }

387        public static void addIntUser(String cmd) {
388          String args[] = getArgs(cmd);
389          if (args.length < 4) return;
390          User user = new InternalUser(args[0], args[1], args[2], args
391          lib.addUser(user);
392          System.out.println("Added user: " + user.getCode() +
393          " - " + user.getName());
394        }

395        public static void rmUser(String cmd) {
396          String args[] = getArgs(cmd);
397          if (args.length < 1) return;
398          User user = lib.getUser(Integer.parseInt(args[0]));
399          if (lib.removeUser(Integer.parseInt(args[0])))
400            System.out.println("Removed user: " + user.getCode() +
401            " - " + user.getName());
402        }

403        public static void addBook(String cmd) {
404          String args[] = getArgs(cmd);
405          if (args.length < 3) return;
406          Document doc = new Book(args[0], args[1], args[2]);
407          lib.addDocument(doc);
408          System.out.println("Added doc: " + doc.getCode() +
409          " - " + doc.getTitle());
410        }
```

```
411      public static void addReport(String cmd) {
412          String args[] = getArgs(cmd);
413          if (args.length < 3) return;
414          Document doc = new TechnicalReport(args[0], args[1], args[2]);
415          lib.addDocument(doc);
416          System.out.println("Added doc: " + doc.getCode() +
417          " - " + doc.getTitle());
418      }

419      public static void addJournal(String cmd) {
420          String args[] = getArgs(cmd);
421          if (args.length < 1) return;
422          Document doc = new Journal(args[0]);
423          lib.addDocument(doc);
424          System.out.println("Added doc: " + doc.getCode() +
425          " - " + doc.getTitle());
426      }

427      public static void rmDoc(String cmd) {
428          String args[] = getArgs(cmd);
429          if (args.length < 1) return;
430          Document doc = lib.getDocument(Integer.parseInt(args[0]));
431          if (lib.removeDocument(Integer.parseInt(args[0])))
432              System.out.println("Removed doc: " + doc.getCode() +
433              " - " + doc.getTitle());
434      }

435      public static void borrowDoc(String cmd) {
436          String args[] = getArgs(cmd);
437          if (args.length < 2) return;
438          User user = lib.getUser(Integer.parseInt(args[0]));
439          Document doc = lib.getDocument(Integer.parseInt(args[1]));
440          if (user == null || doc == null) return;
441          if (lib.borrowDocument(user, doc))
442              System.out.println("New loan: " + user.getName() +
443              " - " + doc.getTitle());
444      }

445      public static void returnDoc(String cmd) {
446          String args[] = getArgs(cmd);
447          if (args.length < 1) return;
448          Document doc = lib.getDocument(Integer.parseInt(args[0]));
449          if (doc == null) return;
450          User user = doc.getBorrower();
451          if (user == null) return;
452          if (lib.returnDocument(doc))
453              System.out.println("Loan closed: " + user.getName() +
454              " - " + doc.getTitle());
455      }
```

```
456        public static void searchUser(String cmd) {
457          String args[] = getArgs(cmd);
458          if (args.length < 1) return;
459          List users = lib.searchUser(args[0]);
460          Iterator i = users.iterator();
461          while (i.hasNext()) {
462            User user = (User)i.next();
463            System.out.println("User found: " + user.getCode() +
464            " - " + user.getName());
465          }
466        }

467        public static void searchDoc(String cmd) {
468          String args[] = getArgs(cmd);
469          if (args.length < 1) return;
470          List docs = lib.searchDocumentByTitle(args[0]);
471          Iterator i = docs.iterator();
472          while (i.hasNext()) {
473            Document doc = (Document)i.next();
474            System.out.println("Doc found: " + doc.getCode() +
475            " - " + doc.getTitle());
476          }
477        }

478        public static void isHolding(String cmd) {
479          String args[] = getArgs(cmd);
480          if (args.length < 2) return;
481          User user = lib.getUser(Integer.parseInt(args[0]));
482          Document doc = lib.getDocument(Integer.parseInt(args[1]));
483          if (lib.isHolding(user, doc))
484            System.out.println(user.getName() +
485            " is holding " + doc.getTitle());
486          else
487            System.out.println(user.getName() +
488            " is not holding " + doc.getTitle());
489        }

490        public static void printUser(String cmd) {
491          String args[] = getArgs(cmd);
492          if (args.length < 1) return;
493          User user = lib.getUser(Integer.parseInt(args[0]));
494          if (user != null)
495            user.printInfo();
496        }

497        public static void printDoc(String cmd) {
498          String args[] = getArgs(cmd);
499          if (args.length < 1) return;
500          Document doc = lib.getDocument(Integer.parseInt(args[0]));
501          if (doc != null)
502            doc.printInfo();
503        }
```

```
504      public static void dispatchCommand(String cmd) {
505        if (cmd.startsWith("addUser")) addUser(cmd);
506        if (cmd.startsWith("addIntUser")) addIntUser(cmd);
507        if (cmd.startsWith("rmUser")) rmUser(cmd);
508        if (cmd.startsWith("addBook")) addBook(cmd);
509        if (cmd.startsWith("addReport")) addReport(cmd);
510        if (cmd.startsWith("addJournal")) addJournal(cmd);
511        if (cmd.startsWith("rmDoc")) rmDoc(cmd);
512        if (cmd.startsWith("borrowDoc")) borrowDoc(cmd);
513        if (cmd.startsWith("returnDoc")) returnDoc(cmd);
514        if (cmd.startsWith("searchUser")) searchUser(cmd);
515        if (cmd.startsWith("searchDoc")) searchDoc(cmd);
516        if (cmd.startsWith("isHolding")) isHolding(cmd);
517        if (cmd.startsWith("printLoans")) lib.printAllLoans();
518        if (cmd.startsWith("printUser")) printUser(cmd);
519        if (cmd.startsWith("printDoc")) printDoc(cmd);
520      }

521      public static void main(String arg[]) {
522        try{
523          printHeader();
524          String s = "";
525          BufferedReader in = new BufferedReader(
526            new InputStreamReader(System.in));
527          while (!s.equals("exit")) {
528            s = in.readLine();
529            dispatchCommand(s);
530          }
531        } catch (IOException e) {
532          System.err.println("IO error.");
533          System.exit(1);
534        }
535      }
536    }
```

References

1. Unified modeling language (UML) specification, version 1.4. Technical report, Object Management Group (OMG), September 2001.
2. A. V. Aho, R. Sethi, and J. D. Ullman. *Compilers. Principles, Techniques, and Tools.* Addison-Wesley Publishing Company, Reading, MA, 1985.
3. L. O. Andersen. *Program Analysis and Specialization for the C Programming Language.* Phd Thesis, DIKU, University of Copenhagen, 1994.
4. N. Anquetil and T. C. Lethbridge. Experiments with clustering as a software remodularization method. In *Proc. of the 6th Working Conference on Reverse Engineering (WCRE'99)*, pages 235–255, Atlanta, Georgia, USA, October 1999. IEEE Computer Society.
5. G. Antoniol, R. Fiutem, G. Lutteri, P. Tonella, and S. Zanfei. Program understanding and maintenance with the CANTO environment. In *Proceedings of the International Conference on Software Maintenance*, pages 72–81, Bari, Italy, Oct 1997.
6. Robert V. Binder. *Testing Object-Oriented Systems: Models, Patterns, and Tools.* Addison-Wesley, 1999.
7. G. Booch, J. Rumbaugh, and I. Jacobson. *The Unified Modeling Language – User Guide.* Addison-Wesley Publishing Company, Reading, MA, 1998.
8. L. C. Briand, Y. Labiche, and J. Leduc. Towards the reverse engineering of UML sequence diagrams for distributed, real-time Java software. Technical Report SCE-04-04, Carleton University, April 2004.
9. Kyle Brown. *Design Reverse-Engineering and Automated Design Pattern Detection in Smalltalk.* Master thesis, North Carolina State University, Raleigh NC, USA, 1996.
10. R. Brun and F. Rademakers. Root – an object oriented data analysis framework. In *Proc. of AIHENP'96, 5th International Workshop on New Computing Techniques in Physics Research*, pages 81–86, Lausanne, Switzerland, 1996.
11. G. Caldiera and V. R. Basili. Identifying and qualifying reusable software components. *IEEE Computer*, pages 61–70, 1991.
12. G. Canfora, A. Cimitile, M. Munro, and C.J. Taylor. Extracting abstract data types from C programs: A case study. In *Proceedings of the International Conference on Software Maintenance*, pages 200–209, Montreal, Quebec, Canada, September 1993.

192   References

13. G. Canfora, A. Cimitile, M. Tortorella, and M. Munro. A precise method for identifying reusable abstract data types in code. In *Proceedings of the International Conference on Software Maintenance*, pages 404–413, Victoria, British Columbia, Canada, Sept 1994.

14. Y. R. Chen, G. S. Flowler, E. Koutsofios, and R. S. Wallach. Ciao: A graphical navigator for software document repositories. In *Proceedings of the International Conference on Software Maintenance*, pages 66–75, Opio(Nice), 1995.

15. James C. Corbett, Matthew B. Dwyer, John Hatcliff, Shawn Laubach, Corina S. Pasareanu, Robby, and Hongjun Zheng. Bandera: Extracting finite-state models from java source code. In *Proceedings of the International Conference on Software Engineering*, pages 439–448, 2000.

16. Patrick Cousot and Radhia Cousot. Abstract interpretation: a unified lattice model for static analysis of programs by construction or approximation of fixpoints. In *Conference Record of the Sixth Annual ACM SIGPLAN-SIGACT Symposium on Principles of Programming Languages*, pages 238–252, Los Angeles, California, 1977. ACM Press, New York.

17. J. Dean, D. Grove, and C. Chambers. Optimizations of object-oriented programs using static class hierarchy analysis. In *Proc. of the European Conference on Object-Oriented Programming (ECOOP)*, pages 77–101, 1995.

18. Dominic Duggan. Modular type-based reverse engineering of parameterized types in java code. In *Proc. of OOPSLA'99, Conference on Object-Oriented Programming, Systems, Languages and Applications*, pages 97–113, Denver, Colorado, USA, November 1999.

19. Matthew B. Dwyer, John Hatcliff, Roby Joehanes, Shawn Laubach, Corina S. Pasareanu, Robby, Hongjun Zheng, and W Visser. Tool-supported program abstraction for finite-state verification. In *Proceedings of the International Conference on Software Engineering*, pages 177–187, 2001.

20. Thomas Eisenbarth, Rainer Koschke, and Gunther Vogel. Static trace extraction. In *Proc. of the Working Conference on Reverse Engineering (WCRE)*, pages 128–137, Richmond, VA, USA, 2002. IEEE Computer Society.

21. M. Emami, R. Ghiya, and L.J. Hendren. Context-sensitive interprocedural points-to analysis in the presence of function pointers. *Proc. of the ACM SIGPLAN'94 Conf. on Programming Language Design and Implementation*, pages 242–256, June 1994.

22. J.C. Esteva. Automatic identification of reusable components. In *Proc. of the 7th International Workshop on Computer-Aided Software Engineering*, pages 80–87, Toronto, Ontario, Canada, July 1995.

23. R. Fiutem, G. Antoniol, P. Tonella, and E. Merlo. ART: an architectural reverse engineering environment. *Journal of Software Maintenance*, 11(5):339–364, 1999.

24. P. Funk, A. Lewien, and G. Snelting. Algorithms for concept lattice decomposition and their application. Technical report, Computer Science Department, Technische Universitat Braunschweig, 1995.

25. B. Ganter and R. Wille. *Formal Concept Analysis*. Springer-Verlag, Berlin, Heidelberg, New York, 1996.

26. J. F. Girard and R. Koschke. Finding components in a hierarchy of modules: a step towards architectural understanding. In *Proceedings of the International Conference on Software Maintenance*, pages 72–81, Bari, Italy, Oct 1997.

27. W.G. Griswold, M.I. Chen, R.W. Bowdidge, and J.D. Morgenthaler. Tool support for planning the restructuring of data abstractions in large systems. In

Proc. of the International Conference on the Foundations of Software Engineering, pages 33–45, 1996.

28. D. Grove and C. Chambers. A framework for call graph construction algorithms. *ACM Transactions on Programming Languages and Systems*, 23(6):685–746, November 2001.

29. T. Gschwind and J. Oberleitner. Improving dynamic data analysis with aspect-oriented programming. In *Proc. of the 7th European Conference on Software Maintenance and Reengineering (CSMR)*, pages 259–268, Benevento, Italy, March 2003. IEEE Computer Society.

30. Xinping Guo, James R. Cordy, , and Thomas R. Dean. Unique renaming of java using source transformation. In *Proc. of the 3rd IEEE International Workshop on Source Code Analysis and Manipulation (SCAM)*, Amsterdam, The Netherlands, September 2003. IEEE Computer Society.

31. D. Harel. Statecharts: a visual formalism for complex systems. *Science of Computer Programming*, 8:231–274, 1987.

32. Mark Harman, Rob Hierons, and Mark Proctor. A new representation and crossover operator for search-based optimization of software modularization. In *Proc. of the AAAI Genetic and Evolutionary Computation COnference 2002 (GECCO)*, pages 1359–1366, New York, USA, July 2002.

33. D. R. Harris, H. B. Reubenstein, and A. S. Yeh. Reverse engineering to the architectural level. In *Proceedings of the International Conference on Software Engineering*, pages 186–195, Seattle, 1995.

34. R. Holt and J. Y. Pak. Gase: Visualizing software evolution-in-the-large. In *Proceedings of the Working Conference on Reverse Engineering*, pages 163–166, Monterey, 1996.

35. IEEE Standard for Software Maintenance. *IEEE Std 1219-1998*. The Institute of Electrical and Electronics Engineers, Inc., 1998.

36. Ron Jeffries, Ann Anderson, and Chet Hendrickson. *Extreme Programming Installed*. Addison-Wesley, 2000.

37. W.L. Johnson and E. Soloway. Proust: knowledge-based program understanding. *IEEE Transactions on Software Engineering*, 11, 1985.

38. Neil D. Jones and Flemming Nielson. Abstract interpretation: A semantic-based tool for program analysis. In D.M. Gabbay S.Abramsky and T.S.E. Maibaum, editors, *Semantic Modelling*, volume 4 of Handbook of Logic in Computer Science, pages 527–636. Clarendon Press, Oxford, 1995.

39. H. A. Muller K. Wong, S.R. Tilley and M. D. Storey. Structural redocumentation: A case study. *IEEE Software*, pages 46–54, Jan.

40. Ivan Kiselev. *Aspect-Oriented Programming with AspectJ*. Sams Publishing, Indianapolis, Indiana, USA, 2002.

41. M. F. Kleyn and P. C. Gingrich. Graphtrace – understanding object-oriented systems using concurrently animated views. In *Proc. of OOPSLA'88, Conference on Object-Oriented Programming, Systems, Languages and Applications*, pages 191–205, November 1988.

42. K. Koskimies and H. Mössenböck. Scene: Using scenario diagrams and active test for illustrating object-oriented programs. In *Proc. of International Conference on Software Engineering*, pages 366–375, Berlin, Germany, March 25-29 1996.

43. V. Kozaczynski, J. Q. Ning, and A. Engberts. Program concept recognition and transformation. *IEEE Transactions on Software Engineering*, 18(12):1065–1075, Dec 1992.

44. C. Kramer and L. Prechelt. Design recovery by automated search for structural design patterns in object oriented software. In *Proceedings of the Working Conference on Reverse Engineering*, pages 208–215, Monterey, California, USA, 1996.

45. M. Krone and G. Snelting. On the inference of configuration structures from source code. In *Proc. of the 16th International Conference on Software Engineering*, pages 49–57, Sorrento, Italy, May 1994.

46. T. Kunz. Evaluating process clusters to support automatic program understanding. In *Proc. of the 19th International Workshop on Program Comprehension*, pages 198–207, Berlin, Germany, March 1996.

47. W. Landi and B.G. Ryder. A safe approximate algorithm for interprocedural pointer aliasing. *Proc. of the ACM SIGPLAN'92 Conf. on Programming Language Design and Implementation*, pages 235–248, 1992.

48. M. Lejter, S. Meyers, and S. P. Reiss. Support for maintaining object-oriented programs. *IEEE Transactions on Software Engineering*, 18(12):1045–1052, December 1992.

49. D. Liang, M. Pennings, and M. J. Harrold. Extending and evaluating flow-insensitive and context-insensitive points-to analysis for java. In *Proc. of the Workshop on Program Analysis for Software Tools and Engineering*, pages 73–79, 2001.

50. C. Lindig and G. Snelting. Assessing modular structure of legacy code based on mathematical concept analysis. In *Proc. of the 19th International Conference on Software Engineering*, pages 349–359, Boston, Massachussets, USA, May 1997.

51. P. E. Livadas and T. Johnson. A new approach to finding objects in programs. *Software Maintenance: Research and Practice*, 6:249–260, 1994.

52. G. A. Di Lucca, A. R. Fasolino, U. De Carlini, F. Pace, and P. Tramontana. Comprehending web applications by a clustering based approach. In *Proc. of the 10th International Workshop on Program Comprehension (IWPC)*, pages 261–270, Paris, France, June 2002. IEEE Computer Society.

53. S. Mancoridis and R. C. Holt. Recovering the structure of software systems using tube graph interconnection clustering. In *Proceedings of the International Conference on Software Maintenance*, pages 23–32, Monterey, California, 1996.

54. S. Mancoridis, B. S. Mitchell, Y. Chen, and E. R. Gansner. Using automatic clustering to produce high-level system organizations of source code. In *Proc. of the International Workshop on Program Comprehension*, pages 45–52, Ischia, Italy, 1998.

55. S. Mancoridis, B. S. Mitchell, Y. Chen, and E. R. Gansner. Bunch: a clustering tool for the recovery and maintenance of software system structures. In *Proceedings of the International Conference on Software Maintenance*, pages 50–59, Oxford, England, 1999.

56. Ana Milanova, Atanas Rountev, and Barbara G. Ryder. Constructing precise object relation diagrams. In *Proc. of the International Conference on Software Maintenance (ICSM)*, Montreal, Canada, October 2002. IEEE Computer Society.

57. Ana Milanova, Atanas Rountev, and Barbara G. Ryder. Parameterized object-sensitivity for points-to and side-effect analysis for java. In *Proc. of the International Symposium on Software Testing and Analysis (ISSTA)*, Rome, Italy, July 2002.

58. H. A. Muller, M. A. Orgun, S. R. Tilley, and J. S. Uhl. A reverse engineering approach to subsystem structure identification. *Software Maintenance: Research and Practice*, 5(4):181–204, 1993.

59. J. Q. Ning, A. Engberts, and W. Kozaczynski. Automated support for legacy code understanding. *Communications of the Association for Computing Machinery*, 37(5):50–57, May 1994.

60. H.D. Pande, W.A. Landi, and B.G. Ryder. Interprocedural def-use associations for c systems with single level pointers. *IEEE Transactions on Software Engineering*, 20(5), May 1994.

61. D. Paulson and Y. Wand. An automated approach to information systems decomposition. *IEEE Transactions on Software Engineering*, 18(3):174–189, 1992.

62. W. D. Pauw, D. Kimelman, and J. Vlissides. Modeling object-oriented program execution. In *Proc. of ECOOP'94 – Lecture Notes in Computer Science*, pages 163–182. Springer-Verlag, July 1994.

63. A. Potrich and P. Tonella. C++ code analysis: an open architecture for the verification of coding rules. In *Proc. of CHEP'2000, International Conference on Computing in High Energy and Nuclear Physics*, pages 758–761, Padova, Italy, 2000.

64. A. Quilici and D. N. Chin. Decode: A cooperative environment for reverse-engineering legacy software. In *Proceedings of the Second Working Conference on Reverse Engineering*, pages 156–165, Toronto, July 1995.

65. Filippo Ricca and Paolo Tonella. Using clustering to support the migration from static to dynamic web pages. In *Proc. of the International Workshop on Program Comprehension (IWPC)*, pages 207–216, Portland, Oregon, USA, May 2003. IEEE Computer Society.

66. C. Rich and R. Waters. The programmer's apprentice: A research overview. *IEEE Computer*, Nov. 1988.

67. T. Richner and S. Ducasse. Recovering high-level views of object-oriented applications from static and dynamic information. In *Proceedings of the International Conference on Software Maintenance*, pages 13–22, Oxford, England, 1999.

68. A. Rountev, A. Milanova, and B. G. Ryder. Points-to analysis for java based on annotated constraints. In *Proc. of the Conference on Object-Oriented Programming Systems, Languages, and Applications (OOPSLA)*, pages 43–55. ACM, October 2001.

69. J. Rumbaugh, I. Jacobson, and G. Booch. *The Unified Modeling Language – Reference Guide*. Addison-Wesley Publishing Company, Reading, MA, 1998.

70. M. Saeed, O. Maqbool, H.A. Babri, S.Z. Hassan, and S.M. Sarwar. Software clustering techniques and the use of combined algorithm. In *Proc. of Seventh European Conference on Software Maintenance and Reengineering (CSMR'03)*, pages 301–310, Atlanta, Georgia, USA, March 26 - 28 2003. IEEE Computer Society.

71. H. A. Sahraoui, W. Melo, H. Lounis, and F. Dumont. Applying concept formation methods to object identification in procedural code. In *Proc. of the IEEE Automated Software Engineering Conference*, pages 210–218, Incline Village, Nevada, USA, November 1997.

72. R. Schauer and R. Keller. Pattern visualization for software comprehension. *Proc. of the International Workshop on Program Comprehension*, pages 4–12, 1998.

73. R. W. Schwanke. An intelligent tool for re-engineering software modularity. In *Proceedings of the International Conference on Software Engineering*, pages 83–92, Austin, TX, 1991.

74. F. Shull, W. L. Melo, and V. R. Basili. An inductive method for discovering design patterns from object-oriented software systems. Technical report, University of Maryland, Computer Science Department, College Park, MD, 20742 USA, Oct 1996.

75. M. Siff and T. Reps. Identifying modules via concept analysis. In *Proceedings of the International Conference on Software Maintenance*, pages 170–179, Bari, Italy, Oct. 1997.

76. Saurabh Sinha and Mary Jean Harrold. Analysis and testing of programs with exception handling constructs. *IEEE Transactions on Software Engineering*, 26(9):849–871, 2000.

77. G. Snelting. Reengineering of configurations based on mathematical concept analysis. *ACM Transactions on Software Engineering and Methodology*, 5(2):146–189, 1996.

78. G. Snelting. Software reengineering based on concept lattices. In *Proceedings of the 4th European Conference on Software Maintenance and Reengineeering – CSMR'00*, Zurich, Switzerland, 2000.

79. G. Snelting. Concept lattices in software analysis. In *Proceedings of the First International Conference on Formal Concept Analysis – ICFCA'03*, Darmstadt, Germany, February-March 2003.

80. G. Snelting and F. Tip. Reengineering class hierarchies using concept analysis. *ACM Transactions on Programming Languages and Systems*, 22(3):540–582, May 2000.

81. B. Steensgaard. Points-to analysis in almost linear time. *Proc. of the 23rd ACM SIGPLAN-SIGACT Symposium on Principles of Programming Languages*, pages 32–41, January 1996.

82. Thomas Tilley, Richard Cole, Peter Becker, and Peter Eklund. A survey of formal concept analysis support for software engineering activities. In *Proceedings of the First International Conference on Formal Concept Analysis – ICFCA'03*, Darmstadt, Germany, February-March 2003.

83. F. Tip and J. Palsberg. Scalable propagation-based call graph construction algorithms. In *Proc. of OOPSLA, Conference on Object-Oriented Programming, Systems, Languages and Applications*, pages 264–280, 2000.

84. P. Tonella. Using the O-A diagram to encapsulate dynamic memory access. In *Proceedings of the International Conference on Software Maintenance*, pages 326–335, Bethesda, Maryland, November 1998. IEEE Computer Society press.

85. P. Tonella and G. Antoniol. Inference of object oriented design patterns. *Journal of Software Maintenance*, 13(5):309–330, 2001.

86. P. Tonella, G. Antoniol, R. Fiutem, and E. Merlo. Flow insensitive C++ pointers and polymorphism analysis and its application to slicing. *Proc. of the Int. Conf. on Software Engineering*, pages 433–443, 1997.

87. P. Tonella and A. Potrich. Reverse engineering of the UML class diagram from C++ code in presence of weakly typed containers. In *Proceedings of the International Conference on Software Maintenance*, pages 376–385, Firenze, Italy, 2001. IEEE Computer Society.

88. Paolo Tonella. Concept analysis for module restructuring. *IEEE Transactions on Software Engineering*, 27(4):351–363, April 2001.

89. Paolo Tonella and Alessandra Potrich. Static and dynamic C++ code analysis for the recovery of the object diagram. In *Proc. of the International Conference on Software Maintenance (ICSM 2002)*, pages 54–63, Montreal, Canada, October 2002. IEEE Computer Society Press.

90. Paolo Tonella and Alessandra Potrich. Reverse engineering of the interaction diagrams from C++ code. In *Proc. of the International Conference on Software Maintenance (ICSM 2003)*, pages 159–168, Amsterdam, The Netherlands, September 2003. IEEE Computer Society Press.

91. Paolo Tonella, Filippo Ricca, Emanuele Pianta, and Christian Girardi. Using keyword extraction for web site clustering. In *Proc. of the International Workshop on Web Site Evolution (WSE 2003)*, pages 41–48, Amsterdam, The Netherlands, September 2003. IEEE Computer Society Press.

92. C. D. Turner and D. J. Robson. The state-based testing of object-oriented programs. In *Proc. of the Conference on Software Maintenance*, pages 302–310, Montreal, Canada, September 1993. IEEE Computer Society.

93. Arie van Deursen. Program comprehension risks and opportunities in extreme programming. In *Proceedings of the 8th Working Conference on Reverse Engineering (WCRE)*, pages 176–185. IEEE Computer Society, 2001.

94. Arie van Deursen and Tobias Kuipers. Identifying objects using cluster and concept analysis. In *Proc. of the International Conference on Software Engineering (ICSE)*, pages 246–255, Los Angeles, CA, USA, May 1999. ACM Press.

95. W. Visser, K. Havelund, G. Brat, and S. Park. Model checking programs. In *Proc. of the International Conference on Automated Software Engineering (ASE)*, pages 3–12, Grenoble, France, September 2000. IEEE Computer Society.

96. Willem Visser, Corina S. Pasareanu, and Sarfraz Khurshid. Test input generation with java pathfinder. In *Proceedings of the ACM/SIGSOFT International Symposium on Software Testing and Analysis (ISSTA 2004)*, pages 97–107, Boston, Massachusetts, USA, July 2004. ACM Press.

97. R. J. Walker, G. C. Murphy, B. Freeman-Benson, D. Wright, D. Swanson, and J. Isaak. Visualizing dynamic software system information through high-level models. In *Proc. of the Conference on Object-Oriented Programming, Systems, Languages, and Applications*, pages 271–283, Vancouver, British Columbia, Canada, October 18-22 1998.

98. J. Warmer and A. Kleppe. *The Object Constraint Language*. Addison-Wesley Publishing Company, Reading, MA, 1999.

99. T.A. Wiggerts. Using clustering algorithms in legacy systems remodularization. In *Proc. of the 4th Working Conference on Reverse Engineering (WCRE)*, pages 33–43. IEEE Computer Society, 1997.

100. N. Wilde and R. Huitt. Maintenance support for object-oriented programs. *IEEE Transactions on Software Engineering*, 18(12):1038–1044, December 1992.

101. R. Wuyts. Declarative reasoning about the structure of object-oriented systems. In *Proceedings of TOOLS'98*, pages 112–124, Santa Barbara, California, USA, August 1998. IEEE Computer Society Press.

102. A. Yeh, D. Harris, and H. Reubenstein. Recovering abstract data types and object instances from a conventional procedural language. In *Proceedings of the Working Conference on Reverse Engineering*, pages 227–236, Toronto, Ontario, Canada, 1995.

Index

Names of main diagrams and graphs appear in small capitals: e.g. CLASS DIAGRAM. Page numbers in bold represent an extensive treatment of a notion. Numbers in italics refer to the *eLib* program. A letter after the page number indicates the appendix.